ACHIEVING
THE IMPOSSIBLE

LEWIS GORDON PUGH

**SIMON &
SCHUSTER**

London · New York · Sydney · Toronto

A CBS COMPANY

First published in Great Britain by Simon & Schuster UK Ltd, 2010
A CBS COMPANY

1 3 5 7 9 10 8 6 4 2

Simon & Schuster UK Ltd
1st Floor
222 Gray's Inn Road
London WC1X 8HB

www.simonandschuster.co.uk

Simon & Schuster Australia
Sydney

PICTURE CREDITS
Courtesy of Margery Pugh: 1, 2, 3, 4, 5
Courtesy of Kim Howard: 6
Courtesy of the author: 7, 8, 9, 11, 12, 13, 28, 30, 33
Courtesy of Veronique Carantois: 10
Courtesy of Else M. Lundal: 14
Courtesy of Gill Stamrood: 15
Courtesy of Monique Andersson: 16
© Reuters: 17
Courtesy of Terge Eggum: 18, 19
© Getty Images: 20, 22
© WWF: 21, 29
Courtesy of Michael Walker: 23
Courtesy of Todd Pitock: 24
Courtesy of Jason Roberts: 25, 26, 27, 31
Courtesy of Fred Kalborg: 32, 34
Courtesy of Yvette Gilbert: 35

A CIP catalogue record for this book
Library.

7-248-2
4737-262-8

hatham ME5 8TD

ed
rces
02341

ACHIEVING
THE IMPOSSIBLE

To my parents, who inspired me so much

The names of soldiers of the British SAS have been changed to protect their identity. The places and grid references referred to in the chapters on the SAS have also been changed in accordance with the Official Secrets Act.

CONTENTS

1

FALLING

Four-point-two kilometres is a long way for a frozen body to sink. I try not to think about it as I stand on the edge of the ice, preparing myself to plunge into the sea. Great depths don't normally hold any fear for me, but this is different.

The water is black, inky black, and so impenetrable that even if my goggles do not mist up, I'll be unable to see even my hand stretched out in front of me. All around me, the ice is cracking up. It's beautiful and terrifying: cracks can appear beneath your feet with little warning. Fall unprepared into one of these and you'll freeze.

And it's cold – unimaginably cold. Other than my red ski jacket, I'm wearing nothing but Speedo swimming trunks, a swimming cap and my goggles: no wetsuit; no nothing. The sea water is minus 1.7°C. It will sap the warmth from my body in seconds.

The one-kilometre swim in the coldest ocean on earth will take almost 20 minutes. If my body fails me, I will almost certainly die. But this is not simply about my body but also about my mind – if it takes me to the right place, I will survive. I do everything I can to tell myself that I *will* make it. I have to stay focused, in control. I tell myself that I *am* going to do this; there is no other place on this earth I would rather be.

Preparation is everything, and I've been preparing for this for years. Ever since I was a little boy, I'd been drawn to the Poles. I knew that one day I would undertake something in the polar regions that no one had ever attempted. During my training I'd learned to elevate my core body temperature. The most effective way I've found to do this originates from my time in the British Special Air Service, the SAS.

I close my eyes and imagine myself in the belly of a Hercules, flying at 1,000 metres, thirty of us waiting for our turn to drop into the dead of night. Once I'd seen a fellow soldier slip at the exit door and get caught, half-in, half-out. It was the terror on his face and his scream for help that stayed with me. 'Don't look down,' we were told. 'Jump as far out as you can. And when you are about to hit the deck, remember – keep your knees together!'

In my mind, the groaning of the ice becomes the steady drone of the aircraft's engines. I imagine myself checking and re-checking my parachute gear; in reality my fingers are feeling for the wires and sensors that are taped to my skin to measure my core body temperature and my heart rate and save me from death just as surely as a parachute saves a soldier.

My heart beats a little faster. I conjure up the smell of the Hercules, that mixture of aviation fuel and sweat. '*Five minutes to drop zone! Five minutes to drop zone!*' On the ice there are instructions too. '*Ten seconds to swim! Ten seconds to swim!*'

The door of the Hercules is pulled open. The men have lined up in front of me. Over their heads I can see the stars outside. My mouth goes dry.

In this state, a strange thing happens. I am standing barefoot and virtually naked on ice, and the air temperature is zero degrees, yet I am heating up. Reacting to the messages from my brain, my core body temperature begins to rise. Without that change the one-kilometre swim would be impossible.

Professor Tim Noakes, one of the world's most respected sports scientists, is standing in a small inflatable boat five metres from where I will begin this swim looking at the data on his computer. In this incredibly hostile part of the world, he is my protector. But I am barely conscious of him and the rest of the small team who have made this journey with me to the top of the world, or of the Russian guard at my left shoulder clutching his AK-47. He and his two comrades are here to protect me from polar bears. But when we spoke earlier in the day, I warned them that they could only let off a round to frighten away a bear, they could not shoot at it; we are the visitors here, after all.

I remove my ski jacket and step towards the water. A rush of air smacks my face. There isn't time for fear now. The jump is everything. The lights at the aircraft door turn red.

'Red on!'

Seconds later they change.

'Green on! *GO, GO, GO!*'

The men in front of me tumble from the plane. I shuffle forward as quickly as possible, and now it's my turn. I can't look back. I jump onto a small ledge, a few inches below the water. I pause for a second, then hurl myself forward.

Suddenly I'm falling – in my mind through the night from the Hercules, but in reality into the icy waters of the North Pole.

2

MY PARENTS

On 15 July 1993, my father passed away. He was seventy-two; I was twenty-three. The call from the Booth Memorial Hospital in Cape Town came just before midnight. Mum was in bed but not asleep and, unknown to me, she had answered the telephone to a nuisance caller a few nights previously so, thinking it might be the same man, she didn't pick up.

'Is this Lewis?' the nurse asked, because by now the hospital staff knew us well. My father had spent the last six years in hospital.

'Yes,' I replied.

'You'd better get over here soon. Your dad may not have long to go.'

Mum picked up the phone in her room just as the nurse was hanging up. 'Only a friend,' I said.

From the time we'd moved from Grahamstown in the Eastern Cape to Cape Town eight years before, I'd watched my mother nurse my father, make daily visits when he was hospitalized, and continue to love him even when his Alzheimer's meant he could give very little in return.

Mum watched Dad go from being this great man, who had risen to the rank of Surgeon Rear Admiral in the Royal Navy and with whom she had shared a wonderful life, to becoming a very different and greatly diminished person. Towards the end my father hardly ate and a couple of his teeth had fallen out. His emaciated body reminded me of photographs of victims of Auschwitz or one of the other concentration camps and he'd had a broken wrist that couldn't be properly re-set.

That last indignity was especially tough on a man who had been an accomplished orthopaedic surgeon. Yet there are memories from this dark time that I treasure: how he always managed to smile on seeing me walk into his hospital bedroom and make so obvious his enjoyment of the ice cream that I brought. He would hold my hand as we spoke and, for a while, it seemed like he was his old self. 'How are you, my boy?' he would say. Even towards the end, when his walk had become a shuffle, I would dress him and we would stroll around the nearby Molteno Reservoir. On those days he would be the father I always knew: polite, interested in what was going on in my life and an inspiration to me.

On other days the paranoia so often associated with Alzheimer's made him imagine things that weren't real. There were times when his memory deserted him and he would forget the most fundamental things. He would tell my mother that the man in the bed next to him, a lovely gentleman called Mr Sessions, was suffering from Alzheimer's but could never accept he, too, had the same disease. My father's problems were caused, he believed, by his medication and he went to great lengths to dupe his doctors. Pills stayed in his mouth until doctors and nurses left the room and next morning I would find them dumped beneath his bed. For me, there was great sadness in seeing a man who had achieved so much, and who always wanted things done correctly, so lessened before his death.

That night in July, I went to the hospital alone. I didn't want Mum to watch him die – I wanted to try and protect her. So I drove as quickly as I could from our home in Camps Bay to the hospital, which was close to the centre of Cape Town. My father had died minutes before I got there. They had pulled a white sheet over his body and, though his death was not unexpected, I stood there in total shock. Standing at the end of the bed, I said prayers and felt utterly forlorn. The man who had been my hero had left me and, even if it was true that Alzheimer's destroyed the father I knew, his death brought a finality that was too much for me. People said time would heal. It has and it hasn't. Every now and then something will trigger a memory that causes me to cry. My father was and remains an enormous figure in my life.

When I returned from the hospital, Mum was sitting in the chair close to the front door. She had heard me leave the house and knew it was the hospital. I didn't know what to say. After struggling to open my mouth, all that came was: 'Dad is dead.' I'm sure it seemed to Mum that I was delivering the awful news in the same stark way that was sometimes Dad's style. Then I broke down and cried. Seventeen years later, I still find it difficult to explain precisely what it was about my father that made me hold him in such awe. Perhaps it was because of my youth – I was only fourteen when Alzheimer's began to take him away from us. Though I can't explain them, the feelings are undeniable.

When I was a boy, my mother read me stories of the great explorers and distinguished military leaders, including the Ladybird collection on major figures in world history: Bonaparte, Nelson, Alexander the Great, Livingstone, Captain Scott,

Captain Cook, Christopher Columbus. They fascinated me but it was the story of Scott and the ill-fated expedition to the South Pole that overwhelmed my imagination. 'They looked like great lumps of sugar floating on the water,' the writer said of the gigantic blocks of ice Scott and his four companions encountered as they sailed into the sea ice off Antarctica.

Dad's part in my upbringing was perhaps more subtle but every bit as influential. My father taught me to understand that dreams need not be vague aspirations that add a little fun and colour to childhood. Not much was impossible, if you had a mind to go after it. What seems beyond you is only unreachable if that's what you believe.

The objects that adorned our house told me that, day after day. On the wall outside my bedroom there hung a beautiful painting by Sir Peter Scott, son of the great explorer. It depicted the flight of geese: majestic, wild and yet beautifully symmetrical. On another wall there was an ancient map of the world, so old there was no mention of the Antarctic, which was not known to exist at the time. A portrait of explorer Captain Cook hung near a bust of Lord Nelson that was on top of a stately grandfather clock with a scene from the Battle of Trafalgar engraved on its face. We also had a beautiful engraving of Jesus College, Cambridge – scholarly, steeped in history and where my father had studied. It wasn't impossible to think that one day I might study there too.

Dad would tell me that the beautiful oak cupboard in the living room had been a butcher's cupboard, once used to hang bacon. Inside that cupboard he had made shelves from the wood taken from the air-raid shelter his parents had built in their back garden in Bournemouth during the Second World War. He wanted my sister Caroline and me never to forget what it had been like for people during the war and those shelves were a reminder of where he had come from and what his parents' generation had been through. Class-mates of his died in the war. The things he thought important *were* important.

In our house, there was a copy of *The Times Atlas of the World*. I think my father wanted me to realize there were worlds beyond the world in which I lived. Nothing excited me more than randomly opening the atlas and seeing places and seas, imagining what they looked like and what kind of life the people had. Later I would go to the atlas to find loca-tions for my adventures. Could I swim from this point to that point? Had it been done before?

My father would pick up one of his beautiful Staffordshire portrait figures of a great explorer or a military figure and teach me history by telling me of the deeds and exploits that distinguished these men. He knew his history and passed on his love of it to me.

Alzheimer's crept up on him. He would talk about having no feeling in his feet and would lift them off the ground in such an exaggerated way that we knew something was wrong. He would drive to Rhodes University in Grahams-town, spend time researching in the library and then walk home. When asked where the car was, he would say he didn't know. Then he and my mum would walk back to the university, locate the car and drive home. This was tough for my mother, Caroline and me because we didn't know what precisely was wrong and, eventually, the illness produced a change in his behaviour that was deeply upsetting.

One day I came home from school and found him tearing up family photographs; this was a man who had written one book about his father's extended family, going right back to the seventeenth century, and was writing another one about his mother's side. Family was very important to him. In the early years of his illness, when forgetfulness and absent-mindedness were the common symptoms, he would say,

'Where are my . . .' and not remember what he was looking for. Eventually he would say 'slippers' and I began to do the same thing. I hardly realized what I was doing but my mother did. Years later I watched the film *I Am Sam*, with Sean Penn and Dakota Fanning, which is about a young girl's relationship with her mildly retarded father. As the girl starts doing well at school, she realizes she is brighter than her father and to lessen the distance that is developing between them she starts to behave in silly ways. I recognized this response because mine had been similar.

There are different memories. One is of him lying on his back in the swimming pool he'd had built in the garden of our house in Grahamstown, after we had moved from England. I might have been eleven or twelve; he was in his early sixties. He would just lie on his back, kick his legs and move slowly but surely through the water. That pool was cold but the temperature never bothered him and I could tell from the way he got out of the water and then straight back to his book-writing that the swim was key to his working day. Fit body, sharp mind – until his illness he was living proof of that.

But his love for the water did not blind him to its dangers. How could it, after his godfather, Dr Herbert Cuff, and his two daughters lost their lives in a drowning tragedy? Dr Cuff worked with my granddad and they wrote a book together. My father told me the story: one day Dr Cuff's daughters went swimming off East Anglia, and got pulled out to sea by the current. Dr Cuff rushed in to rescue them and tragically all three drowned. It left a big mark on my dad. He also told me about the time he was swimming in Australia, while he was there on Royal Navy duty, and got sucked out to sea in a rip current. He and a few other officers were saved by Australian lifeguards. My love for the water would always be tempered by respect for dangers that must never be underestimated.

An affinity with the water was in my genes. My Welsh grandfather, Tom Pugh, was the first Medical Superintendent of the Queen Mary's Hospital for Children in Carshalton near London. In his work as Medical Superintendent, he used to get some of his recovering children into a swimming pool outside the hospital where they would stretch and exercise. Granddad died long before I was born but my father told me many stories about him. Through his work at Queen Mary's, Granddad earned quite a reputation and within medical circles was known as 'Pugh of Carshalton'.

My father grew up in relatively privileged circumstances in a big house on the grounds of the hospital. He was sent to Lancing College, a public school in Sussex, and started at Cambridge in 1939. To be allowed to begin university life at a time when the country was part of a terrible world war was a privilege but the military also needed doctors and engineers, hence the need for graduates in those disciplines. Because of the war, the undergraduate course was compressed into two years and students were advised that if they failed one subject, they could be sent straight to war. I still have the medal he won for coming first in his obstetrics class. It was a sombre time for everyone, even students at Cambridge, as airfields around Cambridge and in East Anglia were targeted by the Luftwaffe; a mile or so from the centre of Cambridge there is a big cemetery where US airmen killed in the war are buried.

After graduating, Dad worked at the Middlesex Hospital in the centre of London when the city was being bombed. He then did his internship in Dublin and lived for a year in a country not involved in the war. One of his abiding memories of Dublin was that the street lighting remained on at night. He returned to England a qualified doctor and joined the Royal Navy. Months later the war ended and my father went off to do the training and examinations necessary to become an orthopaedic surgeon. His career in the Royal Navy, which he then rejoined, was a very successful one, and culminated in the rank of Surgeon Rear Admiral.

Some of the stories from that time have lived on in my memory – like his involvement in the team of military people that tested Britain's first atomic bomb in a lagoon off Monte Bello Islands close to the northwest coast of Australia in 1952. There is a family photograph of Dad in the foreground with the atomic bomb going off in the distant background. You can imagine the impact such stories had on an impressionable boy.

In the post-war years, there was a surplus of warships and they sailed the bomb on one of the ships off the islands and anchored it at sea, clear of the land. That night they had a party on the ship, ate a fine dinner, then raised their plates and threw them back over their heads. Given what was going to happen the next day, there wasn't much point in cleaning up. Early the next morning they left the ship. They took landing crafts to the nearest island and it was from there they detonated Britain's first atomic bomb. What Dad remembered was the hugeness of the explosion, the loudness of the two short cracks, and the sense of being hit by sound. There was also the sight of the cloud gathering and then mushrooming in the sky. Dad was wearing his white protective clothing, goggles over his eyes and gloves on his hands but as the blast went off he put his hands over his eyes to shield them and suddenly saw his hands as if in an X-ray. That was the part he found scariest because they weren't exactly close to the explosion – about ten kilometres away, if I recall correctly. After the test, Dad had to go around the bomb site and examine the dead animals for levels of radiation and assess the damage to the marine life in general.

What has lingered in my mind is my father's excitement at being involved in something so momentous. Political leaders of the day believed the development of an atomic bomb was crucial to Britain's security and it was thought the country would be safe as long as it had atomic bomb capacity. Of course this is with the benefit of hindsight, but it seems to me they were missing a key point: if Britain had an atomic bomb, Russia would want one, so too would China and on it would go, until every military power would have the capability. Then less-developed countries would insist on their right to have an atomic bomb and where will it all end? When will a country with a volatile leadership develop the capability? And how long will it be before a terrorist group gets control of an atomic bomb? My father and his generation had been through a world war, some political leaders had been through two, and they saw things through very different eyes. My own feeling was that witnessing the explosion of an atomic bomb, and having to examine all the dead animals, had a profound effect on my father, as it must have had on all those who witnessed it.

My parents met through the Royal Navy. Margery Jones was born in Cardiff three years before the start of the Second World War, and was moved to Anglesey until the end of the war. Though she was too young to understand the implications of the war, Mum was very much a child of the war years. She didn't like us to leave any food uneaten on our plates and would tell the story of visiting her grandmother in Aberfan shortly after the war. Her grandmother kept two eggs for the visit and, while preparing supper, one of the eggs rolled off a countertop and smashed onto the floor. Her grandmother was distraught, inconsolable, and I've never forgotten that story.

My mother later became a trainee nurse and midwife in Cardiff. After her training, her eye was caught by an ad in *Nursing Times*: 'If you are a midwife, the Royal Navy needs you.' It was the higher salary that attracted Mum, though in her interview at the Ministry of Defence in London she spoke enthusiastically about her desire to travel, which was also true.

She and Dad first met at the bedside of a Chief Petty Officer who was involved in a fatal road accident. The Petty Officer's wife had been having an affair and on this Sunday evening she was out at a club with her lover when her husband learned what was going on. He drove to the club, picked her up there and was then involved in a head-on collision on the return journey to the Navy base. His wife and two occupants of the other car were killed but, although he suffered multiple injuries, he was alive. Dad was called in to assess the man's injuries and found a number of Sick Berth Attendants and my mother attending to him. 'Could you all please leave?' he said. Everyone did except Nursing Sister Jones, who was holding the injured man's hand. Sister Jones could imagine how the accident had happened: a distraught husband drives to the club to bring home his straying wife; he is angry and drives too quickly; there is a terrifying crash and he is the sole survivor. She wasn't prepared to abandon the Petty Officer to a doctor whose bedside manner sounded a little too direct. My father then asked the man if the woman in his car was his wife.

'Yes,' he nodded.

'She's dead,' replied my father.

Sister Jones was taken aback by the matter-of-fact manner and continued to hold the Petty Officer's hand, comforting him as best she could. For years after, Mum and Dad would recall that first meeting. In response to my mother's criticism that he was too direct in the way he spoke to the Petty Officer, my father would say there is only one way to give bad news and he would point between his eyes. 'Straight through here,' he'd say. Dad also said that it was the way Sister Jones endeared herself to the grief-stricken Petty

Officer that endeared her to him too. All it took was that brief scene in ICU (Intensive Care Unit) and my father was smitten.

A few days later he and Mum were on the same table at a dinner in the hospital, a meeting remembered by my mum for a moment of excruciating embarrassment. Unaccustomed to these official get-togethers, known as 'Mess Dinners', she was too shy to tell the waiters she wasn't having wine and, as one course followed another, her different wine glasses were filled. They sat there, untouched. My father was at the top of the table, my mother near the bottom, but when the dinner ended, Dad walked down to where Sister Jones sat. 'My dear,' he said, 'what do you propose to do with all that wine?' He was Surgeon Commander Pugh then, a senior officer, and my poor mother hadn't a notion how to reply.

The embarrassing moment passed and soon they felt comfortable in each other's company. When they discovered their shared Welsh roots, they had plenty to talk about. On the walk back to their respective quarters, he asked her out to dinner. They went to dinner the following evening and enjoyed it. When the Surgeon Commander turned up on the ward the next day and invited Sister Jones to dinner for the second consecutive night, Mum knew she had him on the run.

Three weeks later he asked her to marry him and it didn't surprise her in the least. From their first dinner date, she sensed he was a straight-between-the-eyes kind of man. Mum was thirty-one, not that young, but she had never dated anyone she saw as a potential long-term partner. She wondered whether she was too hard to please. Then my dad came along and three weeks later she was as convinced as he was. They were married soon afterwards; a year later, in 1968, my sister Caroline was born and a year after that I arrived. My father had been married previously and had four children from his first marriage but that relationship had ended in a difficult divorce. Though I remember meeting one of the children, who were all a good bit older than Caroline and me, there wasn't much contact between us and them.

Mum was Dad's best friend and the most generous and wonderful mother to Caroline and me. When we first moved to South Africa and my father was immersed in writing his books, Mum wasn't just a supportive wife but also a work companion who did much of the photography and typed up the manuscript. They worked together on two books then: one about the Anglo-Boer War and the other a history of his mother's family. When I was a small boy, he and Mum spent seven years producing the definitive book on Staffordshire portrait figures of the great and best-known characters of earlier centuries. Working together, they were in their element. I can count on the fingers of one hand the times my parents argued in front of Caroline and me, and even then they would quickly move to another room to resolve whatever difference had arisen.

My memories of my father as Surgeon Rear Admiral Pugh are stored in separate pictures. In most of them he is standing upright in his uniform, wearing the Knight of Jerusalem Cross around his neck and his OBE and other medals on his chest and looking every bit a senior officer of the Royal Navy. He had a beautiful sword and shoes that I was allowed to polish. No shoes were ever shined with as much fervour. Seeing him in full uniform filled me with pride and represented the image of my father that I felt truly became him. He was an Honorary Surgeon to the Queen and was meticulous about everything he undertook.

On a sheet of wallpaper he drew the family tree of his mother's family; it was five metres long and there was nothing he liked more than finding a missing cousin. When we lived in England there was a family outing to Paulerspury in Northampton because my father was descended from Professor William Carey, the famous Baptist missionary of the early 1800s, who was born there. Carey did his missionary work in India and translated the Bible into Bengali and Sanskrit. Four colleges in North America are named after him. You can understand how distressing it was to see Dad, afflicted by Alzheimer's, tearing family photographs to pieces.

After his death, I was curious to find out more about my father. On a holiday to England, I looked up relatives and colleagues who had served with Dad in the Royal Navy. I visited my aunt, his sister, and gleaned as much from her as I could. I went to see Surgeon Vice Admiral Tony Revell in the Navy and he told a story about an important conference of the British Orthopaedic Association organized by my father in April 1967. He was at the Royal Navy Hospital at Haslar at the time and putting on the BOA Conference was considered an onerous responsibility.

'Lewis,' Tony Revell told me, 'there is a story that you will not know because it has remained secret in the Royal Navy. But as your dad has passed on, I can tell you. Your father wanted the event to be as successful as it could be. He had the Royal Marine Band play and a key part of the conference was an exhibition focusing on the surgeons who had worked on Lord Nelson's ships; a year later your father's book *Nelson and His Surgeons* would be published. Various exhibits were on show, including Nelson's uniform coat pierced by a musket-ball, death masks and equipment used by those who treated him – knives, saws, tourniquets. The thing he most wanted for the exhibition was the French musket-ball that killed Lord Nelson at the Battle of Trafalgar. It was held at Windsor Castle.

'Your father made the request to Earl Mountbatten of

Burma, who had been Admiral of the Fleet and who was uncle to the Queen. Permission to exhibit the musket-ball was given and it was agreed two Royal Marines would travel to Windsor Castle, collect it and bring it back to our hospital. It was an unusually warm spring day and on their journey to Gosport, the marines stopped at a pub for a quick drink. Rather than risk bringing their treasure into the pub, the marines left it safely in the glove compartment of the car. They had a drink, then another for good measure and left, only to discover their car had been stolen. Obviously, it wasn't the vehicle they were worried about. They immediately informed your father, who liaised with the police; roads were closed off, helicopters were deployed and an intense search was launched. Eventually the car was located and, to everyone's relief, the musket-ball was still in its case in the glove compartment. The day – and a few reputations – was saved. That musket-ball is now on display at the Maritime Museum in Greenwich.'

People said the nicest things about Dad, confirming impressions I'd already had. And in the course of talking to people about my father, I realized my own memories of him couldn't be enhanced or diminished; they were an integral part of me and remained untouched.

Dad's career in the Armed Forces meant I grew up on Navy bases, first at the Royal Navy Hospital (RNH) at Stonehouse in Plymouth. We then spent a year at RNH Mtarfa in Malta, where my father was promoted to Surgeon Rear Admiral, and returned to England to RNH Haslar in Gosport.

After my father retired from the Navy, we lived near Tavistock in Devon because he had become Chief Medical Officer for Dartmoor Prison. From the middle of December 1979 through to Boxing Day, it rained incessantly. Though the River Tavy flowed past the bottom of our garden, it was so far below the level of our house that there never seemed any possibility of flooding. But on that Boxing Day morning the river was far higher than normal and my mother phoned my dad, who was at the prison, to say the water level was getting dangerously high. Dad couldn't believe it would get high enough to cause flooding but what we didn't know was that a little further down river at Boughthayes, a culvert had collapsed and blocked the river. From early morning the water had started to back up.

My father returned from Dartmoor in the early evening and, though the river was still rising, he was calm. 'The best thing to do in this situation,' he said, 'is to sit down, eat dinner and not worry too much about this.' The house was a split-level bungalow, in which the sitting room, two bed-rooms and a bathroom were at a lower level than the rest. Though we didn't believe the water would flood the house, my mother was very concerned. After dinner, she went to check her bedroom, where two big French doors opened into the back garden, and was shocked to find water gushing in beneath those doors. Outside, the heavy wrought-iron furniture had been dragged down the garden and the water was getting high enough to take the car as well. In the higher level of the house we were still dry but my father decided he had to get the car from where it was parked in the driveway. Up to his knees in water, he walked across the lawn and all the time I was petrified that he would be swept away by the floodwater. He reached the car and, even though the water was rising around it, he got it out of there and onto higher ground.

When he came back, he said we should get ready to evac-uate the house and were to gather only what we absolutely needed. He looked after all the important documents: pass-ports, birth certificates, marriage certificate, insurance policies. My mother took a clean set of clothes for everyone, my sister took chocolates she had been given for Christmas and I took my favourite little carpet with a cat on it from beside my bed. Before leaving the house, my father gathered us together in the kitchen and led us in prayer. It was a simple request to the Lord to protect our home and us. After praying, we rose and looked out the window again to check the level of the water and, unbelievably, it was dropping – as if our prayers were being answered immediately. What was remarkable was the speed with which the water receded: one minute it was all around us and the next it was being sucked back down to the river. First the water disappeared from inside and around the house, then our garden reappeared. 'Never doubt God,' my father said. We heard later that the blocked culvert at Boughthayes was freed and, as soon as it was, the flooding that it had caused disappeared.

All that was left was the mess and it took weeks to get the house back to normal. Builders came, and carpets and floorboards were pulled up and replaced. The timing couldn't have been worse because we were due to emigrate from England to South Africa and the house was for sale. It was taken off the market and three months passed before the builders finished the repairs. My parents were afraid the house would then be difficult to sell. At the time, there was no legal requirement to disclose to a potential purchaser that there had been flooding. In our case, the River Tavy was so far below the level of the house that it was impossible to conceive it might be a problem. Different people came to view the house. When the most likely buyer made an offer, my father spoke up. 'Before I could accept your offer, I must tell you that we had a flood here on Boxing Day. It was caused by a collapsed culvert down river but it happened.' The couple mulled it over and came to the conclusion that the flood had been a one-off accident unlikely to recur and they bought our house.

That was my father. You only had to watch him filling out his tax returns to see the kind of man he was. It was the same when he was writing his books or tracing his family's roots or building up his collection of Staffordshire porcelain. One time in Grahamstown, he arrived home after the longish walk to the bookstore only to realize he had not paid for a book he had picked up. He could have called the store and said he would be in the following day to pay for what he had inadvertently taken, or he could have sent me back with the money, but that wasn't how he did things. Turning straight around, he walked back to the shop, explained what had happened and paid for the book. Now, of course, I wonder if that little moment of forgetfulness was not one of the earlier signs of the Alzheimer's disease that would eventually destroy him.

It was Dad's idea to move to South Africa. His mother's family came from the Eastern Cape and he had spent time in Cape Town while on Royal Navy duty. From his point of view, it was the perfect place to spend one's retirement and a very good place to write his books. It was also a place to enjoy the autumn of his life better. Because my father was set on going, my mother readily agreed. She just said, 'Why not?' What might have been intimidating for another woman was an adventure for her. If her husband had a dream about setting up a new home in South Africa, she was always going to be supportive. As well as wanting to move to South Africa, my father had reservations about Great Britain. It was 1980. The country was going through tough economic times, and had been through crippling strikes under James Callaghan. My father was excited by the change to a warmer climate in a physically beautiful country.

It was Easter before the house was sold and not long afterwards we boarded the Royal Mail Ship (RMS) *St Helena* bound for Cape Town via the Canary Islands, Ascension

Island and St Helena. All our possessions had been loaded onto a container ship and would land in Cape Town about a month later, so it made sense for us to travel by sea, enjoy the journey and arrive at more or less the same time as our belongings. It was cold and wet as we departed Avonmouth, near Bristol, and made our way down the Severn Estuary. At ten years old, I saw the journey and the move to South Africa as one great expedition – something to be embraced rather than feared. Travelling by sea, especially on a journey that had stops at different small islands on the way, simply added to the excitement.

On our trip we spent a week on St Helena in the South Atlantic, which is one of the most remote places in the world and has a population of around 5,000. It is possible to walk the island's entire coastline in a few days, which was a joy for my father, who was an enthusiastic walker. When we lived in Cornwall, we would walk up Kit Hill. Although that wasn't much more than 1,000 feet high, it seemed a long way up to my young legs. Even when Dad wasn't well, we walked up Lion's Head in Cape Town. Always when we walked, it was clear to me how much he loved nature, wild flowers, animals in their natural habitat and the simple pleasure of a beautiful sunset. My love for the environment did not develop out of a vacuum. In the course of walking the entire coastline of St Helena, which we did, we came to understand the richness of the island's history. Under British supervision, Napoleon Bonaparte was dispatched to St Helena and spent the last six years of his life there. Although he was buried on the island, his remains were later exhumed and taken back to France.

For my parents, the excitement of South Africa must have been tempered with some trepidation. They were emigrating to the same country that my father's maternal ancestors had left England for in 1820; for a man so aware of his family tree, history was repeating itself 160 years later. His ancestors settled in the Eastern Cape and that's where we would go. The month-long boat journey gradually introduced us all to the fact that we were moving a long way from home. Mum and Dad were leaving their extended families, separating themselves from networks of family and friends, and there must have been anxieties. They weren't much interested in politics and probably wouldn't have thought too much about the fact that they were moving to a country that was regarded by many as a pariah because of the inhumane system of apartheid. Zimbabwe had just got its independence; it didn't take a great leap of imagination to realize that change would be coming to South Africa too and bringing with it an obvious threat to the country's security. I've always had a healthy respect for the courage of the English settlers who went to South Africa in the nineteenth century not really knowing what awaited them. I now see that my parents had courage too, because they could not have been sure how South Africa was going to change.

For me, the journey from England was magical because it was over water and I could see and hear the sea every minute of the day, yet nothing prepared me for the beauty of our night-time arrival into Cape Town. Some pictures are so vivid they stay in your mind forever. That night, sailing into Cape Town, I was struck by the calmness of Table Bay and the bare majesty of overhanging Table Mountain, which stood out because it was lit up. For a boy who had come from the south-west of England, this was a world on a grander scale. As a first experience of Africa, it filled my senses. I had read about the Statue of Liberty standing guard and welcoming immigrants to America as they sailed into New York. Table Mountain had the same effect on me as RMS *St Helena* slowly steamed past Robben Island into Cape Town Harbour. If this was Africa, I wanted more of it.

3

A SENSE OF PROPORTION

It is hard to overstate the role played by teachers in the lives of their pupils, especially headmasters and housemasters whose personality and philosophy can permeate an entire school. Three men stand apart for their contrasting influences on my life: Tony Wortham, Major Tony Crankshaw and John Ince. Each, in his way, taught me a lot about how to bring out the best in young people – and how not to.

Tony Wortham was the owner and headmaster of Mount House School in Tavistock, Devon. It was an all-boys preparatory school that was predominantly but not exclusively a boarding school. Taking over Mount House when it was small and nondescript, Tony turned it into the best prep school in the West of England and one of the very best in the country. Key to achieving this was his belief that children are individuals and their differences should be celebrated not obliterated.

When Tony Wortham passed you on the corridor, it was natural to say, 'Morning, Sir,' and he would always remember your name to greet you in response. Each dormitory housed eight to ten boys and was named after a famous naval hero: Blake, Nelson, Drake, Raleigh. Our studies were important but not oppressive; our games were many and varied. Each teacher, it seemed, had been handpicked by the headmaster because he or she taught with the same enthusiasm. Tony built a lake on the grounds, big enough for us to learn how to sail and kayak, and when we needed a little more space he would take us into the nearby Dartmoor National Park and set us free.

Because the school was not that far from Dartmoor Prison, there were occasional encounters with escapees. On returning home from the school one evening, our geography teacher, Captain Glossip, found an escaped convict beside the mop and sweeping brush in his cupboard. Another day there was a knock on Mr Wortham's door and a bedraggled man asked if he could have a drink of water. Tony invited him in and asked if the man would prefer a cup of tea? They drank the tea, the man went on his way and, later that evening, Tony learned from the news that the man he had entertained had made an unofficial exit from Dartmoor Prison earlier in the day.

Though I was ten years of age when I left Mount House and departed for South Africa with my family, I remained in contact with Tony. No one was more pleased than he when he heard that Jesus College, Cambridge, had accepted me as a Masters student. He, too, had been to Jesus and he knew what it meant to me to study there. The biggest thrill of all was when he came to visit me in South Africa. He was not far off eighty when I took him swimming in the Atlantic on a day that, at best, could be described as bracing. He loved it. Swimming beside him, the water didn't seem one bit cold. He was eighty-four when he died in 2004.

There was an obituary in *The Times* that talked about what he had brought to Mount House School. 'The pupils,' said the writer, 'learnt how to sail and ski, and to temper learning and duty with a sense of proportion.' If Tony's philosophy could be encapsulated in one phrase that was it: 'a sense of proportion'. *The Times* mentioned how Tony was 'a gentle and spiritual man with whom the youngest new boy felt wholly at ease'. When I left home to begin my first term as a boarder at Mount House, my father had tears in his eyes; it was the only time I ever saw him cry. Though I did miss my family, I soon settled. The atmosphere at Mount House was different from that of a small family, but it was very supportive and just great fun. You never felt lonely on Tony Wortham's watch.

Parents almost always want what they consider best for their children. Part of the reason the Pughs decided to set up home in Grahamstown in the Eastern Cape was that my father's mother had been educated there and he still had cousins in the area. Another attraction was that Grahamstown was a university town with excellent secondary schools, not the least of which was St Andrew's College and its sister college, the Diocesan School for Girls (DSG). In the hierarchy of private fee-paying schools in South Africa, St Andrew's was considered right up there with the best. It also had tradition, being almost 130 years old when I showed up. For my father, whose mother and grandmother had gone to the Diocesan School for Girls, it was a big deal to send me to St Andrew's and Caroline to DSG. The fees were not insubstantial but my parents held the view that a good education was worth whatever price you paid for it. I started at St Andrew's Preparatory School, spent two years there finishing my primary education and then moved on to St Andrew's College, where I endured the first three years of my secondary education. I use the word 'endured' deliberately.

You could board or be a day pupil at St Andrew's. Since I lived close to the school, I was a day pupil. In practice, it didn't make a lot of difference, because the day at St Andrew's began at eight in the morning and didn't end until eight in the evening. All my homework was done in school. When my mother finally picked me up in the evening, there wasn't much time for anything except a little supper and then bed.

As is the way of most private schools, each pupil was assigned to a particular house, which had its own housemaster. Mine was Upper House and Major Crankshaw was the housemaster. Crankshaw was a name Charles Dickens might have given to an unreasonably authoritarian housemaster and, in this case, the name would have been well chosen. If you check on the St Andrew's College website, there is a short history of Upper House in which he gets a sort-of honourable mention: 'Tony "Major" Crankshaw (1980s) was a strong man with a straight view of right and wrong.' Well, that's not exactly how I remember him.

First it should be remembered that I had come from England and, even if both my parents were Welsh, I looked to most South African kids like a 'pom'. St Andrew's pupils were predominantly English-speaking South Africans but there was still a certain antipathy towards England. It was also true that at the age of twelve, I wasn't very big, had enjoyed a sheltered upbringing and wasn't very interested in or good at rugby. Put all of that together and Major Crankshaw's Upper House was definitely not the place for me. Generally I have been very lucky in life but this was one occasion when I drew the shortest of short straws.

It started with the little book, given to every new boy, which contained the names of various people and places at the school. For example, it listed the names and positions of the fifteen boys on the school's senior rugby team. It had the names of the different rugby fields, the names of all the prefects in the school, the names of the boys on the cricket and athletics teams. With the little book came the instruction to learn by heart every name in the book and the promise that you would be subjected to a 'new boys' test'. None except the very bright had a hope of recalling all the names and after failing the 'new boys' test', put to you by a prefect, you were sent off to Major Crankshaw. Typically, the test was given on Sunday evening, the day we went to school for church services, and we would be told to see Major Crankshaw on Monday morning. Perhaps the worst part of the ordeal was the trepidation you felt on that Sunday night, knowing that the next morning you would be punished by the house-master. Everyone knew what form the punishment took. Outside his office, you were never alone and, one by one, we would enter.

'And what have you done wrong?'

'I failed my new boys' test, sir.'

'I am going to give you two of the best.'

He would then reach behind a cupboard, pull out a cane and whack you across the backside or high up on the back of your legs. When he was angry, the blows landed further down your legs and hurt more. It was a grim ordeal, degrading for both the housemaster and the pupils, but to my twelve-year-old eyes he seemed to cope far better with the degradation than we did. This punishment wasn't meted out once or twice in my first year but many times. That little book contained lots of names and, even when you did manage to get it all off by heart, the prefects found other reasons to send you to see Major Crankshaw.

Some of the first years dealt with it better than others. One of my friends in Upper was Adrian Ford and the physical punishment hardly bothered him at all – it was water off a duck's back. He could keep a straight face just long enough to get out of the housemaster's office and then a great big smile would light up his face. Other boys pretended to embrace the culture by saying, 'Thank you, Sir' to Major Crankshaw after receiving their punishment. Even if it might have helped me, I was determined never to say thanks for something I believed was so fundamentally wrong.

There was a boy called Cameron Howie who was very bright and very studious. When he set his mind to learning something off by heart, that's what he did; he didn't forget and he never made a mistake. Through his hard work and with his excellent memory, he threatened to beat the system and always pass the new boys' tests. That wasn't going to be allowed to happen, so he was asked questions that weren't in the book – stuff he couldn't have the answers to – and Cameron joined the rest of us outside Major Crankshaw's office. To me, it was institutional and unwarranted corporal punishment that served no purpose.

At Upper House there was also a culture of bullying. We had a fagging system, whereby a new boy ('a fag') had to work for one of the prefects ('a fag master'). The fag cleaned up the fag master's room, made his bed, cleaned his rugby boots, polished his shoes and did all sorts of menial chores. In return, the fag master looked after his two fags, showed them ways to avoid trouble and taught them how the system worked. If the fag master wasn't pleased with his fags, he could report them to the housemaster or punish them himself. I struck it lucky with my fag master because Craig Rippon was a nice guy who treated his fags – me and another new boy called Richard Smart – kindly. Where possible, Craig protected us. If some other prefect saw us walking on the lawn or committing some small 'offence' that we didn't realize was an offence, he would report us to Craig in the belief that we would then be punished. Craig would sit us down, explain that we had broken a rule and then tell us what we should do in future. More common was the fag master who beat his errant fags.

Perhaps the most ludicrous of all the Upper House practices was the ritual baiting and beating of first-year boys that took place virtually every evening. After dinner, we were expected to pick up litter and clean the changing rooms and corridors after the day's activities. Once that was done, we would assemble inside the changing rooms before proceeding up to the prep room where we would do that evening's homework. Second- and third-year boys would gather along the route of our short journey and, when they shouted 'go', we would sprint to our destination, knowing they had the right to kick us and punch us on the way.

I have never been to the running of the bulls in Pamplona but, from my St Andrew's days, I can imagine it. It might have provided entertainment for the older boys but it wasn't fun for us. Where in the line of stampeding bulls did you place yourself? If you were at the front, you were a target; if you were at the back, you were an easier target. My friend Adrian Ford had a slight limp and mostly ended up near the back so I always tried to avoid being close to him. David Spence, whose father had won a silver medal in the 1960 Rome Olympics at 400 metres, was a very good runner and had the confidence to be at the front, backing himself to avoid most of the blows aimed at him. I tried to get close to David's slipstream but, not being nearly as fast as him, I didn't escape so lightly. To get from the changing room area to the prep room, we ran past Major Crankshaw's house shrieking and shouting.

On different occasions my parents would notice bruising on my arms or legs and, even though I tried to play it down, they were concerned. One morning my father saw the bruises and felt enough was enough. He went to the headmaster at St Andrew's, Mr Arthur Cotton, and asked what on earth was going on? There were dangers for me in my father complaining and, mindful of this, I didn't give up any names but, of course, teachers within the school knew the bullies and three of the more obvious culprits were picked out and caned by the headmaster. My father's efforts to solve the problem just made my life worse. That first year at St Andrew's was terrible and not just for me – plenty of other boys at Upper House suffered exactly the same experience. I suppose the one thing it gave me that was positive was a detestation of bullying. Years later we had an exceptional chief instructor in the SAS, a man who commanded total respect, and nothing disgusted him as much as bullying. Once he detected bullying tendencies in two of the recruits he was training, he watched them closely, confirmed his impressions and immediately kicked them out before they could do any harm.

There was a brutal cycle to the behaviour of Upper House boys at St Andrew's. In first year you were the abused, but in second year you were much less put upon and actually had the licence to mistreat first years. It didn't interest me and when the new boys had to make that hazardous run to the prep room, I made sure I wasn't around. The system revolted me. Often, I would wonder how Major Crankshaw rationalized his use of corporal punishment for what were very minor offences and, in some cases, no offences at all. Perhaps he felt it would harden us and better prepare us for life after school. Upper House enjoyed its reputation for ruggedness; it tended to win inter-house sporting competitions and was the top house for rugby. It goes without saying that when the school's first XV in rugby played its Saturday match, everyone had to attend. There wasn't the same desire to support the hockey team, as it was dismissed as 'mofstok', as in 'mof' for gay and 'stok' for stick.

As the bullying decreased in my second and third years at St Andrew's, so my time there became more bearable. But it was such a waste of my parents' money and that bothered me because I was aware the fees devoured a large part of my father's Navy pension. Over the years I have met many old

Andreans and inevitably end up asking them about their experience of the school. Many have pleasant memories of the school, having been in a different house or gone through the school at a different time. A good friend, Nic Marshall, who would accompany me on many expeditions, didn't experience any bullying at St Andrew's but he wasn't in Upper House and he was at the school fourteen years after I'd left. Michael Walker, a photographer who worked on my Maldives expedition, was at the school at the same time as I was, and he also had bad memories.

Now you will find my name listed with the likes of former Springbok rugby coach Nick Mallett, the current Springbok back row forward Ryan Kankowski and the former South African cricket captain Peter van der Merwe as one of the more famous old Andreans. It is flattering to be thought of as one of the College's distinguished past pupils but, in this case, it doesn't give me any joy. I had the same feeling recently when flicking through a book marking the 150th anniversary of the founding of St Andrew's and finding a photograph of myself diving into the sea off Antarctica. It was written that I have lived up to the St Andrew's motto 'Nec aspera terrent', which means 'Difficulties do not dismay us'. It should have given me enormous pride to see this but, in fact, it didn't. When you have few good memories of a place, it feels uncomfortable to be warmly remembered there. There is one question I would love to put to Major Crankshaw should we meet one day: why was it that in my previous school, Mount House, the pupils were incredibly well behaved and yet there was no corporal punishment but in Upper House, where the cane was constantly used, unruliness was not uncommon?

We left Grahamstown in 1985 because my father needed to be closer to better medical facilities. After some years of not knowing what was causing his forgetfulness and mood changes, his Alzheimer's was diagnosed and we were advised he could get better care in a hospital in Cape Town. We didn't know what awaited us but my memories of that first evening sailing into the harbour on RMS *St Helena* were good and I felt it would be a wonderful place to live. Caroline had just one term remaining at DSG and she remained there as a boarder. All I knew about my new school was that it was called Camps Bay High and it was close to our new house.

Tony Wortham used to say that he could tell what a school was like simply by visiting the toilets. My mind was made up about Camps Bay High School sooner than that. On the morning of my first day, I was perfectly turned out in my new uniform – shirt buttoned to the top, tie neatly positioned, lower jacket button fastened – as if I were at St Andrew's. Entering the school as I was towards the end of my third year, I was very much the new boy and didn't need to draw further attention to myself by wearing the uniform so formally. It wasn't long before I was straightened out. 'Look,' said a girl, introducing herself as Beth, 'loosen the tie, undo the blazer, just chill out.' If there is a better way of helping a new boy to feel comfortable at school, I haven't come across it. Of course it wasn't just friendly Beth, but the school itself that was welcoming. Camps Bay had an atmosphere and an ethos that were perfect for me.

You felt the mood of the school in the corridors. Boys and girls mixed as you would expect them to. The school motto was '*Altissimis nitor*' ('Strive for the highest') and at Camps Bay High School each student really was encouraged to strive for the highest in whatever he or she did. There was a school rugby team but you weren't a lesser person if you weren't good enough or interested enough to make the team, nor did you have to try for the athletics team. If your passion happened to be surfing or acting or cross-country running or chess, you were appreciated every bit as much as the guys on the rugby team. Justin Strong, who was in my class, went on to become the 1991 World Pro-Am Surfing Champion. First, fifth or last – it didn't matter a whit, provided you gave it your best shot. The vibe in the school had its source in a smiling, silver-haired gentleman called John Ince, who had been a teacher at SACS, a well-known school in Cape Town, before becoming headmaster. John knew every pupil by his or her name and made it his business to get to know the parents. If you mention John Ince's name in Cape Town, a smile lights up the faces of those who know him.

Camps Bay High School may be the place of learning with the most spectacular view in the world. It sits on a hill overlooking the rocky Maiden's Cove; a little to the left is the white sand of Camps Bay Beach, but it is the Atlantic that fills your eye. Look out from any part of the school and the ocean spreads out before you, majestic and seemingly endless. I should know because much of my time was spent gazing out, and dreaming the dreams that come from the sea. On the first day of Chris van Jaarsveld's Afrikaans lesson, the desks in our classroom were arranged in a U-shape and, immediately, I had to have one that faced the sea.

Beside me sat Lenjohn van der Wel, who shared my love for the sea and, thankfully, had a better grasp of Afrikaans. He was both my friend and unofficial tutor in the subject. From our desks, we could tell what the wind was doing. If it was a strong, 35-knot wind from the south-east, the sea would look relatively flat but white horses danced on the surface and the spray would be visible all the way to the horizon. The 'southeaster' would whip the top layer of water off the surface. On a summer's day, it could send the water temperature tumbling from a refreshing 16°C to a bitterly cold 10. Then, in winter, the wind came from the north-west and brought with it warm water; the sea could be a lot warmer in winter than in summer. When the 'northwester' was pumping at full throttle, the sea would be fierce and huge waves would crash onto the shore. Like me, Lenjohn looked and saw nothing but the possibilities. He would eventually return to Holland, where his parents came from, and end up taking part in a transatlantic sailing race.

Our house in Camps Bay was a five-minute walk from the school: up a short road, through a small wooded area, across a dried-out riverbed and on to the school's one playing field. Our home was more or less on the same elevated level as the school. From my bedroom, I could hear waves crash onto the rocks below. On very windy nights I would lie in my bed and wonder if the wind was going to blow the windows in or even lift the roof clean off our house. When school ended, the place I most wanted to be was in the sea: swimming, trying to improve my balance on my surf ski and running on the beach. What existed beyond the horizon fascinated me even more than what I could see. How could Portuguese sailors, five hundred years before, have dared to sail around the Cape of Good Hope in search of a passage to the east? I looked out on windy days and marvelled at the bravery of men in small wooden ships. It never surprised me that Bartholomew Diaz, after becoming the first man to sail round the Cape, named it the Cape of Storms. Prince Henry of Portugal would later change it to the Cape of Good Hope, and eventually Vasco da Gama found a route round the Cape and onwards to the east.

Looking out, I knew that Antarctica was 5,000 kilometres south and that some day I would get there. For what reason, I wasn't certain, but there was no doubt in my mind that I would go. I imagined the great ice shelves, the tabular blocks of ice, the penguins, the blue glaciers carving into the sea and whales feeding on krill. Sir Francis Drake came from

Tavistock in Devon, close to where I had lived, and his circumnavigation of the world in the sixteenth century earned him a page in history. Another man from that same part of the West Country was Captain Robert Scott who, in 1912, led an ill-fated expedition to the South Pole. It had been my favourite story as a child. One of the last paragraphs from the Ladybird book my mother read to me ran as follows: 'With fingers that could scarcely hold the pencil, Captain Scott made the last entries in his diary. "Had we lived," he wrote, "I would have a tale to tell of hardihood, endurance and courage of my companions which would have stirred the heart of every Englishman. These rough notes and our dead bodies must tell the tale."' Once I found myself living at the southern tip of Africa, with only the ocean between me and Antarctica, I was sure my destiny was to go there and see what Scott had seen.

Though the dream was very real, there was nothing to support it. What can a boy or teenager do that suggests he will one day travel to Antarctica and push boundaries? So far-fetched was the vision that I didn't tell anyone. It stayed locked in the vault of my inner life, real to me but unseen by everyone else. Though it was clear to me that I would do something special, that wasn't necessarily how others saw my life unfolding. Until I learned to bring intense discipline and application to my work, I was no more than a slightly-better-than-average student.

Camps Bay High School was a magical place. For physical education, our teacher would take us to the beach, mark out a pitch in the sand and organize us into teams for touch rugby. Afterwards we warmed down with a swim in the Atlantic. And for somebody who had come from a macho all-boys school in Grahamstown, the girls at my new school were something else. I fell in love with one in particular: her name was Antoinette Malherbe and she was the most beautiful girl in the whole school. In history class, she would sit at the desk directly in front of me and I would gently tug on her ponytail and pretend it wasn't me. I suppose it's no surprise my love wasn't reciprocated but Antoinette and I did become friends. As well as being gorgeous, she also had personality and the attention of all the older boys in the school. A bit like my dreams of getting to Antarctica, my crush on Antoinette was a dream best kept to myself.

For a school that had such a pleasant and relaxed ambience, Camps Bay was also good academically. Two students from my class ended up getting into Cambridge University, five went on to do medicine and many went to the University of Cape Town, which is arguably Africa's best university. But it is not for academic reasons that the school is so fondly remembered. What distinguished the school was its innate decency, its respect for individuals and the same ability 'to temper learning and duty with a sense of proportion' that distinguished Tony Wortham's school.

In my final year my class was called 10CVJ after our Afrikaans' teacher, Chris van Jaarsveld. Without a grounding in Afrikaans, it was the subject I found hardest, and that was a potential problem because I had to pass Afrikaans to matriculate and continue on to university. Concerned that Afrikaans would be a problem, my mother had a meeting with John Ince and Chris and was reassured by Chris saying, 'I have had worse students than Lewis in Afrikaans and they have got through.'

Chris had AIDS and was one of the first South Africans to be diagnosed with the disease. He had to go into hospital at different times for treatment and John Ince wrote a letter to our parents telling them about Chris's situation. Knowing far less about AIDS then than we do now, some of the parents were concerned about pupils being at risk of infection. Chris's condition worsened, his physical appearance deteriorated and seeing him go into decline was one of the saddest things. He would miss days when he wasn't well but then would reappear until, eventually, he missed a couple of weeks and we were told he had passed away. A new teacher came but we remembered Chris. And he was proven right in the end: I did pass Afrikaans.

Back in Cape Town, years after I'd left Camps Bay High School, I met John Ince a number of times and talked about the old days. We swapped stories about what we'd both done with our lives since he'd retired as headmaster and I'd graduated from the law faculty at UCT. It pleased him that I had made the most of some good opportunities and I teased him that he couldn't have predicted the path I eventually followed. 'Lewis,' he disagreed, 'the one thing that stood out was your determination. You were special.'

Looking back, that's not really what I saw. Every year it was my intention to do a little better than the year before and, in the back of my mind, there was an inner confidence that I would get to university and make something of my life. There was something I had that, in hindsight, I believe was more important than determination. It was well captured in an advert made by one of my sponsors, Investec, years later. It depicts a scene in Antarctica with me walking on sea ice past a line of penguins walking in the opposite direction. Going against the tide has never been difficult for me. It wasn't even a conscious decision but the natural consequence of following my own instinct.

4

INTO THE SEA

My love of the water developed in the swimming pool Dad built at the house we bought in Grahamstown. I wasn't that interested in swimming lengths; even when I had to do them to prepare for some future swim, they weren't something I enjoyed much. In the pool in our Grahamstown garden, I spent hours under the water, pushing off from one side, seeing if I could get to the other without taking a breath and then trying to do a few lengths without surfacing. More time in the water brought greater ease. I taught myself to somersault underwater, do handstands and perform all kinds of tricks on my polystyrene board. I found that no matter how long I spent in the water, it was never enough. Being underwater felt as natural to me as walking in the garden. In winter, the water temperature dropped to a level too cold for any normal person but my father would still do his daily lengths and I would travel beside him on my board, my legs and arms freezing, thinking I had discovered absolute agony.

When I started at Camps Bay, being part of the 'in group' didn't register on my radar. I had good friends but I never cared about being part of the gang or being seen as cool. I was the guy who went off and did his own thing, which at that time was to join the Clifton Life-Saving Club. Clifton Beach was just down from Camps Bay and I loved going to the club, swimming in the sea, paddling my surf ski, running on the beach and being on life-saving duty. In no time I passed the Surf Proficiency Award by proving that I could swim out to sea and rescue people.

Each life-saving club in Cape Town had the right to submit a few members for training to become part of an elite helicopter rescue team. I was seventeen; you had to be twenty-one and so desperate was I to do this course that I lied about my age. Training took place in my final year at Camps Bay, when school exams seemed life-defining, and my poor mother was beside herself with worry. Her husband was hospitalized with Alzheimer's, her daughter was working her way through her first year at university and her son, who had his final examinations the following month, was jumping from helicopters when he should have been studying.

'Mum, this is really important,' I said, 'this is the one opportunity I have to be chosen for the helicopter team.'

I made the chopper squad and remember one occasion when we were called out to a horrible accident involving the former great Springbok rugby player Rob Louw. During a speedboat race, Rob had fallen out and been hit by a following boat. We flew up the coast to Langebaan. One of Rob's arms had been almost severed. His face was grey and he had lost a huge amount of blood. A doctor sat by him, his hand inside Rob's armpit, clamping a severed artery. Getting a man as big as Rob onto the stretcher and into the small Bell Jet Ranger chopper wasn't simple, and we worried that he might not survive the journey back to Cape Town. The doctor took my place in the helicopter for that journey and

I travelled back with Rob's wife, Azille. Thankfully it all ended well, as the arm was sewn back together and Rob made a good recovery.

Another time we were sent up to Melkbos Beach, north of Cape Town. A diver had disappeared and it was feared a shark might have taken him. His distraught girlfriend was on the beach when we landed and she pointed to where he had last been seen. After patrolling up and down for a long time we spotted a red buoy used by divers and hoped that it might provide a clue. I volunteered to jump into the sea and was petrified as I held my breath and followed the rope down into very dark water. When you fear that a shark has been in the area and attacked a human, it's hard to escape the thought that he might still be in the neighbourhood and feeling peckish. I went down as quickly as my body would take me and got to the end of the rope but found nothing, so I got them to hoist me out of there quicker than you'd believe. Sadly, the diver was never found.

Being involved with the life-saving community was an extension of my love for the sea and the joy of swimming in it. From day to day, the ocean changed: one time calm and almost still, the next day it would be rough and threatening. The temperature changed too, depending on the wind. Although I wasn't the world's most technically gifted swimmer, I was strong and good in the water. Nothing thrilled me more than gliding over the surface and seeing the fish beneath, or the kelp, or just the plain sandy bottom. Sometimes the view was so wondrous I would stop swimming and lie face down on the surface, watching everything below and feeling so privileged. Racing people didn't really interest me because the battle was always against the elements. A gusty southeaster, blowing hard into your face, is enough of a rival for any swimmer. Even on the toughest days, I loved the sensation of pulling the water back, taking a breath and hearing the water splash on my ear as my arm came through to take another stroke. Yes, I loved all that. I still do.

When it came to swimming, I wasn't one who learned to walk before he tried to run. At the age of seventeen, tall, skinny and not very strong, I decided to swim from Robben Island, where the former president Nelson Mandela was once imprisoned, to Cape Town. It is seven kilometres and, because of the generally low temperature of the water, it can be a tough swim. If the wind blows, it can be virtually impossible for the inexperienced or underprepared swimmer. Fifty-two people had done the Robben Island to Cape Town swim before I threw my teenage hat in the ring. Most people thought I was taking on too much and, if I'd appreciated exactly what was involved, I would have agreed with them.

Training consisted of a month working with coach Paul Barrett Smith at the Camps Bay High School pool. This was the first time I had received proper swimming lessons. 'Fast guys on the right, others on the left,' said Paul. The ultra-quick Steven Klugman was far right, while I was on the far left. Fellow pupil Barry Diamond, who played water polo, heard what the plan was and said, 'Lewis, you'll never make it.' Barry wasn't the kind of guy who would doubt himself. I just banked his dismissal, knowing that when the going got tougher his lack of faith would keep me going. Even though Paul was totally supportive, secretly he also probably doubted I would make it. Their doubts would, in part, have been fuelled by the thinness of my physique, which is no help when swimming long distances in cold water – something I would soon realize. The first of May 1987 was the day appointed for the Robben Island swim and my parents drove me down to the Oceania Power Boat Club, where I'd agreed to meet the guys from the Cape Long Distance Swimming

Association. If it's to be ratified, each long swim must be supervised by the CLDSA.

Tony Scalabrino skippered the boat; his daughter Maxine and the founder and President of the CLDSA, Peter Bales, were there, as were a number of other long-distance swimming enthusiasts. I would have liked my parents to come, but on the small boat there wasn't room. Luckily for me the day was windless and the sea perfectly calm. Looking into the water, your reflection stared back at you. If ever an underprepared, inexperienced and naive teenager was going to swim from Robben Island to the designated finishing point, Blouberg Beach, this was the day. Not that the guys on the boat believed I would make it because they, too, were concerned about my leanness and relatively light preparation. They called me 'the Biafran' because I was so thin and were agreed that you couldn't swim for three hours in cold water with my physique and lack of preparation.

At this time, 1987, South Africa's apartheid system was in place and Robben Island was home to two prisons: one for political prisoners and the other for criminals. Before we were allowed to start, prison guards came, paperwork and documentation were checked and we were then given permission to proceed to a run-down jetty covered in bird droppings where I would begin the swim. On a beach near the jetty, a group of black prisoners worked with armed guards standing nearby. They smiled and waved as I waded into the water and I did the same in return. Always at the start of a long swim, you think of your preparation and torture yourself for not having done more. If I could have beamed myself away from Robben Island at that moment, I would have done so. Peter Bales swam the first hour with me, which was a help, but about halfway across I began to flag.

It was not because of the distance or tiredness but the

coldness that started at my extremities and gradually worked its way into my body. Breathing on my right side, I would glance up at Table Mountain in the distance, think how extraordinarily beautiful it looked from the sea, and in that way try to keep my mind off the cold. By the standards of the Cape, the water wasn't especially cold; I simply wasn't well enough prepared. For the last hour, it was a protracted hell. A tall block of flats at Blouberg Beach was my target but no matter how many strokes I made they wouldn't come closer. Coldness saps your energy, so at different moments in that last hour I would switch to breaststroke, slowing my progress even further. But I kept on going, one stroke at a time. Towards the end, the guys in the boat got behind me and that helped. When they realized I was going to do it, they offered plenty of encouragement, and Eddie Cassar swam ashore with me. When my feet touched the sand, I smashed my fist into the water and shouted, 'Yes!' I will never forget that feeling of pure joy. All those who said I couldn't do it, what did they have to say now? There would be difficult and far more challenging long-distance swims in my future, but none would give me the same sense of exultation as that first one.

The next day the swim was announced at the school assembly and, for a morning, I was lorded. 'Lewis, what was it like?' I was asked. The following weekend the CLDSA held their annual dinner and I was presented with a bronze medal that goes to all who complete the Robben Island swim. It pictured a swimmer with Table Mountain in the background. That night it sat on my bedside table and it was such a thrill to see it there on waking up the next morning. My parents had waited on Big Bay Blouberg and sadly missed my arrival into Small Bay Blouberg but we were soon reunited and it was obvious to me that they were pleased, although it was not my father's way to make a big fuss. A few days later I heard him talking to a friend on the phone about the swim and how proud he was of what I had achieved. Three hours were spent in the water and, for me, they seemed like the three most worthwhile hours of my life. The challenge had pushed me to my limits but I loved it. It had been physically shattering and totally addictive.

Five years later apartheid ended and Robben Island was transformed from a prison to a popular tourist destination. People wanted to see where Nelson Mandela had been imprisoned for eighteen years. An ex-inmate working now as a guide showed us around when I visited and was asked about the part of prison life he'd found the most difficult; he replied it was when the guards' families came to visit and he heard children laughing and playing. That led him to think of his own children, who were only allowed to visit once a year, and brought unbearable sadness. It felt like someone had kicked me in the stomach, as my mind flashed back to that first of May 1987, when I'd cheerfully waved to the prisoners and had no idea what they were going through. What must they have thought of the white boy who could wade into the water and swim all the way to Cape Town and freedom? The memory of that first Robben Island swim now comes with regret that in my youth and innocence I didn't see any insensitivity in beginning my swimming career in a place that was a bastion of the apartheid system.

But then South Africa was a very different country twenty years ago.

5

AFRICAN ROOTS

We buried my father in the Commonwealth War Graves Cemetery in Simon's Town, near the old Royal Navy base not far from Cape Town. The cemetery was close to the sea and had been a burial place for Royal Navy sailors dating back to the 1800s. My father was laid to rest between two non-commissioned officers and I felt that was as it should be: in death an admiral is no different to the lowest-ranking sailor. Each of us comes into the world with nothing, and when we leave it doesn't much matter what rank we take with us. It was significant that my father was buried in South Africa because it created a stronger bond with the country I had always considered my second home. You cannot easily cut ties with a place where your loved ones are buried.

As a wide-eyed ten-year-old arriving into Cape Town harbour in 1980, I knew little about South Africa and understood nothing of the apartheid system then enshrined in South African law. There might have been television pictures I'd seen of anti-apartheid protests in London but I arrived with little more than a sense that there were black people and white people in South Africa. Ours was not a political family and whether it was his Royal Navy training or just his inclination, my father didn't discuss politics much. He once told a story about visiting South Africa in the late 1970s and how disgusted he'd been to turn up at a hotel and be told that his black driver could not be lodged under the same roof as a white man. But that seemed more a bad personal experience than a statement about the great injustice of apartheid.

The night before we disembarked in Cape Town, the RMS *St Helena* anchored in the sea, a few miles from Robben Island where Nelson Mandela was imprisoned at the time. How little I knew. In Grahamstown, Cameron Howie and Andre Smalberger were friends who attended St Andrew's College. Both were sons of judges, and when there were political trials you would see an unmarked police car travel behind the Howies or Smalbergers as they made the school run. It was a bit different to how things had been in the West of England but, beyond that, the system didn't impinge on my little world. Unlike Cameron and Andre, who were brought to and from school by car, I walked or cycled even though it was nearly an hour's walk. 'Walking is good for you,' my father would say and he was not wrong about that.

As a private, fee-paying school, St Andrew's could accept students regardless of their colour, so it had a sprinkling of black students who were sons of political leaders in the South African government-created homelands. Camps Bay High School on the other hand was a state school and therefore subject to the apartheid laws that decreed total segregation in education, so Camps Bay was an all-white school.

Growing older and more inquisitive, I began to notice the infrastructure of apartheid. On Camps Bay Beach, where I swam almost every day, there was a sign on the grass verge that said: 'WHITE PERSONS ONLY – This beach and the amenities thereof have been reserved for white persons only. By order of the Provincial Secretary.' Similar signs were to be found on public toilets, park benches, public swimming pools and any number of public amenities. There was another sign I remember that said: 'Europeans Only' and that struck me as strange – weren't we in Africa? Up from Camps Bay Beach, in fact directly under the hill upon which our school was built, lay a rocky outcrop called Maiden's Cove. It was for non-whites and, though black people would go there and have barbecues, it was very unsafe for swimming.

How did we live a normal life in such an abnormal society? I'm not sure but the truth is we did. It was all we knew and it didn't seem like it would ever change. Through the first ten years, I didn't have one non-white friend. When we sat on the lovely white sand of Camps Bay Beach and someone said how unfair it was that black people were confined to rocky Maiden's Cove, someone else would say black people didn't see it like that because they really weren't interested in swimming. Ways were found to distort the truth. I have taught swimming to children in many places, but I've never seen kids who liked to swim as much as the black children in Soweto.

At the end of my time at Camps Bay, the choice was between going straight to university or doing my two years of compulsory National Service. If you asked for a deferral to study you would normally get it but I took the same approach as my father: if there is something unpleasant to deal with, get it over and done with. So I opted to do my National Service before university. It was 1988, two years before apartheid would be dramatically dismantled and obligatory National Service for white men was abolished. My love for the sea meant I wanted to serve in the South African Navy and that's what I did.

During my first year, I served on the South Africa Ship (SAS) *Protea*, a hydrographic vessel that surveyed the seabed off the coast of what was South West Africa and would soon become Namibia. Working a few miles out from the magnificent Skeleton Coast, we were also on the lookout for Russian reconnaissance planes. At the time Russia was supporting the liberation movement, SWAPO, and government forces in Angola against South Africa and we were told that anyone spotting a Russian plane would receive a week's paid leave. I spent hours on the bridge, staring into the empty skies, waiting for that Russian plane to come jetting past. It would have served me better to savour the magnificent sand dunes that stood sentry along the coastline.

Life on SAS *Protea* also introduced me to some of the realities of a society organized along racial lines. The commanding officers of the ship were white but the majority of the crew was non-white. As a conscripted sailor, experiencing Navy life for the first time, I was the lowest rank. That meant spending lots of time in the bowels of the ship, where sometimes I was the only white and my immediate superior was Leading Seaman Africa, a coloured sailor who felt every unpleasant job should be given to me. Filthy toilets were my responsibility, so too was vomit in the passageways, and at times it seemed as though Leading Seaman Africa was silently taunting me, seeing if I would react. From where he was standing, the boot was on the other foot now and he was happy to put it into me. It was hard work, but it didn't really bother me. How many non-whites in South Africa had been treated throughout their lives as I was treated on the SAS *Protea*? That was why I wound my neck in when Leading Seaman Africa told me to do the toilets again. What was a week or a month or even two months of being a second-class citizen compared to a lifetime? I got on with it, didn't complain and tried not to give the impression I resented it. Occasionally one of the white officers would see what was going on and stop it but mostly they weren't around and Leading Seaman Africa had the freedom to do as he pleased. They say adversity introduces a man to his inner self but the treatment I received reminded me more of what others had endured. And I definitely wasn't so proud that I couldn't endure a little hardship.

After serving six months on SAS *Protea*, I drew the longest straw available when I was transferred to the South African Navy Museum to give guided tours to tourists. It was not exactly life-threatening military life but it was easy, there was plenty of time off and, as the museum was just a 20-minute journey from our home in Cape Town, it was very convenient too. Commander William Bisset ran the museum and was generous and encouraging. 'Lewis,' he used to say, 'when you've done your National Service, you make sure you go to university.'

Aware of my ambitions as a long-distance swimmer, the Navy allowed me time to train and in return I taught life-saving to National Servicemen. Working with the helicopter rescue team, I realized the need for paramedical training and worked weekends in the Accident and Emergency Department of Tygerberg Hospital in the northern suburbs of Cape Town. It was pretty chaotic, with hundreds of people needing treatment every Friday and Saturday night. Typically, people were injured in car crashes, knife fights, shootings and more random violence. Not surprisingly, the demand for medical care exceeded the supply. It was an eye-opening experience. On my first evening, the doctor in charge took a piece of sponge and cut it in two, got a needle and suture, said, 'This is how you must do it' and stitched the two pieces of sponge back together. There was a long, long line of people waiting to be treated, many of them needing to have knife or glass wounds cleaned and stitched, and I was straight into it. On other occasions I set up drips and made myself useful to the doctor but for many weekends I just stitched people up. Most of those needing treatment were from townships. Though I was almost twenty and had lived for ten years in South Africa, I had never been to a township. Tygerberg Hospital was an important part of my education.

It was the suddenness of the change that caught everyone by surprise. For years South Africa had been a pariah in the eyes of the world. Everyone outside the country and the vast majority of those inside wanted the system of apartheid abolished. Yet when it finally *was* abolished, the reaction was: 'Wow, I can't believe it's happened.' Change came on 2 February 1990, the opening day of the South African Parliament, and the voice was that of the President, F. W. de Klerk. 'We are unbanning the ANC, we are unbanning the PAC [Pan African Congress], we are unbanning the SA Communist Party . . .' he said. De Klerk also announced that Nelson Mandela, leader of the ANC, would be released from prison. Archbishop Desmond Tutu, who had fought against apartheid for decades, listened to the President's declaration and said, 'He has taken my breath away.'

Nine days later, on a beautiful summer's day, Nelson Mandela walked free from Victor Verster Prison in the small wine-making town of Paarl in the Western Cape. Twenty-seven years of imprisonment were over and Mandela's release triggered an outpouring of emotion that showed what change meant to the vast majority of South Africa's population. On the 100-kilometre drive from Paarl to Cape Town, hundreds of thousands came to the roadsides to greet a man seen as the natural leader of the new South Africa. Intrigued by what was happening, I had little understanding of it. Politics, especially the modern politics of South Africa, was a subject that I hadn't explored. Even though history had been one of my favourite school subjects, the syllabus didn't cover the ANC, Nelson Mandela, their struggle and the justification for treating non-whites as second-class citizens in South Africa. The day after his release, Mandela spoke from a balcony at City Hall in Cape Town and, though his public speaking did not carry the power of a Martin Luther King Jr or a John F. Kennedy, he came across as a man of great substance and integrity. What was truly inspiring was the absence of bitterness and the refusal to seek any form of retribution. People listened to Nelson Mandela and believed South Africa could become a peaceful democracy. Some whites feared violent reprisals and considered emigration the safest bet. They left for England, Australia, the US or Canada mostly. Not knowing anything about Mandela, some wondered if South Africa was about to re-enact the scene from *Doctor Zhivago* in which the Commissar arrives and says, 'This house is now owned by the state.'

At the time of de Klerk's speech to Parliament and Mandela's subsequent release, I had begun a five-year law degree at the University of Cape Town. For years UCT had been a liberal university. In the two years of my National Service, there had been many anti-government demonstrations on campus and the police, with sjamboks and tear gas, had made their presence felt. Now all had changed, the sjamboks were being put to one side and South Africa's future was being debated everywhere. There were two schools of thought: one was that the transition would take place peacefully and South Africa would become the rainbow nation of our dreams. The second view was that violence was inevitable, white people would be targeted, and the sensible thing to do was to sell up and get out. That wasn't easy because the new government did not want wealth taken out of the country and laws were already in place making it very difficult to do so.

*

My choice of university course was between history and law and, thinking longer term, I opted to do law. It was the right decision. At the time, the system in South Africa meant you had to do an undergraduate BA degree for three years and then a two-year law degree, the LLB. Politics and law were my undergraduate subjects but you also had to do English, Afrikaans and Latin. Just so we didn't get the idea that university was going to be all fun, our week started with a lecture on the history of Afrikaans literature at 8 a.m. on Monday. But by now I was beginning to get to grips with Afrikaans and, as I improved at the language, the classes became more interesting.

It was in the Afrikaans' lecture, on that first Monday, that I met David Becker, who would become my best friend. He was slightly built but obviously athletic and very energetic. Squash was his big game and he was one of those runners who saw a marathon as a standard challenge – the 90-kilometre Comrades Marathon was more to his liking. Friendly, outgoing and with a zest for life, he was one of the most popular guys in our year and an avid sports' follower. Rugby, cricket, football, American football and golf were particular passions but it only needed one human competing against another to get him interested. His days were more full than most people's, yet he found the time to get involved with a student fundraising programme that helped the disadvantaged. David had spent a year in a school in the USA on an exchange programme and had that worldliness that comes from travelling. We both felt it was a fascinating time to be law students in South Africa.

The first free democratic election in South Africa took place after apartheid was dismantled. It was a momentous day, 27 April 1994. Some students from my class at UCT worked at polling stations and the university closed for the day, ensuring everyone had the opportunity to vote. My polling booth was at Jan van Riebeeck High School in the Gardens, a suburb not far from the centre of Cape Town. When I got there, a long line had already formed inside the school and was meandering out into the schoolyard. There was a joy all around. Instead of the usual irritation when people have to queue, there was euphoria. People from every background stood in line, chatting excitedly, a few people were actually dancing and everyone felt they were part of a day they would never forget. For all of us, it was the first time we'd stood together in South Africa as equals and it was liberating. There was also irony in the setting because Jan van Riebeeck, after whom the school was named, was the first white settler in South Africa.

With so much joy and optimism in the air, I wanted the queue to move slowly but, alas, it was all too well organized and the line moved quickly. Whenever I wonder about South Africa's future, I think back to that April day in 1994 and recall the belief and the optimism felt and expressed by so many. On that day there was no violence. Desmond Tutu called it a miracle and coined the term 'Rainbow Nation' to describe the multiracial coming together in the new South Africa. Even then, we were all conscious that the peaceful transition to democracy happened because of Nelson Mandela's willingness to forgive and a charisma that inspired so many others.

After the election came the drawing up of a new constitution. By then, I was in my fourth year as a law student and studying Constitutional Law. We talked about what rights should be enshrined in the new constitution: the right to life and the right to freedom of speech, freedom of religion, freedom of movement? We argued over the death penalty and to what extent the right to education, healthcare and housing should be absolute. Our new political leaders and constitutional lawyers were having the same debates. Some of our lecturers assisted in writing the new constitution, thus enabling us to feel connected to this great moment in South African history.

Though the transition was mostly peaceful, there were murders and violence. Adrian Ford, my old friend from the Eastern Cape, arrived home one day to find his father murdered. Often living in isolated places, farmers were most vulnerable. The killing of Adrian's dad hit home because as a young boy I had camped on the farm and Mr Ford had driven Adrian and me wherever we wanted to go. I visited Adrian after the murder and saw the revolver strapped to his leg, which he felt was now necessary, and I thought not all the changes in South Africa were for the better. Near where we lived in Camps Bay, a lady was murdered. Another lady was raped and then brutally murdered by five men in nearby Seapoint. Such crimes created a terrible fear and drove many white people away.

Though many young white people left South Africa around this time, fears about the future of the country were nothing more than a marginal factor in my decision to return to England. I believed in the country. What doubt existed was created by a holiday in Zimbabwe in 1996, not long before I eventually departed for England. Driving through the Zimbabwean countryside, admiring the beauty, I suddenly heard sirens. Coming down the other side of the road was a presidential motorcade. There seemed to be a hundred or more police and army shepherding him. There were guns everywhere and the police outriders, travelling at the front, were aggressively forcing oncoming cars to pull to the side of the road. What struck me was that when President Mugabe drove past in his state car, none of the people by the roadside cheered or welcomed him. There was plenty of evidence of poverty and hunger in the countryside and I wondered what had happened to a nation that had once boasted a very efficient agricultural economy. Would this become South Africa's future? As much as I believed South Africa's situation was very different, there was also the thought that Nelson Mandela was the glue that held the country together. What would happen when he was gone?

6

PUSHING BOUNDARIES

In South Africa it is common for students, especially those in the cities, to continue to live at home while attending university. So I, too, lived at home during my student days and it meant I could continue my life-saving work and swim as often as I wanted. I drove to and from UCT and generally was back home by four o'clock in the afternoon. I would swim every day and take once-a-week runs to the top of Table Mountain. All the time, I was becoming stronger. To give my training focus, I always wanted some project on the horizon. After that gruelling first Robben Island swim, I planned a swim from Robben Island to Cape Town, followed immediately by a run to the top of Table Mountain, and I started to train specifically for that.

It went well – at least, sort of well. The plan was to swim from Robben Island to Three Anchor Bay, then jump out and run to the top of Table Mountain. Volunteers from the CLDSA supervised the swim. Their willingness to help people do long-distance swims in the Cape area is a good example of the volunteerism that underpins amateur sport. Tony Scalabrino skippered his boat on that swim to Three

Anchor Bay and would accept nothing from me except the price of his fuel. I was indebted to both him and the CLDSA. Halfway across, I picked up on minor disharmony in the boat, as people talked and argued about the best route to Three Anchor Bay. When you're in the water and sense that the guys in the boat are not sure where they're going, it's disconcerting at first and then deeply frustrating. And they did get themselves into a muddle, because we ended up not at Three Anchor Bay but at Rocklands, a small bay further down the coast and so rocky Tony couldn't bring the boat ashore. By my estimation, the mistake kept me in the water for about an hour longer than necessary. Unable to land at Rocklands, Tony went off to the nearest slipway, taking with him my running shoes, which were still on the boat. Desperate to get on with it, I set off barefoot for Table Mountain and had run almost ten kilometres by the time my mum caught up in the car with the missing shoes.

Afterwards it was hard to know which was greater, my tiredness or the rawness on the soles of my feet. I was also conscious that lessons needed to be learned. Although the confusion over the route from Robben Island hadn't stopped me achieving my goal, it had made it more difficult and could have destroyed everything. The lesson was straightforward. The guys on the boat weren't to blame because it was I who decided with whom I travelled and it was I who had to take full responsibility for things going wrong. In planning the swim and run, I was confident my team would be able to get me to Three Anchor Bay and didn't for a second think there would be a problem. I got it wrong and vowed that in future more attention would be given to assembling the right team and preparing them adequately for the event.

*

Each challenge was the creator of the next. After the swim and run, I wanted to do a swim, a run and a cycle along the lines of an ultra-triathlon. Robben Island was again the starting point and the seven-kilometre swim to Blouberg Beach was much less difficult than it had been for the pencil-thin seventeen-year-old three years before. Kevin Fialkov, who had taken over as my swimming coach, accompanied me on the swim that day, and both of us got through it in a comfortable two and a half hours. The run from Blouberg to the top of Table Mountain was approximately 30 kilometres but, as the last 1,000 metres was steeply uphill, it was harder than that. Adding greatly to the difficulty of the run and cycle was the searing heat – temperatures were close to 40°C – and, of course, I wondered how healthy it was to be running and cycling in such conditions. Thoughts like that are banished as soon as they surface because you're really just searching for a weakness that will enable you to slow down or stop. At the summit, I had to run down to the Table Mountain Road, located 500 metres below, and from there I set off on my 70-kilometre cycle to Cape Point. On that downhill run I slipped and dislocated the middle finger of my left hand. When your body is warm and the adrenalin is flowing, you don't think for too long in those situations. I quickly pulled the finger back into place and carried on. Now, two decades later, I'm reminded of the fall by the slight crookedness in the finger and, on cold days, the touch of arthritis that affects it.

Swimming, running and cycling, it took me twelve hours and every last ounce of energy to get me to Cape Point. Kevin Fialkov's son Laurie drove the car behind me on the cycle to make sure that if I collapsed there was someone around to sweep me up and take me home. That night I was too exhausted to sleep properly and, whenever I did drop off, a recurring nightmare had me back on the bike, struggling towards Cape Point. When it woke me, I didn't know whether to be happy knowing that it was all over or disappointed I wasn't getting to sleep.

As majestic as the great Cape Peninsula landmarks are I now longed to take on a challenge beyond South Africa's borders and started looking through *The Times Atlas of the World* for some new frontier to cross. To me the great lakes of Central Africa – Lake Tanganyika, Lake Victoria and Lake Malawi – were particularly interesting. Because of its elongated shape, I began to consider the possibility of swimming across Lake Malawi. No one had ever done it, which might have had something to do with the numbers of hippos and crocodiles that call Lake Malawi home.

At this time I was swimming in the outdoor, seawater swimming pool at Seapoint and had come to know Otto Thaning, a heart surgeon from Cape Town. Otto was the most technically gifted swimmer I had ever seen. He is almost thirty years older than I am, but if you watched him glide through the water, making graceful yet powerful strokes, you wouldn't have thought it. Saying Otto didn't look his age was like Noah looking out from his Ark and saying, 'It looks like rain.'

Otto had trained under Dr Christiaan Barnard, who performed the world's first heart transplant in 1967 and as a result became one of the most famous people in the world. Chris Barnard, with his boyish good looks, was thought of as 'the film star surgeon'. When Otto recalled his time with Chris and a friendship that endured until Chris's death in September 2001, you just listened in fascination.

'In terms of intellect, Chris was exceptional,' Otto said. 'He was also very charismatic but the thing that separated him from everybody else was his driven nature. He accepted only 100 per cent, from himself and from those with whom he worked. With Chris, it was not that less than 100 per cent wasn't good enough but that if he didn't get it, a vibrant, electric shock went through him and you knew about it. In some respects, he was at times almost impossible to work with. I was one of the very few who spent their entire training working under him; others got broken down, some left for a time and came back, others never came back. I ended up having a good relationship with him and, when he retired from public medicine, a group of us from his original unit went into private practice together. When he passed away, the hospital we worked at in Cape Town changed its name to the Christiaan Barnard Memorial Hospital in his honour.

'Chris had the sharpest mind of any man I had ever known. Technically, he was a good surgeon but what made him different to everyone else was his ability to operate and think at the same time. Most surgeons, especially in cardiac work, which can be complicated, like to stop and think and draw up battle plans and then proceed. Chris didn't need to do that. He was the one to do the first transplant because he had the courage to do it. There were at least two other surgeons in the US who were ready but, in my opinion, they just didn't have the guts. If they failed, they would have been academically and professionally dead. Chris wasn't going to be held back by fear, because he had an inner force that overcame everything. When he walked into a room, people turned their heads and said, "Who is that?" He had an incredible presence, an aura you couldn't miss. I often think how lucky I was to have been able to work with him, know him, like him and ultimately survive him – because you had to survive Chris.

'He came from a humble background. He was the son of a Dutch Reformed Church pastor in the small town of Beaufort West in the Western Cape who found himself thrust onto a pedestal and suddenly everyone wanted his opinion: about the afterlife, the soul, psychology, astrology. He used to say, "I know nothing about these things but they expect me to have the answers." It didn't matter how many times he said it wasn't his area of expertise, others came along with similar requests. In the end Chris probably started to believe he was extraordinary. If all the most beautiful girls in the world and the great and the good of society come to you, then you can be forgiven if you end up thinking you are special. In a way, I think Chris was seduced by fame. He acknowledged that once to me, and expressed regret that he had not spent more of his later years with his patients.

'Then, of course, you got the awful cycle of failing marriages and broken dreams. As mortals, we like gods; we create them, put them up there and, when we get them as high as we can, we start to tear them down. Marilyn Monroe, Elvis Presley, people like that – we create them to destroy them. Late in his life, after the divorce from Karin, his third wife, Chris became quite lonely. I remember going to see him alone in his apartment and taking him back to the hospital to see an operation that a colleague of mine was performing and being so cheered to see him totally absorbed in his familiar environment. It was gratifying to see the passion ignited once more in those shining eyes because that was the Chris I knew.'

As a student, Otto had captained the Transvaal swim team and was one of the best in the country but his medical career came first. What he didn't lose was his love of the water. When I suggested swimming across Lake Malawi, he jumped at the idea.

The plan was for me to travel to Malawi a couple of days before Otto and attempt to hire the boat, arrange some of the logistics and find out what I could about the difficulties we would face. In all, four of us would make the trip to Malawi: me and my girlfriend at the time, Kim Howard, followed by Otto and Peter Bales from the CLDSA. We flew into Lilongwe and travelled from there to Salima, a town on the western shore of the lake that would be our base camp.

A classmate at UCT, Kim was like Otto in that she had a sense of adventure. Like me, she had very little money. She raised the money for the flight by waitressing at a restaurant in Hout Bay. We shopped around for the cheapest tent money could buy. Kim suggested we each get a little synthetic mattress; in the end we got one mattress that she would use – that's how tight our finances were.

After landing at Lilongwe we hitch-hiked the hundred-odd kilometres to Salima and were blown away by the friendliness and generosity of the people. We never had long to wait for a ride and, of course, there were plenty because everyone was going just to the next village. Perhaps comparisons aren't fair but, coming from South Africa, it was impossible for us not to make them. Here were people who had not grown up under a repressive regime and it showed. Malawi is one of the poorest countries in Africa, yet I've never seen another country in which a smile seemed to be the national symbol. In between lifts we wouldn't be standing at the roadside for more than a minute before groups of children would gather round us. Even though they didn't speak English, and we certainly didn't speak Chichewa, the main Malawi language, we had no difficulty in communicating. The only confusion arose when we explained that I was going to swim from one side of Lake Malawi to another – they understood what we were saying but didn't believe it was possible.

After arriving in Salima, we were sweaty and dusty and our rucksacks felt like ton-weights on our backs. Someone told us the lake was further up the road, over the brow of a little hill, so we walked on. As long as I live, that first sight of Lake Malawi will never be forgotten. We were in a region of equatorial heat when we walked over a slight rise in the road. The blue lake that spread out in every direction was so vast that it looked like it couldn't possibly be surrounded by land. I thought about David Livingstone when he turned up here in the mid-1800s, the first non-African to see the lake, and what he must have thought on first seeing it – probably the same thing that Kim and I were thinking: this is nature at its most breathtaking. Whatever tiredness we felt was banished by the splendour of the setting and the chance to pitch our tent in the campsite on the lakeshore.

Conveniently, those already camped had taken places well back from the beach, leaving us to set up close to the edge of the water – prime site, we said. There was only one tent where we were but there was plenty of space and we settled down for the night feeling like we were close to heaven. But after we dropped off to sleep, the tent shivered – a little wind, we thought – and within minutes, the heavens opened and we were being battered by torrential rain and demonic winds. The rain poured into our cheap little tent and the wind threatened to take it flying away over Malawi's western borders. I got out to check what could be done, telling Kim to take hold of the two upright poles inside the tent and not let go.

Outside, the people near us were much worse off. Their tent was down and they hadn't much idea how to secure it. After helping them to avoid disaster and getting soaked in the process, I remembered Kim, whom I'd left holding our tent poles. She was very upset, having spent at least fifteen minutes in the cruciform position not knowing where I'd gone. 'You just abandoned me,' she said. There was nothing I could say because she was right and it definitely wasn't going to help to mention that everyone who had pitched their tents in the sheltered area at the back of the park had been well protected from the storm.

Next morning we woke to a beautiful African day of blue skies and warm sunshine. By this time we were two wiser tourists and left our 'prime' location by the water and pitched the tent at the back with everyone else. Lake Malawi was originally called Lake Nyasa, meaning 'Lake of Storms', and someone way back then knew what they were talking about. Kim and I checked with locals who hired out boats but met with incredulity when we explained our intentions. 'You want to swim across this lake?' they asked and, fearing that it would all be a waste of time, prices were jacked up.

On our third day, Otto arrived with Peter Bales. Still in search of a boat, we were directed to Stuart Grant, a Scot who lived by the lake and made his living exporting tropical fish found in Lake Malawi, called cichlids, to Europe and America. We were told Stuart might have a boat for rent. He lived in a quiet, isolated part of the lakeshore but Otto had hired a car and off we went to meet Mr Grant.

Stuart was seated at a desk, looking into a computer screen, and didn't look up when we were shown into his office. Beyond it was the big warehouse containing hundreds of concrete tanks, each slightly smaller than a domestic bath, full of cichlids ready for export. It was an extraordinary scene because, as Otto and I introduced ourselves, Stuart hardly lifted his eyes from the computer screen.

'Hi,' I said, 'I'm Lewis; this is Otto.'

'Yeah?'

'We're looking for Stuart Grant.'

'That's me.'

'Sorry, we've come from South Africa,' I said, raising my voice a little, 'and we're looking to hire a boat for two days – something to take us to the other side of Lake Malawi?'

'A boat, yeah,' said Stuart, still not bothering to look up.

Otto and I glanced at each other, wondering how to get his attention. Otto raised his voice. 'We're going to swim across Lake Malawi. We need the boat to go with us while we're swimming?'

Suddenly, Stuart Grant came alive. 'You're what?'

'We're going to swim across the lake. We believe no one's ever done that,' I said.

'Yeah, swim across the lake, that's great. You can take the *Lady Di*, and Justas can guide you across the lake . . . *Justas!*' he shouted at the top of his voice. Into the room came the Malawian, Justas Chirwa, who would pilot the boat.

'What about hippos and crocs?' I asked.

'There are hippos and crocodiles,' Stuart replied. 'The hippos are more dangerous; they kill a lot of people in Africa. But the lake is very deep and the hippo doesn't go into deep water. So swim fast at the beginning and again at the end when you're in shallow water! Justas will also rev the engines. You'll be fine. One bit of advice: you should swim from east to west – the wind is more likely to help you that way. Go in the boat this afternoon, swim back in the morning. But there won't be any accommodation on the other side.'

'Lewis has a tent that will take two people,' Otto said. 'But Peter and me?'

'I'll take care of that,' said Stuart, and he gave them what looked like a big curtain and some mosquito netting. 'You'll be fine with this.'

In the end, the boat was hired with the minimum of fuss and no paperwork. Stuart Grant couldn't have been more helpful.

We travelled across the lake that afternoon on the *Lady Di*. Four hours it took us and we worried about how long it would take to swim the same distance. It was a beautiful journey. Four of us on the boat with our guide, Justas, travelled across one of the biggest lakes in Africa, thinking of the swim we would do the next day and knowing we would be the first people to attempt it. 'This is why you were born,' I thought to myself. The sense of adventure thrilled me.

Though we were still in Malawi on the eastern shore of the lake, it seemed like another world. There is a route from Nairobi in Kenya to Cape Town taken by lots of backpackers and quite a lot of cargo-carrying trucks but they travel on the western side of the lake. The eastern side, close to Mozambique, feels unchanged from fifty or a hundred years before. Because of the shallow water, we anchored the *Lady Di* in a place called Cape Ngobo and went ashore in a small fibreglass boat. Lots of children came to inspect us. They were dressed in the poorest clothing and lived in mud huts in a village close by but they were extraordinarily welcoming. Such was their fascination with Kim's blonde hair we wondered if they'd ever seen blonde hair before. If Kim moved her head quickly and her hair swished from one side to the other, they went crazy, laughing and screaming with delight. So taken were they with us that Justas had to draw a line in the sand and tell the children they weren't to come any closer. These were kids aged from two to sixteen and Kim was brilliant with them. We had a wonderful evening around our campfire until the children's mothers came and took them home. At one point some local people brought us dried fish to eat but Otto said that although the fish would probably taste great, it would have been dried in the open air with lots of flies buzzing about; the locals might have immunity to the flies but we didn't. We took his advice and turned in for the night: Kim and I in the tent, Otto and Peter wrapped up in Stuart's curtains and sleeping under the stars.

Otto has spoken many times since about that wondrous night, how different and far more beautiful the sky is from an isolated beach in Central Africa, and how Peter and he listened to the wonderful beating of drums as local fishermen went out in their boats after midnight. They were going to

work but with joy in their hearts. You think of all the men
and women walking over London Bridge or driving across
Manhattan Bridge early on a midweek morning and how
few of them feel that same sense of fun and joyful anticipation. I think it was wonderful that one of the top heart
surgeons in South Africa should have been sleeping under
the stars in curtains and loving every minute of it.

The blissfulness of the night was ended by early morning
realities – our belongings had been stolen from the *Lady Di*
and we still had a 25-kilometre swim in front of us. I had
taken just a few things ashore and left most of my stuff on the
boat. What concerned me were the things I needed for the
swim that were gone: my lucky yellow costume, my goggles
and all my suntan lotion. I had a replacement for the costume but I'd worn the yellow one for my three Robben
Island swims and had it in my head that it brought me good
luck. Otto had a second pair of goggles that I could use but,
between us, we had only a minimal amount of sunscreen –
not nearly enough. We were going to be in the water for
about ten hours, the sun would be beating down on us for
that time and the water wasn't going to provide much protection. We wondered what to do.

Justas was distraught about the robbery. 'This is just unac-
ceptable, so bad that it happened in Malawi. We must go to
the local police and try to find whoever did it.'

I felt there wasn't time. 'Let's just crack on with the swim.
The sun will be up soon.'

Justas, Peter and Kim stood on the *Lady Di* as Otto and I
waited for the signal. 'Are you ready?' shouted Peter. 'Okay,
go!' He dropped his arm, started his stopwatch and we ran
into the water and swam as fast as we could, both of us
remembering that hippos like shallow waters. Fear certainly
drove me. For the first minute or two, I never looked up but
sped through the water at an incredible rate. Then I could

hear Peter shouting, 'Lewis, Lewis!' I looked up but couldn't see the boat – it was behind me, but it shouldn't have been. In my desperation to get into deep water, I'd not looked where I was going and my stronger side (every swimmer has a stronger side!) had taken me in a semi-circle back towards the beach. What must Justas have thought? Here were two guys who had come from South Africa to swim 25 kilometres across this lake and one of them starts by going a little forward and then swimming in a circle back towards the shore. Hippos have a strange effect on me.

I settled down after that and fell into a normal rhythm. There was much that was beautiful about the swim: the clean freshwater felt good; it was gorgeously warm, especially in the slightly cooler early morning; and the lake couldn't have been calmer. There were also parts that weren't so good: Otto's spare goggles leaked in one lens and filled up with water every five minutes or so. Through the course of a close to 10-hour swim, that meant pulling the lens away from my face and letting it empty about 120 times – annoying to say the least! Beating down on my insufficiently protected legs, back, arms and face, the sun became my biggest enemy. By the halfway point, I was somewhere between human and lobster.

I hadn't reckoned on how much swimming in the less buoyant freshwater would tax my lower back. After five or six hours I was feeling it; after seven hours I was in agony. Adding to the frustration was the sense that I was holding up Otto. His gliding rhythm took him through the water at a slightly quicker pace than mine and it meant he was constantly pulling ahead of me. With the boat present in case anything went wrong, we needed to swim close to each other but Otto was going at his natural pace and couldn't comfortably swim any slower. Every so often, when he had moved 40 or 50 metres ahead, he would stop, dive five or six feet below, where the water was cooler, and stay there for as long as he could to cool down. By the time he resurfaced, I would have reached him and we would repeat the routine. I hated not being able to keep up but that day he was stronger. As the day wore on, the temperature rose: the water went from lukewarm to warm until it was completely uncomfortable. Every so often we would swim through a film of plankton, identifiable by the greenness of the water and the sudden rise in water temperature. Plankton absorbs the heat of the sun when it's on the surface of the water and then you don't want to be swimming in the vicinity. For me, the last four hours were murderous and poor Kim and Peter, who were passing us food and drinks, had to suffer my grouchiness.

We got there eventually, and it was an event worth waiting for. A kilometre or so from the shore, I heard the commotion. Soon children in dugouts were paddling towards us and their excitement was infectious. Otto was ahead of me. When he got near enough to the shore to stand up, there was a sea of smiling black faces in front of him, all of them cheering and clapping. Then the sea parted and a man in a starched white uniform appeared. He had a tray in one hand, a napkin on his wrist and two folded-up wicker chairs in the other hand. Walking up to Otto, he said, 'Sir, would you like a cup of tea, compliments of the Livingstonia Beach Hotel?'

Otto felt he had been transported back to Victorian England. 'Yes, thank you, I would.'

The chairs were placed on the sand, Otto seated himself and afternoon tea was served. I arrived about three minutes later, utterly wasted and unaware of what was happening.

'Otto, how on earth did you organize this!?' I said.

'Lewis,' he replied in an aristocratic English accent, 'would you care for a cup of tea?'

Otto and Peter flew back to Cape Town the next day and

Kim and I set off on a week's holiday in Malawi. It should have been a wonderful week but 9 hours and 50 minutes of being grilled by a burning sun had taken its toll on my poor body. No lobster was ever as pink or as raw. So bad were the burns on my face that some of them bled. Kim, at least, was sympathetic, insisting that I sleep on the mattress even though it had been meant for her. For much of our holiday week, I could hardly move. In time the sunburn disappeared and the memory of a great trip remained.

So many lessons were learned too – painful at the time but valuable for the future. I had researched the trip but not well enough. No attempt had been made to work out how much harder it would be to do a long swim in freshwater with so much less buoyancy. My aching lower back told me how important a mistake that had been. I learned, too, about leaving valuables unattended on the presumption that they wouldn't be stolen. Presumption was ever the enemy.

The Malawi trip was also inspirational. I went there because Lake Malawi is one of the great African lakes and because its shape made it possible to swim from one side to the other. Nothing about the country or the lake disappointed me. If ever you get the chance to go to Malawi, seize it. A lasting memory was of meeting Stuart Grant, the Scot who had chosen to live in the heart of Africa. His cichlids business employed seventy local people and was run in a way that was sympathetic to the lake and the surrounding environment. Stuart spoke fluent Chichewan and was also proficient in Chitumbuka, the language spoken in northern Malawi. He reminded me of David Livingstone, whose tracks he had followed to Lake Malawi. Livingstone was a missionary and an explorer but, more than that, he was a humanitarian. History books credit William Wilberforce with ending slavery but Livingstone played no small part in the movement. Before his death, Livingstone asked that his heart be buried in Africa. His body, repatriated to England, was laid to rest in the company of kings and queens at Westminster Abbey. In 2007 Stuart Grant died suddenly following a stroke. His body and soul are buried on the shores of Lake Malawi.

Lake Malawi turned out to be a tougher swim than I'd expected. Far from being discouraged, the experience whetted my appetite for more. Okay, done that, what next? I was young, enthusiastic and fearless.

Cape Point, on the south-eastern tip of the Cape Peninsula, was a landmark that inspired awe because of its physical beauty and fear in the swimmer because of its unpredictable swells. It lies about 70 kilometres south of Cape Town and it seemed the next perfect challenge. The American swimmer Lynne Cox had swum around Cape Point some years before me. Because of the likelihood of rough seas and the sudden change in water temperature, it is a tough swim. In organizing swims there is a danger that because of the effort that goes into setting it up, you go ahead with it even when there are good reasons for aborting. The day of the swim we towed a boat the 70 kilometres from Cape Town to Cape Point and were in two minds about going ahead once we got there because the swells were so great. Two of the team thought it was too dangerous and didn't want to do it.

'You are being silly,' said Clem Gutche, an experienced lifeguard. 'These are big swells coming through here.'

I felt it was just about okay. 'I've just got to get the timing right when I'm coming in at the end.'

The swells were fierce but it was still a magnificent swim because of the astonishing beauty of the coastline. Two big lighthouses stand sentry on the tip of the Cape and the ruggedness of the landscape testified to the power of the sea. Having started in water that was a very comfortable 18 degrees, you went round the Cape and, in the space of thirty strokes, you were in water that was a bracing 11 degrees.

For a swim such as this to be official, it must start on land and finish on land; achieving the latter was always going to be extremely difficult. We headed for Diaz Beach, I swam and the Zodiac, the inflatable boat that was accompanying me, went in as close to the beach as it could. Ahead of me, I could see five-metre waves crashing against the shore and realized that if I got it wrong one of those waves would slam me onto the sand with a force that could do a lot of damage. Worse still, one of them could throw me onto a rock. Near the shore, I let a big wave go past and swam as hard as I could after it, hoping to beat the next wave to the beach. Fat chance. I looked back and there was a monster coming up behind me. It picked me up and tossed me down its face, and suddenly I had no control over what was happening.

I was no more than 25 metres from the shore. My friend Laurie Fialkov was waiting for me to land; I could see him clearly but it was impossible to get to him. There were some big rocks that I was desperate to avoid and, to buy some time, I went underwater every time a massive wave approached. I tried to get down to the sand so that I could dig my hands into it and withstand the force of the waves. It was so turbulent that I lost my sense of where things were: was I facing the surface or the bottom? Every time I got to the surface gasping for air there was another big wave coming and I had to go down again. All of this seemed to last a lifetime but it was minutes. Eventually I became so exhausted after resurfacing that I just lay on top of the water. So be it. Whatever happened happened. I had no more strength or air in me. Fortunately, the next wave took me and miraculously threw me onto the beach. There were no broken bones, no gashes or burns from being hurled onto stones or gravel, just complete and utter exhaustion. Laurie came running over to me and I think he was as surprised as I was that no damage had been done. The miracles did not end there because the lighthouse man who had been following my swim through his binoculars ran down with a cup of tea and a blanket after I landed on Diaz Beach. They were very welcome, for it had been an epic swim with a hair-raising end. The next day there was a report in a Cape Town newspaper saying I had been reckless to attempt that swim, especially in those conditions. At the time I bristled at such criticism but now, with the benefits of hindsight, I accept it probably wasn't the wisest decision.

After Malawi Otto Thaning was also keen to take on another challenge and it wasn't long before we identified our next target. If you say to people you love climbing big mountains, they will ask if you've done Everest. Similarly, if you tell them you like long-distance swimming, they will talk about the English Channel. 'Have you swum the Channel?' The distance from Dover in the south-east of England to the nearest point in France is just 35 kilometres and with good conditions it is not a particularly difficult swim – except that good conditions and the English Channel aren't always on speaking terms. You might hit upon a day when the Channel is perfect for swimming but more likely you will end up sitting in Dover waiting for the wind to calm down. When you travel from as far away as South Africa, and you only have a few days in which to do the swim, you need luck on your side.

Otto and I swam Lake Malawi in early February 1992 and planned our trip to England for August of that year. I was in my third year at the University of Cape Town, and the cost of flying to England and coming up with the money to hire the boat that would guide us across the Channel were way beyond my resources. I told Otto as much. 'Don't worry. I will find a sponsor and we will be able to do it,' he said. At the time, anyone from South Africa who attempted the Channel swim was sure of newspaper and television coverage and, I suppose, there was some possibility of attracting sponsorship. But, in my heart, I thought Otto was taking on the expense of both our trips. We didn't speak about it but I'm sure there was no sponsorship. I am indebted to Otto for this and plenty more.

He talked about a book he'd read, *It's Cold in the Channel*, which tells the story of Matthew Webb's historic first Channel swim. It was 1875. Webb spent 23 hours in the water, he needed a horse and cart to take him out of the water on the French side and, when he was visited by a doctor, the physician did his examination and said, 'Look, he's got a pulse, that is about all I can say.' It was Otto's way of telling me not to be complacent in any way. After Malawi, I couldn't be. Even then, I was beginning to realize that swimming long distances in cold water demanded a maturity that you couldn't have at twenty-two and that put me at a disadvantage.

Everything I'd read or heard about the Channel seemed to add up to one thing: the sea is boss. I trained for six months with the Channel always on my mind. I swam off Camps Bay Beach, at the outdoor Seapoint Pavilion Pool, and thought about what I needed to do to make sure Otto and I had the best chance of making it. There were four imperatives:

1. We had to do the training – both the long-distance work and the hours – in cold water.
2. We had to choose the very best pilot. A good one would know the currents and get us to the right spot in France; a bad one might take a chance with the weather because he would still get his fee irrespective of whether we made it or not.

3. Our seconder, who would feed us, talk to us and encourage us from the boat, had to be the right person.
4. We had to choose the right day. In this we were restricted to a degree because our time in England would be relatively short.

When you are preparing for something as demanding as a 35-kilometre swim across one of the more difficult channels, the danger is that you concentrate on the physical training to the exclusion of all else. I was determined this wouldn't happen.

We decided that Peter Bales would again second us. We found a pilot, Richard Armstrong, with a good record and I booked the hotel that would be our base in Dover. After an overnight flight from Cape Town to London, we got to Dover in our hired car around midday. Conditions were good. We went for a short swim off the beach and, compared to what we were used to back in Cape Town, the water temperature was pleasantly high. After the 12- or 13-degree water at home, the 17-degree temperature in the Channel actually seemed comfortable. We had lunch and then Richard Armstrong came to meet us. 'Conditions look okay for tomorrow, a bit rough at first but good after that, so I propose one of you goes tomorrow and the other the following day,' he said.

Channel Swimming Association regulations insist that each swimmer must have one boat because it could be dangerous to have a pilot responsible for any more than one person in the water. Because there was the prospect of favourable conditions the next day and because I wasn't as experienced or as accomplished a swimmer as Otto, I asked if he would mind me going first. Otto's generosity came into play again. 'Of course not. You go first,' he said.

That was the good part. Richard then said we would leave at 4 a.m., so that most of the swim would be done in daylight and we could get back to Dover from the French coast some time around midnight. A 4 a.m. start meant I would have to be up at 2.30 a.m. and, not having slept much on the overnight flight from Cape Town, it all suddenly felt a bit daunting, but I tried to banish the negative thoughts because they didn't help. That afternoon there was just enough time to buy some bananas, chocolate and drinks from a nearby shop and a tub of grease from a Boots pharmacy. I went to bed around nine and slept for what seemed like a minute before I was woken from a deep sleep by the alarm. 'Where am I? Why am I here? Oh, no!'

I got ready pretty quickly and walked down to the harbour. Ferries were still coming and going at this unearthly hour; the statue of Matthew Webb on the seafront was a reminder of what lay in front of me; and Dover Castle, all lit up on the cliffs, looked majestic. Richard's boat was a small wooden vessel that he'd once used to fish. The changing nature of that industry and the opening up of British waters to the giant Spanish fleet put paid to Richard and many small operators, so he had become a kind of seafaring sherpa, helping those who wished to swim the Channel. We headed out from Dover harbour a little before 4 a.m., and made our way to Shakespeare Beach, where I would swim from the boat to the beach and begin my marathon from the land. The short journey in the boat told us what kind of day it was going to be. We were hardly out of the harbour when the waves began to crash against the side of the boat, and in less than a minute we were all holding on to the sides. 'Richard,' I thought, 'are you really sure about this?' Peter Bales was beside me and my questioning look told him what was on my mind. 'Don't worry, Lewis, it's going to be okay. You've just got to trust Richard.' Conditions were expected to be tough through the early part of the swim and then much better afterwards. I prayed they would be because the turbulent sea in front of me wasn't one you'd want on a twelve-hour swim. 'This,' I thought, 'is why the Channel swim is held in such regard.'

We had an official from the Channel Swimming Association on the boat to verify that the swim was done according to the rules. After I'd swum onto Shakespeare Beach, he shouted, 'Are you ready? Get set, go.' With that my Channel adventure began. I was both excited and nervous. I'd trained properly and was going to enjoy the experience but there was no telling how long it would take or whether, in fact, I would even get to France. Lake Malawi, with its warm, tranquil water, now seemed like a doddle, which it wasn't. If this went well, it would be a ten-hour swim; not so well, and it would take fifteen hours. My plan was to start at a sensible pace, to forget about the time it would take and to get through the tough conditions without the loss of too much strength. There is only one objective on a Channel swim and that is to get to the other side. People only want to know if you make it across.

From the very beginning, the waves are throwing me about and I have the awful feeling of spending as much time going up and down as going forward. I try to stay relaxed, not fighting the waves but rolling along with them, and accept it is going to be a long, long day. One of the nice things about starting the swim in pitch darkness is that every minute in the water is another minute closer to daybreak, and it's comforting to see the sun coming up. One, two, three hours and it's still rough and I'm still being thrown about. Occasionally, I take a stroke, turn my head to suck in air, a wave crashes over me and I get a mouthful of saltwater. Yugh! Swallowing a little water is not bad but if you swallow too much you have a problem. I look behind, hoping that the white cliffs of Dover will appear much smaller, but they're still big and I can still make out Dover Castle. Three hours of fighting the waves becomes four and then five. Even though I am trying to conserve energy all the time, it's not working. I'm feeling it. If the conditions don't get better, there's no way I am going to reach France. Then, just as despair is creeping up on me, the waves begin to get smaller and my mood brightens. 'Ah, this is better.' By the end of the sixth hour, the sea has transformed into a millpond and I now have a great chance.

Peter throws me a drink and food on the half-hour, as CSA rules are that the swimmer can't leave the water or even hold on to the boat while eating. I tread water, eat the chocolate and bananas I'd bought the previous evening and take long slugs from my energy drinks. After about ten hours I start to feel sick – too much saltwater rolling around inside has that effect. Though feeling horrible, I have to get something inside me and try taking a drink. It is all I need to make me throw up everything that is already there. It is not pretty because my projectile vomiting discolours the water. It is actually quite hard to tread water and be sick at the same time. Peter watches but can do nothing. After everything has come up, I start dry-retching, which is actually worse than vomiting. This is a pretty miserable situation but when I look towards Peter, he just giggles, as if I've done something funny. It is the perfect response because if he'd been sympathetic I might have begun to feel sorry for myself. Instead, I smile back at him and we keep going. He tells me I have about another five hours to go and, not hearing correctly, I think he has said there's another two hours left. Two hours? I'm ecstatic because that means I'm getting there. I swim aggressively, driven by the excitement of almost being there and, after an hour, I ask him how much longer, expecting the answer to be in minutes.

'I reckon you've got another three and a half or four hours,' he says.

I can't believe what I hear.

'You're not serious?'

'Yes, Lewis, you have some way to go. Just keep going.'

I want to die, or at least scream at Peter, but I don't have the energy. Instead I put my head down and carry on. After being in the water for more than twelve hours, I can see the white cliffs of Cap Blanc on the French coast but I force myself to stop looking up. The more I look, the more I'm convinced that the coastline isn't getting a fraction closer. To distract myself from the coast, I count each stroke: one, two, three . . . all the way to a hundred. Counting is a simple device to counter the pain of physical exertion but it works. Weary of counting, I let my mind anticipate the pleasure of reaching the beach in France, feeling the sand beneath my feet and ordering the food I will eat once I'm back at the hotel. For some reason, it's going to be a chicken burger for dinner. Don't ask me to explain why, because that's not something I normally eat, but I can't stop thinking about it now and what I will have with it – chips, probably. After thirteen hours in the water, my tongue has started to swell with all the seawater and my throat is raw and sore, but still I'm thinking of food and how wonderful it will be to flop down on a bed with a full tummy.

I'm forced back into the moment by the concern in Peter's voice. 'Lewis! Lewis!' he shouts. 'You're just off the coast of France now but you're being pushed west by the current, away from where you need to be. You've got to give it everything for the next half an hour; otherwise you're going to be swept down the coast.' After fourteen hours, the thought of not making it is too much, but Peter is deadly serious: I've got to find some energy. My head goes a little deeper into the water and I try to quicken my stroke-rate, but I have so little energy left that instead of my hands knifing through the water, I'm just slapping them downwards. Then I see small waves ahead of me, little distant ripples at the top of the water that tell me the French beach is there at last. Each stroke is now a separate challenge and I concentrate on making one, then another, until I can see sand beneath me and feel utter relief when my feet touch it. I stagger up and, like a drunken man, I wade onto dry land. France! On the beach I collapse and kiss the sand. Though I'm thrilled to have made it, the dominant emotion is relief. Fourteen hours and fifty minutes it has taken me and all I want to do is rest.

From the boat, Richard is shouting, 'Swim back, swim back to our boat.' They are only about a hundred metres out from the beach and they need me to come to them because they can't bring the boat in any closer. But the Channel has been crossed and my body, obedient for hour after hour, has had enough. I don't budge. They shout that it's only a little swim but it's no good. I'm done with swimming for the day. Eventually Richard gets the message and puts the little Zodiac in the water and comes to fetch me. An old French fisherman walks past where I'm lying, looks at me and says nothing. Back on the old boat, Richard says, 'Well done, son, well done.' He wraps a blanket around me and, as there's nowhere to sleep on the boat, I settle down on the only place available – a hard bench in the wheelhouse. Think of the 14 hours 50 minutes in terms of an office worker getting to his desk at 9 a.m. and leaving ten minutes before midnight. Though shattered, I'm unable to sleep on the long journey back to Dover and it is close to midnight when we reach the harbour. Somehow I walk back to the hotel and, of course, the restaurant is closed, there's no room service and no chicken burger. Walking through the empty bar, I pick at peanuts in a small aluminium bowl; they're not quite as tasty as the chicken burger I'd fantasized about. Otto is slightly taken aback to see me so wasted. He helps me into the bath, washes the grease from my back and then tries to get a little sleep because, at about 3 a.m., it will be his turn to answer the alarm and get himself down to the harbour for his 4 a.m. start.

Otto drew the short straw. His swim was infinitely tougher than mine. In terms of the conditions, his experience was the reverse of mine: fairly flat for the first few hours and then very, very rough after that. Because Otto is such a strong swimmer, he battled the elements for ten hours and got within five kilometres of the French coast but the combination of big waves and strong currents made it impossible for him. Before the guys in the boat decided they had to call it off, Otto had spent another one and a half hours in the water and not progressed one metre closer to France. Conditions made it difficult to stay close to Otto. Sometimes he would be in the water, high up on a wave and looking down on the deck of the boat; at other times he would be looking up at the underside of the boat. After telling Otto it was futile, the team spent 20 minutes trying to get him safely into the boat. Word came back to me that Otto's swim had been abandoned and I waited at the harbour for him to return. He looked so battered, so humbled by the ocean, but, being Otto, he put on a big smile. 'Look, Lewis,' he said, 'this is why the Channel is such a challenge. It just means I have to stay in full training for another year because I'm going to do it next year.' I took him to his shower and felt terrible for him. We were due to spend another week in England. I don't know if Richard should have had a clearer idea about how the day was going to turn out and whether it would have been better to wait until the following day or the day after that. It was hard to know because a year later Otto returned to Dover and waited eight consecutive days for the winds to drop. They never did and he returned home without getting in the water. A year later, he tried for the third time and, in calm waters, he flew across the Channel in just over ten hours.

When we arrived back at Cape Town airport, my mother and sister were waiting for me and Otto's partner Sisca was waiting for him. It felt awkward. It would have been lovely if both of us had made it but the fact that one of us hadn't put a little dampener on the trip.

My dad was still alive at this time but very poorly. Immediately after getting back to Cape Town, I went to the Booth Memorial Hospital to tell him that I'd swum the Channel. He was delighted. He died shortly afterwards and sadly never saw me do a swim.

Not long after my father's death, I decided to swim around Cape Agulhas, the southernmost point in Africa. Cape Agulhas is where the Indian Ocean meets the Atlantic Ocean and it is usual for the sea to be pretty rough around there. It wasn't the possibility of rough seas that discouraged people from swimming around Cape Agulhas but the fact that it was home to Great White Sharks. Some of the greatest concentrations of Great Whites in the world can be found around Cape Agulhas. It was 1994, some years before the invention of electronic anti-shark devices that could be attached to boats and greatly lessened the possibility of being attacked. I look back now and think, 'What was I playing at?' Swimming in those waters without an anti-shark device is something I wouldn't dream of doing now but my mindset was very different back then. I remember thinking, 'If I die, so be it.' People might have mistaken this for courage but it wasn't that. Courage presupposes fear. At the time, I missed my father so much that death brought little fear; if the worst came to the worst and I got taken by a Great White, I would simply join him.

After driving up to Cape Agulhas, I went in search of a man with a boat who could escort me around the Cape. Even at this point, I was learning to interview people and often would come to an instinctive assessment about whether they could be trusted to do the job properly. Peter Bales was again with me to ensure that the swim was conducted according to the rules of the Cape Long Distance Swimming Association and we were invited round to the house of the man who would pilot our support boat. He earned his living by taking tourists out to dive with Great White Sharks but before that he used to catch Great Whites. In his house there were pictures of some of his biggest catches and there was one Great White that was as big as a flipping mini-bus. Not only that but there was a smile/sneer on its dead face and it sent a shiver down my spine. I went to bed that night with the image of that Great White in my head. The next morning, conditions could hardly have been better and, fortunately, the swim around Cape Agulhas passed without incident.

7

WHO DARES WINS

Before I ever considered the University of Cape Town, my father suggested the South African Marines might be a career for me and took me to the Navy base in Simon's Town, where I met the Commanding Officer, Captain Thompson. It was all very polite, and Captain Thompson couldn't have been kinder, but it wasn't for me. At the time I had spent seven years of my life in South Africa after living the first ten in England and it was to the British Army that I looked instead. In my teenage innocence, I wrote a letter to the British Army Headquarters, Whitehall, London, England:

Dear Sir,
I would like to join the British Army and, specifically, I would like to join the Special Air Service. Can you please send me an application form?
With much gratitude,
Yours faithfully,
Lewis Pugh

I didn't get a reply. That didn't bother me. Throughout my life, there would be plenty of rejections but, mostly, they just made me try harder. When my father suggested the South African Marines, it was because he wasn't sure I would qualify for university and he knew I shared his interest in the military. When we lived in Grahamstown, he took me to Rorke's Drift in Zululand where, on 22 and 23 January 1879, a small company of British soldiers (139) successfully defended a garrison against an attack by 4,000 to 5,000 Zulu warriors. 'This is where the battle took place; this is where the Welsh soldiers are reputed to have sung as they fought; this is our heritage,' my father told me. Eleven Victoria Crosses were awarded for bravery to men who had fought at Rorke's Drift, which was the most ever earned by a regiment in a single battle. When my father took me to see Captain Thompson, he didn't realize that he had already planted the seeds that had me looking in another direction – the UK and the British Army.

Towards the end of my university life in Cape Town, I went to Britain on a short holiday and spent two days in Cambridge, as I wanted to see where my father had been to university. All I did was walk through the colleges and the narrow cobbled streets in the heart of the city. The place enthralled me, from the beauty of the buildings to its tradition and antiquity. Jesus College was special for me because it had been my father's college. Even though it was wintertime, I took a punting trip on the River Cam, around the back of the colleges, and listened while a young guide told stories about some of the famous alumni. 'On the left, ladies and gentlemen, is Trinity College, where Sir Isaac Newton matriculated in 1661 and then became a Fellow of the College in 1667. Trinity, with thirty-one, has won more Nobel Prizes than Italy.' That night I went to sleep with the thought that one day I would come back to Cambridge to study. I wanted to cycle through the narrow streets with a rucksack full of books on my back, walk down the narrow lanes, be taught by some of the sharpest minds in the world and on a summer's day sit in the field behind King's College and just watch the cows eat the lush grass. In the evening I would go for a beer with a few fellow students to one of the older pubs and do what pretty much every student in Cambridge's history has done.

People who knew me would probably have laughed, believing Lewis wasn't perhaps a fine enough scholar to go to Cambridge, but I wasn't as far off as they thought. Through my years at UCT, I was in the top third of the class but I knew that if I was to get into Cambridge I needed to be in the top few students. That was a big ask but, with my final year remaining, it wasn't impossible. I returned to Cambridge as a student in 1999.

After completing my law degree at UCT in 1997, I did my year of articles with a firm called Dawson and Associates in Cape Town. They were a good firm to work for and Peter Dawson, the senior partner, was a fair man. Much of the work assigned to me was relatively straightforward: filing legal papers, going to and from court and occasionally looking up a point of law and drafting an opinion based on what I'd found. If I'd stayed in Cape Town, there was every opportunity to progress in a law firm, become a partner eventually and enjoy a relatively comfortable lifestyle. But the lawyer's life didn't excite me. Much of a lawyer's time is spent waiting for a client to instruct him. It is not like being an executive running a company, or some other business manager taking initiatives and leading a team. Unsure of what I wanted from life, my instincts whispered that it wasn't to be found in law. The question that constantly presented itself was this: are you really passionate about your work as a lawyer? No was always the answer.

Clarity came simply. To get to work at Dawson and Associates, I walked past the South African Parliament. It is an impressive building, with a statue of South Africa's first Prime Minister, General Louis Botha, at the entrance. Written in both English and Afrikaans, the inscription beneath the statue read: 'Louis Botha − farmer, warrior, statesman', and I wondered what I would like written alongside my name. 'Lewis Gordon Pugh, attorney-at-law'? That didn't seem enough.

With that realization came an acceptance that I would have to do something else with my life − but what? There were some interesting options. In my final year at UCT, I'd taped every lecture, applied myself conscientiously to my work and ended up top of my Masters class, so if at some point I still wanted to sample life at Cambridge University that possibility now existed. There were other factors that drew me towards England, not least the fact that I felt British. I half-hoped that working in a major London law firm would perhaps change my feeling about being an office-based lawyer. Something else pulled me towards London. Part of me was still the young boy who had once written to the Ministry of Defence requesting an application form to join the British Army. The idea of becoming an officer in the British Army was one that I just couldn't put out of my mind.

I landed at Heathrow Airport in January 1998 with about £2,000 in my bank account − enough to keep me going until I found a means of earning money. The first thing I did was pitch up at the British Armed Forces Recruiting Office off Trafalgar Square and announce that I would like to undergo officer training. 'The maximum age for anyone

wanting to go to Sandhurst [the British Army officer training academy] is twenty-five years. I'm sorry but you're too
old.' No exceptions would be made and the alternatives
didn't look promising. 'You can join as a Private, but I think
that as a qualified lawyer, you would find that quite frustrating. You would be training with guys directly out of school
with nothing like your academic qualifications.' A few years
later they increased the age for officer training after the war
in Iraq and Afghanistan created new pressures and someone
realized there are people who don't know until their mid-
twenties that they want to serve in the Army. But the
recruiting officer was still helpful. 'If it's adventure and
excitement you're interested in, perhaps you might want to
consider the TA [Territorial Army] reservists. Every section
of the British Army has a TA arm, from the Army Medical
Corps to the Parachute Regiment.' But the TA was an
option for someone with a job and some free time, so getting
a job was my priority.

At the Law Society's offices just off Fleet Street, I learned
about the conversion course an overseas lawyer would have to
do to be able to practise in London. It meant three months'
study at the College of Law, followed by three exams. The
course was enjoyable and I passed the exams without much
difficulty. That was just the theory part of my conversion to
English law. Another requirement was to do articles at an
English law firm for fifteen months. I was fortunate to get a
job at Ince & Co, which was the top maritime and insurance
law firm in the UK. Its headquarters were close to Tower
Bridge in the City and around 200 lawyers worked out of the
London office. Contracts for the hire of ships and the trans-
porting of cargo tended to include a clause stipulating that
any dispute would be settled in the High Court of England.
Others provide for disputes to be settled by arbitration in
London and Ince & Co tended to get a lot of the business.

London was working for me in other ways as well. I was accepted by Goodenough College, a postgraduate hall of residence for overseas postgraduate students in London. Located on Mecklenburgh Square, near Russell Square, Goodenough College was an amazing place, as it housed 700 postgraduate students from all over the world, young men and women who each seemed to me to have a more interesting background than the other. David Becker, my close friend from law class at UCT, had also moved to London and we were together at Goodenough.

It was there that I met and began dating an Eastern European, Anna Kotzeva, who had read law at Cambridge University and whose love for her experience at Cambridge refuelled my desire to study there – a desire that she encouraged. She had come to England with her family when she was twelve. Her parents had been scientists in Bulgaria and Anna won a scholarship to a top public school before reading law at Cambridge. We got on really well.

Goodenough was run by a retired British Army General, Tim Toyne Sewell, and his empathy with young people and his zest for life were part of what I loved about my time at Goodenough. I organized two relay teams from the college to swim the Channel and Tim, who loved swimming, insisted upon swimming with one of the teams. He loved being involved with young people and we loved having him around.

Work at Ince & Co went well. I shared an office with one of the partners, a Scot named Alan Weir whom I liked a lot. There was one case we worked on that was fascinating. Descendants of Holocaust victims had sued a Swiss bank for money, jewellery and art deposited by their parents before or during the Second World War. The bank repudiated the claims and referred them to its London insurers. But the insurers felt sure the bank must have known these claims were possible and should have disclosed that possibility when the insurance contract was being drawn up. The insurers hired Ince & Co to help them prove the bank had known about the likelihood of the claims before taking out their policy and that is what we did. Alan was a ferocious advocate with a good eye for detail. We went through dozens of history books, scoured old newspapers and came up with enough evidence to show that the bank knew more than it had revealed when the contract was drawn up. As a result of Alan's work, the claim was seen off.

As much as I enjoyed some cases, the nagging thought that I wasn't quite cut out for life in a law office never went away. One day, walking down the King's Road, I noticed a little display for the Parachute Regiment outside Chelsea Barracks. The notice said: 'Join the Parachute Regiment', and there were TV monitors showing soldiers parachuting into Holland during the Second World War. Another notice said: 'One night a week, one weekend a month, and two weeks a year, join the TA.' A year had passed since the recruiting officer suggested the TA and still I felt a pull towards the Army.

With its relatively low level of commitment, I thought the TA would be perfect, as I could continue to work at Ince & Co while getting a first taste of British Army life in my spare time. 'Yes,' the recruiting sergeant said, 'we are recruiting at 10 Parachute Regiment.' Soon I began to learn the way things worked: 10 Parachute Regiment was the TA arm of the Parachute Regiment in central London. He gave me some leaflets and said that if I was interested, I should come back the following Wednesday night with a pair of shorts, a T-shirt and running shoes. I was interested. Two Wednesday evenings were as much as I could take. We ran around a track, did some push-ups and sit-ups but it was all too relaxed for my liking. Many of the recruits were allowed to hang out at the back of the group and not really push themselves. Perhaps it would improve over the following weeks but I didn't have that sense and I wasn't interested in wasting time in an environment where you could get away with giving only 50 per cent of what you had.

I went and had a look at the Royal Marine Reserves and it wasn't noticeably better. Someone suggested that maybe 21 SAS was what I was looking for. I hadn't realized the SAS had a TA arm but immediately knew it was the challenge that I had been seeking. Where the SAS is spoken about within the Armed Forces, it is referred to as 'The Regiment' and the allure is not lessened by the secrecy surrounding it. I wanted to join but didn't know what to do or where to go – the information isn't out there. You don't just sidle up to the recruiting officer in the nearest barracks and pick up the SAS brochures. Desperation and naivety led to a call to directory enquiries.

'I'm sorry, I wonder if you would have a telephone number for the SAS?' I asked, not fully understanding why I felt like a weirdo.

'Yes, we have a listing for SAS Airlines. Would you like me to put you through?'

'No, I'm looking for the Army SAS.'

'I'm sorry, there's no number listed for the Army SAS. Would you like me to put you through to the British Army's general enquiry number?'

'Yes, please.'

'Putting you through.'

'Hello, could you please put me through to 21 SAS?'

'I am sorry, sir, we cannot.'

'Could you then please give me the number for the SAS, so I can call them?'

'I'm sorry, sir, we cannot give you their number.'

Perhaps I'd been away from Britain for too long and had

forgotten how things worked. Tim Toyne Sewell had been Commandant of the Royal Military Academy at Sandhurst; he would surely know people. I knocked on his door at the College. 'General, this might sound like an unusual request, but can you please try and get me a number for 21 SAS. I want to join but don't know who to contact.' Tim said to leave it with him. He called me soon afterwards and gave me the telephone number. I called, a recorded message advised me to leave my full name, address and telephone number and I would be contacted in due course. For three weeks, I heard nothing. Perhaps I was being checked out, even watched to make sure I was whom I said I was, or perhaps the answer machine hadn't worked properly. A month passed, six weeks, and by then I'd given up hope. Then a letter came in the post; it was on one sheet of paper and had a short message: 'Arrive at Duke of York Barracks in Chelsea on this date, at this time, bring two forms of ID, a pair of running shorts, a T-shirt, running shoes, a towel, and a swimming costume.' In getting that letter, it felt like the first hurdle had been cleared. It would be the first of many and by far the easiest.

What I knew of the SAS could have been written on the back of a postcard. There was the storming of the Iranian Embassy in 1980, the raid into Argentina to destroy their fighter jets during the Falklands War, the work behind enemy lines during the Second World War and their fearsome reputation. It was, at best, a layman's knowledge and a layman who hadn't read *Bravo Two Zero*, the book written about the Regiment by former SAS soldier Andy McNab.

Without any idea of what to expect, I turned up on the appointed Saturday morning at the Duke of York Barracks at 9 a.m. and found myself with a group of forty men of varying shapes and contrasting appearances. Some had the lean, athletic look that you expected of prospective SAS soldiers; others were utterly clueless. One guy actually turned up in a tweed jacket and red corduroy trousers, which would have been funny if it had been some kind of prank but he didn't seem to think he was out of place. We never saw him after that first morning.

From the first minute of that Saturday morning introduction, no one was in any doubt about who the bosses were. The instructors told us to call them DS or 'Staff', as in 'Directing Staff', and they wasted no time in convincing us we had entered a pretty challenging environment. First we were escorted from our meeting point into the barracks proper and then taken into a brick-faced building. Toned and naturally aggressive, the instructors conveyed a hint of menace that every recruit understood as: 'Don't even think of messing with us.' No one did.

Then the guy who seemed to be the chief instructor called out, 'Right, have any of you guys got any knives or weapons on you?' The question staggered me. Why would anyone walk into an Army base with a weapon? Even though the silence indicated no one had any weapons, the guy doing the ordering said, 'Okay, we're going to search you anyway.' Two of them took the first guy and rammed him hard against the wall, as you might a terrorist suspect. No one said anything, everyone noticed. They frisked the recruit head to toe and very thoroughly. Then they went through his bag and made him produce his ID before moving on to the next recruit. Every recruit was searched and eventually they found a guy who had a pretty big knife in his bag. 'Why the fuck do you come in here with that?' barked the instructor. 'Come out here; bring your bag.' The recruit followed the instructor out of the building and we never saw him again. In the bag of another recruit they found a copy of McNab's *Bravo Two Zero* and it might as well have been a knife given the reaction. 'You think this is what the SAS is about? You really think that?' the instructor said, his words dripping with scorn.

They then took us for a run, telling us that if we didn't keep up with the instructor we would be 'binned'. It was an expression that we all got to know because it was always being used. Each of us knew that the easiest thing in the world would be to get binned. We ran out of the base in pairs, along the street, over Chelsea Bridge and then into Battersea Park. A number of the guys had found the run to the Park tough but it was merely a warm-up and the real run, eight kilometres inside Battersea Park, was about to begin. We did two laps of a two-kilometre circuit behind the DS and then it was every man for himself, on your own, maximum effort. We were told there was a set time and anyone outside the time would be binned. In anticipation of something like this, I was physically fit and managed to come in about sixth in the group. The last ten or twelve were outside the time limit and we never saw them again. Back at the barracks we did a circuit of punishing exercises and an equally tough sprinting session. At the end of the session, one of the instructors told us to report back at the barracks the following Wednesday evening.

Throughout the morning there hadn't been much said between the recruits but after showering the guys started talking. 'You've got previous, right?' one said to another, meaning 'you've been in the Army'.'Yeah, I was in 10 Para.' Another had served two years with the Honourable Artillery Company and another six years in the Royal Marines. Eventually someone looked my way and, though I had spent two years in the South African Navy, I shook my head and said, 'Nah, no military experience.' The South African Navy wasn't going to cut it with these guys and it was better for me to be just one of the boys who'd never been in the Army.

On our first Wednesday evening, we each swore the Oath of Allegiance to the Queen and the O/C (Officer Commanding) Training Wing talked us through what was involved in SAS training. If we got through 'Pre-Selection', involving a number of evenings in London, we would then do 'Selection', comprising weekends in the Brecon Beacons. Those who weren't eliminated on one of those weekends would then take part in 'Test Week', an intense week of physical and mental challenges, again in the Brecon Beacons. Test Week would be the first time that 21 SAS, the TA arm of the Regiment, would work with 22 SAS, 23 SAS and the SBS (Special Boat Service). Even though we were TA, or part-time soldiers, we had to be just as strong as the guys for whom the SAS was their only way of life. If we got through Test Week we would undergo that part of the training known as 'Continuation', which involves learning how to fight, how to use every weapon a SAS soldier may have to use, how to operate on every conceivable terrain and how to gather intelligence behind enemy lines. Learning to use the weaponry was a big part of Continuation and we would be taught to use everything from an SA80, the standard British Army weapon, to a GPMG (General Purpose Machine Gun) and the AK-47, favoured by many liberation armies. Those who got through Continuation would then do a two-week battle camp, including an interrogation section, after which each survivor would be presented with his SAS beret.

The way it was presented to us was that we were part-timers attempting a challenge designed for tough, committed men who had only one aim in life: to be part of the most elite special forces unit in the world. At every opportunity, they more or less told us not to worry because most of us wouldn't survive the training and wouldn't have to prove ourselves in the field. I couldn't have been more excited and fully understood why the entry requirements were formidable and had to be the same for everyone. Given the danger of the missions undertaken by the SAS, there had to be complete trust in the man working alongside you and that could exist only if you knew he had undergone the Regiment's arduous training. In later years I heard someone demur about the Territorial Army SAS and it struck me they didn't understand there was no such thing as 'SAS Light'.

The need for discretion within the SAS is absolute and something that every recruit must buy into. David Becker, my closest friend, was the only one who knew what I was attempting, although in time I would tell my mother. Because you couldn't tell people what you were doing, there were dangers. For those first Pre-Selection Wednesday evenings, I had to leave the offices of Ince & Co at 5.30, and there was always the fear that my boss would need something done that meant a later departure. Had I been late for one of those Wednesday evenings, I would almost certainly have been binned. Leaving our Tower Bridge office at 5.30, it was a brutally quick three-kilometre walk down to Monument, across London Bridge, into the rail station and onto a train and then another über-fast walk from the station in Hordley to the TA Centre. One or two evenings, I made it just in time and recall an occasion at Ince & Co when we were busy and it wasn't on for me to leave the office as early at 5.30. So I put my jacket on the back of my chair and left a notebook and pen on my desk, as if I'd just slipped away to the loo or something when in fact I had escaped out the back door.

Yorkie was our principal instructor, a no-nonsense guy from the north of England. He existed to push us hard and make us realize that what we were attempting was close to impossible. To find the chinks in our physical or mental armour, he taunted us, showed little sympathy when we didn't keep up and ridiculed our feebleness – praise was for pussies. Like the other instructors, he homed in on the guys who were content to be at the back or were happy to be just inside the time limit. If you were looking for a peaceful life, you didn't want Yorkie or any other DS on your back. Yet

Yorkie was fair and I couldn't but respect him; in the end, I even liked him. More people wanted to join the SAS than the Regiment could ever accommodate and his job was to make sure only the best recruits made it through the selection process. There was nothing personal about it; he didn't have favourites and his only loyalty was to the Regiment. If you didn't like him, you had a choice: you could keep quiet and get on with it or you could stay at home. And if you did quit, the one certainty was that you wouldn't be missed.

Of course it was a tough, macho and totally unforgiving environment but I loved it. It was an opportunity to get to know better who you were. I had been bullied in my early years at St Andrew's College and, even if I believed there wasn't much I could have done to avoid what happened, there were still doubts. Was I a little soft? Did that make me an easy target? If that softness existed, SAS training would find it out. Though I loved being outdoors, my sports had tended to be individual rather than team games: swimming, kayaking, cycling, running. I had great individual friendships but had never been one of the boys. For many years, that had been my strength. Now I was one of the boys, one of the recruits, and unless I could fit into the group, a tough challenge would become even harder. But these were challenges that I embraced and, of course, the training was mostly physical and predominantly outdoors. If you made it through Pre-Selection, much of the subsequent training would be done in the Brecon Beacons and, provided I didn't fall by the wayside, the mountain terrain of the Beacons would be exhilarating.

Pre-Selection Wednesday evening sessions took place at the TA Centre in Hordley. There was a drill hall but the first battles for survival took place on the streets of Hordley. Through the streets we ran, up and down hills; we did push-ups and sit-ups, and sprints; we ran with a fellow recruit on our back. Each succeeding Wednesday evening our numbers would be one or two down. Guys who weren't physically robust and couldn't cope with the demands or guys who had come with a Walter Mitty view of what the SAS was about were out. We were being asked if we were the kind of men who could pick up a weapon and kill a fellow man. Did we have the mental toughness to sit in a forest for two weeks, when there's a cold, wet sleet, and spend four hours on, four hours off, with our binoculars trained on one spot?

To begin to find out, our instructors made us wear rucksacks (in the SAS we called them bergens) with 25 pounds of equipment inside them. It might not sound that much, 25 pounds, but it was hard work to lug that around and still keep up with Yorkie. People on the streets of Hordley would look at us and wonder what was going on, not knowing they were watching an SAS training evening. We weren't permitted to wear anything other than civilian training gear. When a few of the ex-paras proudly wore their purple T-shirts with the Parachute Regiment emblem, Yorkie told them to 'get that effing T-shirt off'. We weren't ex-paras or ex-Royal Marines or ex-anything; we were just a group of recruits all starting at the same place. That, for me, was reassuring.

On the second Wednesday, Yorkie said that Pre-Selection would have a milling session on the final evening. He described what would happen, relishing every detail, as if that was the night the instructors would finally discover our true mettle. Back at Goodenough College a few evenings later, I went round to David Becker's room. 'David, I've never been in a serious fight in my life and four weeks from now my future will be decided by how well I fight. There's going to be a bloodbath and it scares the hell out of me.'

'Lewis, I've never told you that my grandfather was ban-tamweight champion of South Africa, so boxing has been in our family. You're going to need to learn some basic moves and I can teach you.'

'But I can't defend myself. It must be all-out attack, no defence.'

'Okay, so you need to learn how to hit hard. I can show you that.'

David is not a big guy and I had always thought of him as calm and very unwarlike. I just didn't know the complete David Becker. He took me to the basement gym at Goodenough College and we worked on the punch bag. David taught me to get my body behind my punches, the importance of where and how to set my feet and, most important of all, how aggression can be switched on. Often all it takes is a guttural noise from within and it will trigger your aggression; you associate that sound with all-out attack and you become naturally aggressive. We sparred together in the gym and, with my height and reach advantage, I was able to land a lot of punches and he defended himself as best he could. The sessions with David taught me a lot and gave me the confidence to believe that when it came down to it in the milling session I would have a chance. I'd still be scared, I'd worry that I was going to get a pasting, but at least I would fight back and show the aggression they were looking for.

Yorkie stood in front of us. 'Right,' he barked, 'here are the rules for milling and you guys had better listen because I'm only sayin' this once. You put on the boxing gloves and the headguard; the rest is simple. This is milling, not boxing. You don't defend yourself; you attack your opponent with max-imum aggression. If one day you're caught behind enemy lines, we need to know if you have the guts to fight your way out of it. It doesn't matter a toss if you get punched and knocked down, what does matter is that you get back up and you keep fighting. One rule: you don't hit below the belt. Do that and we'll bin you.' His voice then dropped a decibel or two. 'Milling is not a requirement to get into 21 SAS. You don't have to do this. If you're not keen on this element of the training, just put your hand up.' I really didn't want to participate in this but, like everyone else, my hands stayed very much by my sides. I suspected that if I opted out of milling, some other reason would be found to bin me at a later date. We'd been hearing about this milling session for weeks and the more I heard the less it appealed to me.

One of the instructors put down some gym mats. Yorkie bellowed out again: 'Okay, I want everyone to line up in order of height: tallest on my right, all the way down to the shortest stump dwarf in the room. Right. Get in your position.' Guys hunched their shoulders to make themselves look smaller than they were. The tallest was Welsh, a big, strong guy. Next was a lawyer from New Zealand, then two more. I was fifth tallest. On my right was this hard-looking guy, very muscular with a tattoo covering most of his right calf. Without seeming to be aware of what was going on around him, he rotated his head in a clockwise direction like it was the last act of mental preparation before the eruption of violence. I couldn't help thinking it was going to be the tallest against the next tallest, third against fourth, and me against the monster on my right. We'd had a run earlier that evening, and a few guys got binned but they were allowed to hang around for the milling. One of them, Paul, I'd got to know and now he was mouthing at me, 'Give it to him. Stuff him up!'

I'd hardly ever been in a fight in my life. Once in a rugby match there was a bit of a punch-up but that didn't constitute experience for what I was about to face. Though it was tempting, it was also too late to duck out of this. Yorkie then got the ball rolling. 'Okay, gentlemen. First fight of the evening – you two guys,' and he pointed at Huw, the tall Welshman, and Gordon, the New Zealand lawyer. Huw just battered Gordon: one man knew how to box; the other wasn't allowed to defend himself. I can still see it – thud and Gordon's head was jolted backwards. Huw had been an engineer in the Royal Marines and had an air of knowing what this was all about. The fight ended after two long minutes for Gordon, and Huw's hand was held aloft by the referee. Yorkie then shouted, 'Next pair.' This was a much more even fight, with both men throwing a huge number of punches and making no attempt to defend themselves. I was shocked at the aggression levels and realized that without aggression, you didn't stand a chance. Another hand went up, there was another winner, and my stomach churned at the likelihood that I was next.

By now Mr Tattoo was like a crazed animal. His head was still revolving but now it was accompanied by a growling sound coming from the back of his throat. If it were merely a question of intimidating me, the Tattoo-man had won round one. As I stood up to follow my opponent, one of the instructors grabbed my shoulder. 'Not you,' he said. He then shouted at another recruit, 'Your turn.' Tattoo-man pulverized his opponent and a shiver went down my spine. 'Thank God.'

Alex Wales was Tattoo-man's name and, after his hand was raised, he walked to his place with a smile on his face that could have come all the way from Siberia. Though mightily relieved to have avoided Alex, I was also wondering why I had been passed over. Did they see the fear in my eyes, the absolute sense of dread? Were they about to come and tell me that with the best will in the world I wasn't cut out for the SAS? They went through the remaining guys, and still I wasn't called to fight. A voice inside my head said, 'Speak up, speak up. Tell them you haven't fought; make it seem like you're disappointed.' Another voice said, 'You've just been lucky, that's all; accept it.'

When everybody had finished, Yorkie walked to the middle of our boxing square and, like the announcer on fight night in Las Vegas, began: 'Gentlemen, the fight you've all been waiting for.' In a flash I realized what was happening. Earlier that evening a new recruit had turned up, a short but extremely powerfully built Australian, who was next to me when we were doing push-ups. 'Down, up; down, up; down, keep it there, up,' shouted Yorkie. Though it went on and on, the new Australian was cruising them out. My arms burned, shook a little even, and when I gave him a 'how-much-longer-is-this-going-to-last' look, he gave me a nonchalant 'no-idea' look in return.

So here we were pitted against each other and Yorkie was revving it up. 'In the blue corner, representing Australia, Shaaaane Jenkins. His opponent, representing the Republic of South Africa, Lewisssss Pugh.' Shane only came up to my shoulders but his arms were the size of tree-trunks. They clearly wanted some southern hemisphere spite. Because I was softly spoken, they probably thought I wouldn't be able to produce the aggression necessary to survive; before the fight I might have agreed with them. But the long wait and my sense that they thought I wouldn't be able to hack this made me pretty mad. I went in there and threw everything at Shane. Some punches were wild and missed the target but a few caught him smack in the face; he caught me with a couple of good punches too. Where it came from, I'm not sure, but I let out a growl and started pounding his face with punches. He slipped and we both ended up on the floor, punching and grappling. Even though I'd been very conscious of the recruits cheering and yelling out in the seconds before we started, the background noise disappeared as soon as we'd begun. As we were on the floor, the ref shouted, 'Break, break.' We separated, got to our feet and started belting each other again. The rule was no defence, just all-out attack, and it sucked the energy out of me.

Again, we ended up on the floor. This time the ref left us to it. My arms grew heavy and I gasped for breath, but Shane was still as strong as the moment we started. It felt like we had been beating the daylights out of each other for an eternity – it was probably two minutes. I was sinking, his punches were still coming rapid fire and my arms ached. Desperate, I swung hard at his balls and connected but it made no impact. The ref shouted, 'Break,' and we stopped and got to our feet. 'That's got to be it,' I thought, but, no, we started again. After more punches, I was just fighting on instinct. Shane still seemed okay. We grappled with each other again, Greco-Roman wrestling, and again I went for his balls – whack – with everything I had and it slowed him down. After what seemed a lifetime, the ref shouted, 'Break. That's it.' He then raised my arm and in the Las Vegas voice said, 'The winner is Lewissss Pugh.' I couldn't believe it. I had never felt as much fear in my life and, even though I hadn't really wanted to do it, it had been exhilarating. Almost in spite of myself, I had enjoyed it. And Shane didn't suffer any long-term injury: he's married now and has four kids.

At the end of the evening there was a debriefing. Each recruit was in turn called into an office where three Directing Staff (DS) sat behind a desk. I walked in, stood to attention and one DS, a Kiwi doctor, immediately started, 'Pugh, that was a good fight. Lots of aggression, but what did we tell you about hitting below the belt?' I tried to think quickly and gamble on this DS's feeling towards Aussies. 'Sorry, Staff [we called the instructors 'Staff'], he is Australian.' They all laughed. One of the other two then said, 'Fair enough, Pugh. You have passed Pre-Selection. You are through to Selection. Send in the next recruit.'

Of the forty or so recruits who showed up on the first Saturday morning at Chelsea Barracks, twenty-five made it through Pre-Selection. A few had been binned that first morning and then there'd been a drip-drip of casualties along the way. Pre-Selection was what it was: a process we had to survive in order to get the chance to become members of the SAS. On those evenings in Hordley it was no accident that we worked out in civilian clothes because that is what we were – civilians. Our squadron, A Squadron 21 SAS, had many men who worked in the City during the day – bankers, stockbrokers, lawyers, accountants – who probably were like me in wanting something more from their lives. There was a certain amount of ribbing from other squadrons because of the way some of the A Squadron guys spoke or the cars they drove or whatever, but it was good natured. Most people knew that the SAS badge had a white vertical dagger with light blue wings on either side set against a dark blue background: a number of the SAS's founders were Cambridge and Oxford graduates, and those, of course, are the respective universities' colours.

Getting through Pre-Selection brought its rewards; namely, we were given our uniforms. You went into the quartermaster's office and he called out what it was you were receiving: 'Here is your bergen, two pairs of trousers, two shirts, a woolly jumper, a cap, a poncho, a smock [overlaying jacket], two mess tins [from which we would eat food], two water bottles.' The issue of uniforms and equipment was important in that it made us feel one step closer to where we wanted to be, although Selection promised to be far more demanding than Pre-Selection.

No longer would the challenge be purely physical because at Selection we had to learn to map-read. No longer were we being asked to run from A to B, instead we were given a map and told to find the best possible route from A to B and then complete the journey in the quickest time possible. Map-reading required good judgement. If you didn't learn to read a map properly, it didn't matter how fast you could run. Our Wednesday evening session was a one-and-a-half-hour map-reading class followed by a stiff physical workout. Some recruits never got the map-reading. At first I found it difficult but then the penny dropped and it seemed easy enough. Initially we went out in groups in the Brecon Beacons and learned from our instructors how to use the compass and read a map. Later we navigated our way across the mountains in pairs or we were sent out on our own with a map and grid references. To be as good as I could be, I went to Wales for a few weekends on my own and practised my map-reading on some of the routes favoured by the SAS. I learned where the terrain was marshy and unsuitable for running, and found routes that looked slightly longer on the map but were, in fact, the best ones.

During the training weekends you never ran with just a map, compass and grid references. On your back was a bergen that had to contain at least 45 pounds of equipment not including your food and water. In other words, the bergen had to weigh 45 pounds at the end of your six- or eight- or ten-hour trek. We never went anywhere without our weapon, an SLR, because whatever we learned to do had to be done while carrying it. 'And if I see anyone carrying their weapon like a bloody handbag,' Yorkie would tell us, 'that person will be binned on the spot. You carry the weapon in both hands at all times. Am I making myself clear? The second it takes to raise your weapon is the second that can end your life.'

Those extra weekends on my own in Wales helped my map-reading and improved my fitness. Selection might even have been fun if it weren't for my boots. With our uniforms, we were issued with Army boots and it was obligatory for us to wear them until we were over halfway through Selection; after that we could replace them with our own boots, provided they looked similar. The Army boots didn't suit my feet and on long runs through the Brecon Beacons they sand-papered the skin from my heels and toes. Running downhill, my feet would pound into the front of the boots and crucify my toes. As a result, my performance in the runs suffered; I was inside the time limit but always towards the back. After every weekend in Wales, one or two more men were binned. I wasn't sure my feet would stand up to much more.

One of the instructors, the Kiwi doctor, cottoned on to the problem. 'Those feet are becoming badly infected. You've got to get yourself some good boots, otherwise you're not going to make it,' he said. Already I'd spent money on new thermal gear and a new warm jacket and I didn't fancy spending another £150 on boots that might or might not work. My feet were so badly messed up, the idea of breaking in new boots was not appealing; there had also been recruits who'd bought new Army boots and been binned the very next weekend. As Selection involved every other weekend, there wasn't enough time for my feet to recover. After the halfway point, my feet were again a mass of blisters.

At about this time a South African friend, Anthony Smit, came to visit. He had been in the South African Army for years. I told him I was attempting an Army selection course and about the problems with my feet. He assessed the situation.

'Lewis, I've seen this a number of times. You're going to get eliminated not because you're not tough enough but because your feet are getting so infected, you will not be able to move quickly enough. You've got to sort out those feet and get new boots.'

We went down to Covent Garden and went from one outdoor store to another and, given that it was killing me to walk in ordinary shoes, it was a difficult job to find boots that felt comfortable. Eventually there was a boot/running shoe that felt easier than anything I'd tried.

'Buy it,' said Anthony.

'It's brown,' I said. 'The rules say our boots must be black.'

'You can paint it.'

'But it doesn't cover the ankle properly.'

'Buy it!'

Back at Goodenough College, Anthony decided my feet had to be sorted out. From the tenderness of the area around my big toe, it was obvious that the blister under my toenail had become infected. The wounds on my heels were raw but visible and treatable. 'We need to deal with the problem under your big toenail,' Anthony said, as he produced a small Swiss Army knife and then held it in the flame of a cigarette lighter to disinfect it. 'Drill a hole through the top of the toenail,' he said, handing me the knife. Slowly, I revolved the tip of the blade through my toenail until it got through to the other side. Once a hole through the nail had been created, blood and puss surged through and the relief was amazing. Sometimes you only realize how bad the pain was when it is taken away. My feet still needed lots of treatment but a dark corner had been turned.

It was just as well, too, because the next weekend we had an especially tough run (known in the Regiment as the Fan Dance) along the Old Road, then up to the summit of Cefn Y Bryn, before we began the long descent down to The Griffin Inn. Our instructors said those outside the time limit would be binned but refused to tell us what the limit was. With new footwear and no pain in my feet, I went from being a backmarker to running with the front guys through-out the run. Blackie, a tall, well-built guy without an inch of body fat, was in front of me all the way; no matter how hard I raced, I couldn't peg him back. Towards the end, a recruit from C Squadron, Paul Hamilton, came from behind to challenge me for second but, with one final surge, I held him off. Yorkie came in soon after us.

'My God, Pugh, what happened to you? You've been doing a bit of training?'

'Yes, Staff,' I said. After running so well, I was now con-vinced I could get through Selection.

Doing the SAS training, I could never be upfront and honest with people about what I was up to and it always seemed best to say as little as possible. Anna Kotzeva, the girl I'd met at Goodenough College, wondered about the week-ends when I just wasn't around and on one occasion thought that I might even have been seeing someone else. Colleagues at Ince & Co saw me as someone who kept to himself and even my sister Caroline, who lived in London, knew noth-ing of my extra-curricular activities. The fewer people who knew, the better. I tried to conceal the truth while telling as few lies as possible. Law was my profession, Ince & Co were my employers but the SAS training had become my passion. It enriched my life in a way that my job couldn't.

One weekend, a fellow recruit and I came together on a long downhill run through the Brecon Beacons. His name was Terry Elliot. We'd been running and trekking through the mountains for twelve hours when we met, signing in at the various rendezvous points, called RVs. We came to an RV next to Lake Gwyn and it was obvious there was a prob-lem, as there was a lot of commotion and the chief instructor who was present was barking out orders. Recruits were being lined up and having their bergens weighed. 'I told you that you had to have forty-five pounds in your bergen, minus food and water!' The instructor then picked up an offending bergen and flung it into the lake. Terry's was the first to be weighed and his came in under the required 45 pounds. It, too, was thrown into the lake.

I was next but felt pretty confident my bergen was the correct weight. The scales said 43 and, by now, the instructor was raging against our dishonesty. 'You,' he shouted at me, 'you're the swimmer?! Well, let's see how good you are at swimming.' Twisting like a hammer-thrower, he cast my bergen as far into the lake as he could. It landed about 15 metres in and was sinking quickly. By then I was already in the water, fully clothed, and in desperate pursuit of my bergen. It was quite a job to swim it back to the shore. Luckily my clothing was in a plastic bag in the bergen and had stayed dry. Not pleased that I had been underweight, the instructor put a rock in my bergen, which put the weight up to at least 60 pounds. 'At the end, it will be weighed again and that rock better be there,' he barked.

Terry had already moved off towards the next hill and, exhausted, I put one foot in front of the other and moved off after him. When I got to the other side of the hill, Terry was sitting on the grass trying to get the water out of his bergen and somehow dry his clothes.

'Were you bust too?' he asked.

'Yeah, sure was,' I replied.

'I'm certain his scales were wrong. I weighed mine on the squadron scales this morning. It was 45 pounds. I've taken nothing out of it. His scales were wrong. I mean, we can't all be underweight.'

I hadn't considered the possibility that this was another test for us, a little injustice to see how we responded. Now that Terry mentioned it, it did seem like a distinct possibility. We sat there, bitching about the system, boiled up some water and made ourselves a cup of tea. Inside Terry's bergen were two sodden Bakewell tarts; he'd had them for two days, saving them for the time when he needed them most. 'Lewis, mate,' he said, 'you've got to have one of these.' How sodden they were didn't matter; we wolfed them down and I was touched by Terry's generosity. It's hard to explain to a civilian the closeness that can develop among a group of soldiers. It's hard to say why two grown-ups would laugh uncontrollably because the Bakewell tarts were soggy. Perhaps it is sharing adversity that brings men together. Of all the regiments, the SAS is defined by the extreme danger of its missions and the extreme adversity that its soldiers must encounter; as a result the kinship can be extraordinary. Sharing those two tarts with Terry, I thought of another partner I'd shared an office with at Ince & Co. We were in that space from 9 a.m. to 6.30 p.m. five days a week.

'Morning, Lewis,' he said at the start of every day.

'Morning, Oliver,' I replied.

Though not much was said, we were polite to each other at all times. After three months, I knew nothing about him and he knew nothing about me. Was he married? Did he have kids? What did he do at the weekend? Three months and I couldn't have answered one of those questions.

It was different for Terry and me on that long trek through the Brecon Beacons. We were exhausted, right at the end of our tether, and we still had 15 kilometres to go but we kept each other's spirits up and we kept on going. Through the really tough Voluntary Withdrawal Valley (so-called by SAS instructors because so many recruits give up in that valley) we spent an hour covering a relatively short distance. Another three hours got us to the last RV and, though we were shattered, we were inside the time limit. Terry's sleeping bag was still wet from Lake Gwyn so he simply flopped down on his roll mat and slept like a baby.

Selection was very tough. At the end of it the twenty-five eager and determined recruits who had survived Pre-Selection were down to just seven. By now the surviving seven from A Squadron 21 SAS all knew each other well and had heard enough about SAS training to know that the next phase, Test Week, would make Selection look like a Scout Camp. The good bits of Test Week were that we were based at Gwenddwr Military Camp on the edge of the Brecon Beacons, we each slept on a bed and under a roof, and there was plenty of food. The tough bits included pretty much everything else.

Each day began at 4 a.m., when we were out of bed, into the 'scoff house', as we called the dining hall, and devouring as much breakfast as was humanly possible. Such was the need to eat huge amounts of food that recruits hadn't the time to make conversation while eating. We started with two days in Erwood Valley, a hilly region of mid-Wales where much of the terrain is marshy and thick mists are common, and then spent the following four days in the Brecon Beacons. Each day we had to cover 40 to 50 kilometres with a weight-laden bergen on our backs and our weapon held in both hands. If only it had been a straightforward 50-kilometre trek through the mountains, but it wasn't. You were given a set of grid references, which pointed to the location of the first RV, and once you'd reached that, you were given the next grid references and on you went. The distance between the rendezvous points could be anything from five to ten kilometres.

Test Week took its toll on recruits. Terry Elliot and Chris Fry, who had been my colleagues in A Squadron 21 SAS since that first Saturday morning in Chelsea, were both binned and that was before we got to the greatest challenge of the week, Endurance or Long Drag. Our chief instructor at Test Week described this final challenge as 'a walk in the park' and, in the strictest sense, that was true. But it was no ordinary walk and Brecon Beacon National Park wasn't any old park. After five consecutive days on which we had run and trekked for anything between eight and twelve hours every day, we now had to run 80 kilometres through tough mountainous terrain. About 120 recruits began Test Week and the first five days had seen approximately half fall by the wayside. Those still standing were limping with blistered feet, bashed-up toes and swollen knees, and there were raw shoulder burns from the constant friction of bergen straps on skin. My worry was the pain in my right knee, which had grown through the week; I wasn't certain it would withstand an 80-kilometre trek through the mountains.

The evening before Endurance we gathered in the scoff house and listened as the Officer Commanding 22 SAS (training wing) congratulated us on getting this far and briefed us on the route we would follow for Endurance. It began at Trefor Reservoir and from there we would run to the top of Cefn Y Bryn, down to The Griffin Inn, around Cadair Berwyn and then Aberedw Hill, down to Llyn Isaf, then up to the top of Cadair Berwyn, down to Lake Gwyn, through VW Valley, on to Cwmtillery Reservoir and then back to Trefor Reservoir.

When do you start a mountain run that is going to take the best part of twenty-four hours? We set off at 2 a.m. and if all went well we would finish at around midnight or a little after. Each recruit was sent off on his own but as one slowed or another quickened little groups formed. It was essential to spend much of the journey in the company of others. By doing so, you are reminded that your exhaustion is no different to that felt by the man at your side but, more than that, the camaraderie shortens the journey and helps to keep you going. However tough you like to think you are, it is remarkable how well people respond to simple words of encouragement – something as simple as the person alongside telling you not to give in, that you can do it.

Llyn Isaf was the halfway point but it was still 40 kilometres from the finish and my knee was beginning to ache. Every time I used it, pain shot through the joint and it grew progressively more severe. I tried every way of moving that lessened the strain on the knee with obvious consequences for my progress. My run became a walk and my walk became a shuffle. Because of the ways I was trying to protect the knee, my right hip began to seize up. At the Llyn Isaf RV, the DS said, 'You must be Pugh, 21 SAS?' I nodded. 'You are last. If you don't speed up, you will simply not make it. You've been out for just over twelve hours and it's not looking good.'

You know things about the SAS – don't sound like a baby because it's not a kindergarten – and you respond accordingly but you sometimes forget. The chief instructor was at the Aberedw Hill RV. As I came through, he shouted, 'Pugh, what the hell is wrong with you? You'd better speed up, son.' There was no point in going into any detail about my injury but I wanted him to know the reason why I was lagging behind.

'Staff, my knee is very sore,' I said.

'Your knee is sore? I don't give a f*** about your knee! What happens when you've got an enemy patrol hunting you down?'

My knee throbbing, I limped, hobbled and otherwise dragged myself to the top of Cadair Berwyn and hated every step of the descent because, whatever was wrong, the knee couldn't deal with the strain of going downhill. Nor was the experience doing much for my love–hate relationship with the majestic barrenness of the Brecon Beacons. On a clear day especially, but mostly on any day when I was healthy and not wasted by too much physical effort, I loved the landscape and the mountainous terrain. How could you not love it? But as darkness fell on that Thursday evening and I fell further behind, I hated its every inch. After getting through

VW Valley, a forest was indicated on the map but it had been cut down recently and I could shorten my journey by running through it. In the darkness I couldn't see the tree stumps beneath my feet and I fell many times, an occurrence worsened by the 70-pound bergen on my back. Running through the forest turned out to be not such a clever move, as I could not find the route I'd imagined and eventually had to double back and go right round it. Cwmtillery Reservoir was the penultimate RV, about ten kilometres from the finish, but the previous 70 on the top of the 200-plus we had done over the five days before Endurance had destroyed my knee. A couple of hundred metres from the RV at Cwmtillery, the knee just went from under me. I decided to crawl towards the RV, the bergen on my back.

To get to the RV I had to cross a road and, as it was now pitch dark, I remember thinking that if some Welsh farmer came driving round the nearby bend, I'd be dead. Thinking how the farmer might describe the accident to his friends – 'To me it looked like two giant tortoises mating on the road' – I tried to smile inwardly. Fifty metres before the RV, I hauled myself up and tried to walk as if nothing were the matter. Two DS were in a Land Rover, and one of them pointed a torch in my direction.

'Okay, stop,' he said, and then he got on the radio to the chief instructor, whose replies were clearly audible.

'What condition is he in?' asked the chief instructor.

'Bad condition,' said the DS, who ran the torch up and down my body.

'It's your call then, out.'

The DS looked at me again, unable to make up his mind. 'Do you want to carry on?' he asked.

'Yes, Staff,' I replied.

He thought for a moment. 'Okay, your final RV is 321 764. Double away.'

Being stationary for a minute or so hadn't helped at all and as soon as I set off, the pain shot through my knee. This caused me to hobble and, shocked by what he'd just seen, the DS jumped out of his Land Rover.

'I'm sorry, mate, I am going to pull you. Your leg is totally stuffed.'

'Please, Staff, I've come so far; I can get there.'

'No, mate, it's over.'

Twenty-one hours in the mountains, seventy kilometres behind me, just ten remaining – I was distraught. All those Wednesday evenings in Hordley, the weekends of map-reading my way through the mountains, the work I had done on my own and all for nothing. Recognizing the devastation written on my face, the DS was sympathetic. 'I couldn't let you go on with that knee – not in darkness when it's easy to get lost. But I'm binning you. If you'd stopped, you'd never be allowed another shot at joining the SAS. By binning you, I've given you the chance to come back and try again.' This was an important distinction but at that moment I couldn't see beyond the carnage – physical and emotional. Next time? Who cared about next time? But it was futile to argue. They put me in the back of a truck and drove me to Gwenddwr. Other recruits were returning at the same time as exhausted as I was but giddy with triumph. They had made it. Thank God it was almost midnight because it was easy to walk quietly past with my head down. Inside the camp, I collapsed on my bed and waited for sleep to take away the pain temporarily.

We were taken back to London by bus the next day and the feeling of abandonment accompanied me all the way. The Regiment had abandoned me and left only devastation in its place. In my mind, I was the guy who didn't make it. For weeks afterwards it stayed with me, affecting my mood at work with Ince & Co and affecting my relationships. I was relieved that I had told so few people about my attempt to join the SAS. David Becker and my mother knew, so did General Tim Toyne Sewell, and that was it. Of the forty A Squadron 21 SAS recruits who showed up on that Saturday morning at Chelsea Barracks, only a guy we knew as Gary Blackie got through. He was tall, muscular and tough, and could run forever in the mountains. But at the very next stage, training in the use of weaponry, Blackie was binned. Under pressure, he couldn't get his weapon loaded quickly enough. A few guys from C and E Squadrons of 21 SAS made it through. As they were also part-timers, they proved it could be done and convinced me that I mustn't give up.

8

VASBYT*

The SAS wouldn't go away. The experience had been arduous and the ending was heartbreaking: I had failed. Like a toothache, the pain infiltrated every aspect of my life over the following weeks. I could talk as much as I wished about the knee injury and how unlucky it was to get so close but it didn't change the reality. I had been binned because SAS training is brutal. Even though I was motivated and well prepared, I was betrayed by my own body. Everyone who doesn't make it has a tough-luck story to tell.

At the time, I was a maritime lawyer preparing to take a year out to study at Cambridge University, something that excited me greatly, and there was plenty of other stuff to occupy me. I could have just let the SAS go and got on with my life. But that was impossible. The Regiment ran like a

---

* The Afrikaners have a word called 'vasbyt'. The literal translation is 'bite hard'. Imagine a lioness running across the veld and grabbing a wildebeest under the neck, kicking and hoofing. The lioness holds on because her life, and the lives of her cubs, depends on it. To the Afrikaners 'vasbyt' means to never, ever, ever give up – to have grit and determination. This was a time in my life when I had to bite very, very hard.

steam engine through my head, last thing at night, first thing in the morning: this was something I had to be part of. It was not about earning the sandy-coloured beret; it was so much more than that. I loved training with the men of A Squadron 21 SAS because in that environment friendship was real and your mates were genuine, strong and principled. They were as hard as any men I'd met but they were also humble. You rarely met their kind in a London law office and, if you did, you didn't easily get to know them.

When we went to Wales on training weekends, I discovered a mountainous landscape that thrilled me. Sure, there were days and nights when the rain pelted sideways into your face and your feet found every inch of swampy ground but the elements were only a reminder of what countless generations had to cope with as they tended their sheep and waited for the wind or the rain to pass. My ancestors, on both my father's and mother's sides, were Welsh. Out on the Brecon Beacons, I found it easy to feel connected to the land of my fathers. My cousin Grif Griffiths is a lawyer in Brecon. During my weekends off, I would stay at his home, spending long days in the mountains and pleasant evenings catching up with him. But all the good times were destroyed by having failed in the last hours of the final day of Test Week. Inside, it gnawed at me: 'Lewis, failure is something you can't accept.' Some of the guys who got through weren't as strong as I was but, when it came to that last 80-kilometre march, their bodies had held up.

If there's one thing our instructors discouraged, it was self-pity. It is a weak man's emotion. No matter how tough things got, none of the commanding officers were interested in sob stories. Injury was your problem, not theirs. After being binned, I got my right knee checked out and the medics didn't need much time to work out that I had been suffering from a severe case of ITBS (iliotibial band syndrome), a condition caused by my flat feet and the great distances I was covering

with a heavy load on my back. It is not an uncommon condition and a podiatrist gave me insoles to create an arched
effect inside my boots and shoes. Recovery depended upon
the knee getting plenty of rest and my willingness to do a lot
of stretching exercises.

As depressed as I was to have failed, I still couldn't give up
on the SAS. I'd experienced a cruel but temporary disappointment and it was up to me to make sure the setback
didn't become permanent failure, an irremovable scar. I have
met men who did the SAS training and they tell how they
got their beret but as the conversation develops, they say
something that indicates they couldn't have made it. Their
sense of self-esteem got so wrapped up in making it into the
SAS, they began to spin an untrue story and told it so often
they ended up believing it. Given the aura that has attached
itself to the Regiment, perhaps it is not a surprise that Walter
Mittys are desperate to get in.

Because my elimination was the result of an injury, the
rules allowed me to apply again but not to start at the point
of my exit. They said I would have to begin midway through
the Selection weekends and, if I got through Selection, then
I would be allowed to have another shot at Test Week.
Everything went fine until the final weekend of Selection,
when a heavy dose of influenza laid me low; it was so severe
I could hardly stand and every inch of my body ached. Two
days before departure for Wales I tried to stay calm, telling
myself it wasn't my fault. I was gutted, as there was no
chance of recovering in time.

I rang one of the DS. 'Staff, I'm not going to be able to
make Test Week. I'm dying with the worst flu I've ever had.'
As I spoke, I could detect a damning judgement in his
silence. He was thinking the Regiment were wasting their
time with me: on being given a second chance, this guy
chickens out because of bloody flu.

'Why not wait until tomorrow before deciding?' he said, straining to be diplomatic. I felt like a chicken.

The next morning I got an appointment with my doctor and begged him to give me something – anything – that would allow me to get to Wales. 'This isn't something you can rush, Lewis. Flu runs its course. Take this medicine and stay in bed.'

Feeling worse than I had the previous day, I made another call to the DS. 'Staff, I've been to the doctor; I'm not going to be able to make it.'

Now diplomacy was forgotten. 'Look, Pugh, you've got to listen to me. You've got nothing to lose here. You're on a second chance. You only get two goes. You might as well try and maybe you will make it.' It was hopeless. I knew that my condition meant I wouldn't be able to survive a weekend of timed runs in the Brecon Beacons.

'Staff, I'm telling you honestly, I can barely move and, if I went, I couldn't possibly make it.'

There was a momentary silence at the end of the line. 'Okay, Pugh, it's your call.'

And so the dream of being in the SAS was dead. Something I had wanted to be part of since my mid-teenage years wasn't going to happen. This was more disappointing than the first time because I wasn't even getting the chance to fail. The flu eventually passed, and I felt strong again and more upbeat. 'Maybe they would be sympathetic and accept it wasn't me chickening out,' whispered one voice inside my head. 'Don't be daft, Lewis, no one gets a third chance in the SAS. You are only ever allowed two goes,' replied another. Feeling miserable about how my SAS experience had turned out, I decided the only way to end it was to beg for that one final chance.

By now I was at Jesus College in Cambridge doing a Masters in International Law and the nearest military base was

Cockford. I went there and explained my situation. Because I hadn't actually completed two Test Weeks, they considered my request. The instructor in charge weighed up my case. What was a tricky decision for him was life defining for me. 'We've never done this before,' he said. 'In fact, I don't know anyone in fifty-odd years of the SAS who has been given a third chance, but we're going to give you another go. Although it's your third time, we're going to pretend it's only your second because you've been to Test Week only once.'

Elated doesn't begin to describe how I felt. This time I wouldn't fail. Again, I started midway through Selection. By now a couple of the guys who had been fellow recruits on my first Selection were instructors and their exaggerated kindness spoke of pity more than admiration. 'This poor bloke, he keeps coming back. He's never going to make it,' I imagined them saying to each other. I got through several weekends but then disaster struck on a trek through the Beacons. There was a thick fog, and somehow I ended up in a rocky area that played havoc with my compass. A recruit from 23 SAS in Scotland, on a pre-Test Week training weekend, had also become lost and for about an hour we walked in circles, the blind leading the blind. We would look at our compasses, follow the needle as it pointed north and, then, 100 metres later, the needle said we were actually going west. The fog was like pea soup and we didn't have a clue which way to turn. There is a procedure for those who get lost on SAS Selection: you walk down a hill until you come to a river, you follow the river downstream until you come to a road, you follow the road until you come to a house and you ask the owner if you can please use their phone to call the Army. We arrived at a farmyard, where dogs were barking, and discovered other recruits had got there before us. 'You guys lost too?' one of them said to us. We nodded, thankful that they had contacted the Army and even more thankful that we weren't on our own. A Land Rover came and took us back to Gwenddwr Military Camp. The journey passed in silence. We felt like idiots and expected to be sent packing that evening.

Once we were back in Gwenddwr, I went to the scoff house and ate alone. The chief instructor from 21 SAS walked in. At his side was the Permanent Staff Instructor (PSI) from 22 SAS and it was clear the PSI was taking control of the situation. After so many weekends on Selection, we knew each other. He was ruthless. Despite being a smoker, he was so fit and strong that on the long runs few could keep up with him. Without much fuss, he motioned me to one side. 'How the hell did you get lost? I'm binning you.'

I pleaded, 'Please don't, Staff. I've sacrificed so much to be here. I desperately want to do this.'

He was slightly taken aback and looked at the chief instructor, who was from the TA. The chief instructor didn't say anything but somehow conveyed sympathy for my situation.

'How many goes has this guy had?' asked the PSI.

'One,' said the chief instructor, who may have been trying to protect me or may not have known I was on my third chance. Either way, I was staying quiet.

'One more cock-up, Pugh, and you're out of here. Do you understand me?'

I survived the rest of Selection and got to Test Week. I was again reminded of the extraordinary toughness of SAS training. It had rained a lot in the days before we were due to start. My cousin Grif from Brecon said it was the worst rainfall he'd seen in the area during his life. Roads were passable but only by slowing and inching your vehicle through a foot of surface water. On the first morning, the rain was still bucketing down. Everyone seemed to think they were going to cancel

Day 1 because the land at Erwood Valley is marshy at the best of times and would be one enormous swamp after the prolonged rain. As well as that, the streams we had to cross on our march would be swollen and dangerously fast-flowing. We all thought they couldn't possibly send us out in those conditions and we were like kids unexpectedly informed that school was closed for the day. We couldn't have been happier.

The evening before we were due out, there was a briefing at which we expected confirmation of the cancellation. Instead we were reminded not to forget our transponder beacons, which we had been given the previous day, and we were advised to put them in our bergens. 'Make sure you've got a fresh battery in it,' said our O/C, 'because tomorrow's weather forecast is shite and if you get lost or carried away in a river or are unable to get out of a swamp, the transponder will allow us to find your body.' He smirked, but not everyone thought the joke was funny. 'See you on parade at 5 a.m.,' one of the other instructors then said. Reports of a Day 1 cancellation had been greatly exaggerated.

Erwood Valley is a part of Wales close to my heart. A few months earlier my mother had come from South Africa and I had taken her to the valley. She was moved by the beauty of the place and by being back in the country of her birth. Once an endangered species, red kites soared all above us and their presence in Erwood Valley was a reminder that so much can be done to protect nature and the environment. Trends can be reversed: birds that were once scarce were now plentiful in a former habitat. Often all it takes is the will of people to make it happen. Mum and I were thrilled by our visit. We were far more excited than the many recruits who assembled at 5 a.m. at Gwenddwr Military Camp on that first day of Test Week.

It was dark, the rain was lashing down and we were already soaked by the time we got into the back of the army truck to Lake Celyn, the starting point for that day's timed march. When the truck came to a stop and the canvas was pulled back, it revealed a picture as bleak as any you've ever seen. Rain was pouring down, water cascading over the wall of the nearby reservoir, and the gentle little river at the bottom had been transformed into a raging force of nature. We were sitting in the back of that truck still thinking they wouldn't go through with it and they would have to call it off. So miserable were the conditions, the instructors stayed inside their Land-Rovers – no point in them getting drenched. 'Okay,' shouted one, 'first recruit, yes, you, Hunt, get yourself weighed. Forty-five pounds in your bergen excluding food and water. Your first grid reference is 274382. Okay, off you go. Next. And, lads, make sure when you're crossing rivers you take care.'

Hunt departed; the next to go was John Ferguson, who was training to be a priest. I was third off and enjoyed the thunderous sound of water spilling from the top of the reservoir. Soon the rain stopped, I caught up with John and we ran over a hill together. According to our maps, we had to cross a small river after descending the hill – but it was no longer a small river. Now it was 20 metres wide and flowing furiously. We watched Hunt trying to wade across, his bergen held high over one shoulder, his weapon in his other hand. Two steps, three steps and then on the fourth step he lost his footing and was swept downstream. His head bobbed up and down for a bit, his bergen was ripped from his grasp and by the time he scrambled to the bank it was 50 metres further down. He sprinted after it, but the river was too fast. Only then did we notice that Hunt had also lost his weapon, an offence for which there would be no forgiveness. He was not going to be in the SAS.

'This is treacherous,' I said to John. 'The alternative is to run a few kilometres upstream and try to find an easier place to cross but that will mean we won't be inside the time limit.

We get a red card or we cross here.' On Test Week, you get a red card if you finish outside the time limit; a second red card means you're out. We had been instructed how to wade across a river – you walk sideways, never crossing your legs, always facing upstream. It was straightforward enough in theory except that we had never attempted a river crossing in such conditions.

'Lewis,' said John, 'let's say a short prayer.'

I wasn't going to disagree.

'Dear Lord,' said John, 'please protect us on this river crossing. Please keep us safe. Amen.'

'Amen,' I said.

We ran to what appeared to be the safest place to cross. 'Okay,' I said, 'you go first. I'm going to take off my bergen. If you slip, I will be in there in half a second to fish you out. Just make sure you keep hold of your bergen and your weapon.' He inched across, doing everything correctly, leaning forward into the water as it gushed into and around his knees and thighs and eventually his waist. Close to the far bank, he dived and got there safely. 'Well done,' I shouted. Knowing John had done it helped me and, moving gingerly, I made it across too.

Climbing up the valley we waited for a minute on some elevated ground overlooking the river as Mike Farmer came up to make his crossing. He didn't fancy it at all and, winding himself up like a hammer-thrower, he flung his weapon over the river into the far bank. It landed like a spear, the barrel torpedoing into the sodden earth. Unknown to Mike, one of the instructors was watching from a Land Rover higher up on the hill. Mike got across and followed us up the hill. At the same time the instructor got out of the Land Rover and signalled Mike to stop. 'What the hell do you think you're doing?' he screamed. 'Are you seriously trying to get into the SAS? You know you never, ever, let go of your weapon. Not under any circumstances! What happens if you're in the field and come under fire after throwing your weapon across a river? Right now you go back down to that river, you go across it with your bergen and weapon and then make the crossing properly.' That took time – enough for Mike to get a red card that evening. He got another the following day and we never saw him again.

In a valley south of Lake Celyn, another stream had doubled in size and the swollen water surged downstream as if speeding for the last tide out to sea. In normal circumstances it would have been possible to jump the eight feet but with a bergen on your back and a weapon in your hands it wasn't easy. Three hundred metres from the stream, John and I watched a recruit jump and, although his feet reached the far bank, he slipped and fell back into the water. In a second he was swept downstream towards a large waterfall. Danger lay in the rocks at the bottom of the waterfall. John and I were too far away to do anything but another recruit, closer to the stream, sprinted and cut an angle that allowed him to jump in front of his fellow recruit. Somehow he got him out – just in time, as seconds later he would have gone over the falls. It was one of the bravest things I've ever seen.

That evening a number of recruits reported losing their weapons and bergens. The loss of a rifle is a very serious issue in the Army and searches were organized for each lost weapon. At least forty per cent of those who set out that day got red cards and by the end of our second day our numbers were very depleted.

When they had sent us off that morning, I thought it was wrong. What justification could there be for ordering men to do a march in conditions that could so easily have led to serious mishap? A few years later my view on that had changed completely. It was the correct decision because that day in Erwood Valley became part of who I am. No matter what the conditions were later, I had dealt with worse and that thought instilled a lot of confidence. Later on I knew that if the Regiment asked me to do a job in atrocious weather conditions, they wouldn't be any worse than Erwood Valley that day. I had survived before and I would do so again. And there would be comfort in knowing that on a foul night the enemy would be tucked up in bed, convinced that nobody would dream of hunting them down in such conditions. The other point about getting through that terrible first day without picking up a red card was the morale it gave you for the following four days. I survived those four days without drama and found myself facing my old adversary, the 80-kilometre Endurance march that would decide whether or not I had a future in the SAS.

Last time, I had gone through Selection in summer; now it was late January, the heart of winter, and the forecast was for pretty inhospitable conditions. We were briefed around one o'clock in the morning, and it was a serious talk from our instructors about the magnitude of what we were facing. This time there were no jokes about it being a walk in the park because the conditions ensured it couldn't be that. Instead we were reminded of the dangers and how, if any man went down with an injury or sickness, it was the responsibility of those who were with him to put up his basher (a canvas sheet for sleeping under), give him food and make sure he was okay before leaving him to call for help.

It is 2 a.m. and there isn't much talking in the vicinity of Trefor Reservoir in the Brecon Beacons as recruits ready themselves for a trek that none can be sure of completing. As if the 80 kilometres of mountain terrain are not challenging enough, it is also pitch dark, the wind is howling and a sleeting snow is driving into our faces. And it's so damn cold. I concentrate on the first part of the journey, the trek to the top of Cefn Y Bryn, content to follow the recruit who walks five metres in front of me, just as the recruit in my slipstream follows me. Our pace is determined by our bergens. Packed with food and water, they weigh over 70 pounds and, going uphill, that load feels no lighter. I know Cefn Y Bryn so well now that I make sure that at the top I stay well back from the cliff on the right-hand side. On windy nights, recruits have been blown over that cliff to their death. Once over the top, we descend to The Griffin Inn and our first RV. Already there are casualties. I hear a recruit speaking to one of the instructors, 'This is too cold, Staff, too extreme. I'm VW-ing.' Once you voluntarily withdraw, that's it. You will never be given another chance. In front of me, a well-built and obviously strong Royal Marine just stops. He's had enough.

Seeing others give up encourages me and I need it because my knee is hurting again. It isn't a surprise and this time I've come armed with strong painkillers and anti-inflammatory tablets. In fact, I have been taking them for the previous three days and, to a degree, they are working. But the knee slows me and when we reach the RV at Llyn Isaf, which is the halfway point, I have just two recruits behind me. I know this because of the kind words uttered by the DS stationed at the last RV. 'Pugh, you are one of the last three. You'd better speed up or you're not going to make it.' I check my watch: it has been almost twelve hours exactly. To get inside the allotted twenty-four hours, I've got to go a lot quicker on the return journey because exhaustion will slow me at the end. I pop another painkiller and tell myself to keep going. Quickening my pace, I catch up one recruit, then another and finally we are a group of about eight. They are all from 23 SAS and stationed in the north of England and Scotland. Not knowing the Beacons nearly as well as I do, they are happy for me to guide them. They are unaware of all the weekends I've spent on these mountains: three Selections, one Test Week and a number of other weekends training with my friend James Maxwell. There are shortcuts everywhere and even in the snow and sleet I find them easily. There is a Major among the 23 SAS guys and he is especially appreciative. 'Thanks, mate, this is great. You're saving us so much time,' he says every so often.

The conditions take their toll on us. During the day, the weather gets progressively worse until the sleet and snow is driving horizontally into our faces. Through the last 20 kilometres, we are a collection of zombies, each one walking with his head bent, focusing only on the patch of ground one metre in front of him. Part of me wants to give up but another, louder voice tells me to keep going.

I think of my father's cousin, Carey Heydenrych. Carey fought in the Second World War and was involved in the famous Great Escape. He came to our house in Cape Town and gave me a copy of the book in which he told his story. He volunteered in South Africa, was trained as a fighter pilot and was later shot down off the Norwegian coast attempting to take out a German ship. He survived, was captured, attempted to escape, was re-captured and was then taken to Stalag Luft III, where he became involved with the group of prisoners who tried to tunnel their way out of the prison. Each man was given a number for the order in which they would escape and Carey was number 132. They had a network of three tunnels – Tom, Dick and Harry – and the plan was to tunnel underneath the perimeter fence and not resurface until the tunnel had reached a nearby wooded area. Unluckily, they miscalculated the distance and instead of the tunnel opening up into the woodland, it came up in a piece of open ground between the perimeter fence and the trees. That slowed the escape as each prisoner had to wait for the watchtower searchlight to pass and then make a run for the trees. While Carey was waiting his turn in the tunnel, a guard saw one of the prisoners make his escape and raised the alarm. Aware of what was happening, those in the tunnel desperately tried to get back to their quarters. Some made it; some didn't. Many of those who escaped were rounded up and shot in cold blood. Only three prisoners made good their escape. Carey was fortunate; he did not get out.

Near the end of the war, prisoners from Stalag Luft III were taken on two forced marches in brutal weather so the Germans could try to use them as bargaining chips in their surrender negotiations. Carey became close friends with another pilot who walked alongside him and helped his friend through when he had a bad bout of dysentery. Then, when Carey got sick, that friend did precisely the same for him and they both survived. It was an inspiring story. On my last legs in the Brecon Beacons, I think of what Carey went through and it keeps me going. 'Is this as bad as what Carey had to endure?' I ask myself and the answer is always no. And, most inspiring of all, Carey wrote a full account of his war experiences without once expressing bitterness towards the Germans.

If Carey could cope with what he'd been through, I have no right to complain about my summer uniform (21 SAS didn't have winter uniforms in stock when I went looking) on this murderously cold night. It cheers me that among all these 23 SAS guys, I am the only recruit from 21 SAS. Now we are climbing Cadair Berwyn, a convex mountain that doesn't show its summit. You climb and climb and climb but never seem to get to the top. Eventually, we get there and see the tent that serves as our RV. It is being blown every which way, two DS are inside and, through a partially open flap, we shout our names and are given the grid references to take us to the next RV.

Boosted by getting to the summit of Cadair Berwyn, we speed things up on the descent to Lake Gwyn. We've only gone a little way when my knee buckles beneath me. It feels as if someone has suddenly driven a six-inch nail through the outside of my right knee. The fall is something over which I have no control. 'Guys,' I shout, 'my knee has gone. Please wait a minute while I take a painkiller and get some food into me.' They stop to assess the situation. Each of them is desperately tired and all are worried about the time limit. Now I am no longer the recruit who has guided them for so long, the guy who made sure they avoided the bogs, the one who found sheep tracks and showed them all the shortcuts through the storm. No, that guy is gone. I am now the man who has become a burden. They exchange glances and come to a decision without a word being spoken. This isn't their problem. 'Sorry, mate,' one of them says, 'we can't afford to wait.' There are no words that adequately convey how I feel on seeing my comrades disappear. 'Best of luck, then,' isn't what I want to say but, in any case, they are gone before I can utter a word.

What of the instruction we'd been given before setting out? The chief instructor told everyone that time spent helping an injured colleague would be subtracted from our finishing time. Didn't they believe this would happen? I try to figure it out: they are freezing cold, some probably suffering the early symptoms of hypothermia, and I know from swimming in cold water, hypothermia affects decision-making. Still, I want to yell, 'Bastards', but I haven't the strength. Six hundred metres above where I am lying is the RV and two instructors but they might as well have been on another planet. In the howling wind there is no way they would hear my screams for help. I feel like I have been left to die on the side of a mountain and think that only someone who has suffered this experience can ever know how terrifying it is. I am petrified.

Can I claw my way back up the mountain to the RV tent or should I try to work my way down and off the mountain and out of the storm? About five metres from where I lie, there is a small hole and, turning my back to the wind and the sleet, I edge towards the hole and wriggle myself into it. I curl up as best I can, take two painkillers, an anti-inflammatory, some food and some drink and begin to feel drowsy. Sleep, I know, is the drug that can hasten the hypothermic man to his death and I try to fight it. I try to stand up but I can't. Exhausted, frozen, sodden and demoralized, there is then a moment of pure clarity: 'Lewis, if you don't get yourself off this mountain, you are going to die. You will merit one paragraph in the *Daily Telegraph*: "A British soldier lost his life when training in the Brecon Beacons last night. The soldier has not been named as his family has yet to be informed."'

Move or die – it is so simple. The prospect of dying is like an injection of adrenalin. I roll onto my stomach, get into the push-up position and somehow lever myself upwards. I lift my bergen onto my back, convert my weapon into a walking stick and begin the long, slow trek down the mountain. There is no way I am going uphill. If I'm seen using the weapon as a walking aid I will be binned on the spot but there isn't a choice. I think what my response will be: 'Sorry, Staff, I'm just trying to stay alive.' All the way down from Cadair Berwyn, I walk without bending my right leg.

By concentrating on taking one step at a time, and not slipping on the ice, I eventually get to the next RV. The DS looks at my limping gait, 'You okay, Pugh? Listen, just keep going. You can make this.' It's funny the extraordinary effect simple words of encouragement can have on the lowly. They give me a magical boost and I realize my leg isn't as painful walking on the relatively flat terrain after the descent. But then I get to VW Valley and it almost kills me. I slither into the valley, wade across the swollen river, and crawl my way out of it. I get to another RV, then on to the RV at Cwmtillery Reservoir, where I had been binned before. Some of the recruits who had left me have fallen back and seeing them in front of me is good. I don't say one word when I reach them but they know and I know that my silence says everything. Bastards. At that penultimate RV, the DS tells me I'm cutting it fine if I'm aiming to finish within the 24-hour limit. He then calls out my grid reference, '731 424'.

I reply, '731 424, Staff.'

He says, 'Okay, Pugh, move it.'

I see Kember, a former Guardsman whom I know and like. He looks totally disorientated, drunk on hypothermia. I don't see him again and he doesn't make it.

This is déjà vu. I'm almost the last man on the trail and I'm right on the limit, pulling my gammy knee towards the finish line. There is a road up ahead that shortens the journey but, if I'm caught using it, I will automatically be binned. SAS soldiers don't use roads when fields and forests and mountains provide so much more cover. Besides, roads can be booby-trapped and are convenient places to set up an ambush. I've never used a road in all my training in the Beacons; the risk wasn't worth it. But tonight, it is. I get to the road and make quicker progress. Suddenly, there are lights coming round the corner. I fling myself down an embankment and, with the bergen on my back, I cartwheel away from the road. Have they seen me? I listen for the sound of braking; the truck slows, as if someone thinks they've seen something, but it then picks up speed again and is gone. Thank God. I leave the road and carry on. All the time I'm checking my watch and calculating how far I have to go, and I'm encouraged by my progress. I'm going to make it. I reward myself with a five-minute nap but I wake suddenly to realize 25 valuable minutes have slipped away. Why the hell did I fall asleep?! Now it is a desperate race to get to the finish in time. I run, swinging my right leg as if it were one long inflexible plank of timber that my hip has to carry, but I'm not going to be beaten now – not after all that has happened.

I almost sprint into the final RV and shout my name: 'Pugh, Staff.'

'Not much to spare, Pugh,' he says. 'Twenty-three hours and 58 minutes. Well done.'

I am so relieved. Tears well up. I feel joy, relief, pain and, most of all, total exhaustion. But I have made it. A few seconds after calling my name, and a couple of metres from the RV, I collapse. My body has taken all that it can and my spirit no longer puts up a fight. The shelter of the truck is just metres away but I can't get back on my feet. A Colonel walks towards me. I can see a crown and two stars on his epaulette. I do not have the strength to stand and salute him. He says, 'Come here, son,' and takes the bergen off my back. He then picks me up and puts me into the back of the truck, then picks up my bergen and weapon and hands them to me. 'Well done, lads,' he says to all of the guys in the back of the truck. 'And lads, please help this guy. Get some food into him.' Someone hands me some food and I eat ravenously.

Back at Gwenddwr, my friend Woody helps me out of the truck and, though he too is exhausted, he carries both our bergens into the barracks. I'm still hungry but I haven't the energy to eat and it is a colossal job to take off my boots and my sodden clothing. My feet are swollen and infected but, feeling wasted, I'm numb to the aches and pain. All I want is sleep and, within seconds of lying on the bed, I am gone.

The next morning we are woken at seven and called out on parade. I realize now everyone else is hobbling too, as if we had all been in the fiercest battle. The PSI speaks to us. 'Those guys who finished last night can be proud of what they achieved because that was one hard day and night. Some officers from the Norwegian Special Forces were here

as observers and they said they had never experienced anything so severe as last night. Because the conditions were so
bad, we have decided to pass those recruits who finished last
night but were outside the time limit. Now you've got to
clean your weapons and get your quarters tidied up.' A few
recruits who had come in almost an hour late and been shattered by the experience are now ecstatic. Though part of me
thinks it would have been nice to know this last night, I am
glad I made it inside the twenty-four hours.

But, now, I don't much care about anything. I've passed
SAS Selection and even if my knee is shattered and my body
bruised from head to toe, even if my back is chafed from
friction caused by the bergen, and there are severe infections
under both big toenails, I'm not one bit bothered. Bodies
heal themselves; what matters more is the state of your spirit.
There are other bridges to cross before I can earn my SAS
beret but passing Test Week is a pivotal moment and I've
done it. I climb onto the coach for the return journey to
London and I float all the way home.

Part of my respect for the SAS lay in the environment it
creates. On every training exercise, I enjoyed the compan-
ionship of my fellow recruits far more than I had in the
corporate world of law firms. Many times I have wondered
about this and here's what explains it. The SAS has clearly
defined ideals and it was customary for our superiors to brief
us on the core beliefs that underpinned the Regiment. In law
firms, there weren't any similar principles and we were never
told what the company stood for, apart from the generally
accepted goal of making financial profit. You were expected
to bill for seven hours every day and those who didn't were in
trouble. In the SAS we were constantly reminded about what
Colonel Sterling had in mind when he established the
Regiment, what he expected of his soldiers: the unrelenting

pursuit of excellence, humility, self-discipline, a classless society and a sense of humour. Never did a senior partner in the
law firm give us his vision for the company or his understanding of what the company stood for. Partners got worked
up when one of their fellow partners didn't bill sufficiently
and, unless that guy got his billing up to the level of his colleagues, he would soon be pushed out.

When working at the law firm, when I needed to have
some typing done I would take it to one of the secretaries a
little after five o'clock; she would say she was sorry but as she
was leaving at 5.30 there wouldn't be time to get it finished.
In the SAS, you were only finished when everyone's work
was done. At the law firm many of the partners believed that
a new European Union law forbidding employees to work
more than a 49-hour week wasn't practical. The managing
partner approached all the solicitors and asked them to sign
contracts excluding them from the new EU law. The argument was that the firm had to provide a service to their
clients and, as ships sometimes collide in the middle of the
night, someone might have to work night and day on the
case to get things sorted out. Similarly, there were court cases
that compelled lawyers to work very long hours for the
duration of the case. 'We live in the real world, not Brussels,'
the managing partner said. A number of the solicitors
weren't sympathetic to that argument and didn't want to sign
the contract. It became a big issue. I thought, 'Forty-nine
hours. I've worked that on any number of weekends away
with the SAS.' I signed the contract.

The reason others didn't sign it was the lack of team spirit
in the firm. There were good reasons why team spirit wasn't
what it should have been. In law firms there are 'fee earners',
comprising solicitors and partners, and 'support staff' who
are secretaries, human resource personnel, court clerks, pho-
tocopiers and other members of the office staff. Meetings

would be held for the fee earners to which no support staff member would be invited. The great divide was best illustrated by the divergence in salary. An equity partner might earn £500,000 in a good year while an ultra-efficient secretary would earn £30,000. How can you expect a strong team ethic when one member of the team earns sixteen times more than another? Who could blame the secretary for looking at her watch at 5.30 and deciding it was time to go?

It is very different in the SAS, where there is an understanding that if the mechanic doesn't do his job properly, the trooper driving the Land Rover can end up in extreme danger behind enemy lines. Everyone wears the sandy beret and that ridiculous disparity in salary does not exist. And despite the very obvious dangers involved in the life of the SAS soldier, he and those who support him have, in my view, much more fun and job satisfaction than their counterparts in the corporate world.

I met many fine men in the SAS – people who once encountered were not easily forgotten. Paul Hamilton, who tried to pass me in the race for second place on the infamous Fan Dance run of my first Selection, became a close friend. He was a prison officer. When we ran together he would talk to me about how important it was to treat prisoners with respect and to ensure they were not physically or verbally abused. He had blond hair, a barbed-wire tattoo around his bicep, and was about the best mimic I've ever heard. Running together in the mountains, he would slip behind, wait for a little while, and shout, 'Pugh, what the hell do you think you're doing?' exactly as Yorkie would have said it. 'Pugh, you had better start running at four kilometres per hour or I will bin you.' Paul eventually left the prison service and joined the Metropolitan Police in London but combining police work with SAS training proved too much and he unfortunately didn't get his beret. Later I heard he'd joined SO19, the Metropolitan Police's elite firearms unit and, as he was very good with weapons, that was going to be right up his street.

Terry Elliot is another fine man whom I remember – the same Terry who shared his soaked Bakewell tarts with me. He was short and balding and had a big heart. The instructors liked him and it seemed to some of the other recruits as though Terry was getting preferential treatment. It wasn't true and it wouldn't have mattered anyway because when it comes to Test Week there is only one person who can pull you through – you. Or, as our instructors constantly reminded us, 'The mountains will choose you.' No truer words were ever said. Terry got two red cards in Test Week, was binned and never returned to try again.

Eddie Payne was another character everyone had a lot of time for. In civilian life he was a lawyer. He was a lad's lad with an outgoing personality. His father had served in the SAS. Eddie had served in the Honourable Artillery Company (HAC), and had enjoyed the reconnaissance work. No one in 21 SAS knew that Eddie resigned from the HAC because he did not think he could kill a fellow man. Although I hadn't known that, it didn't surprise me when eventually it came out because Eddie was a thoughtful person – perhaps too much of a thinker. Some time after resigning from the HAC, Eddie rolled up for the SAS. In so many ways, he was an ideal candidate. He easily got through Pre-Selection, passed Selection and then got through Test Week. Sometimes I would see him on the mountain, he moving in one direction, me in another – it was always me on my way to the turn and he on his way home. He enjoyed the physical challenge and he was good at it.

After Test Week, he went on to Continuation but by that time his transfer papers had arrived from the HAC. I wasn't present that day because my Continuation was at a different time but I heard reports of what happened. It was evening parade and all the recruits were present with Yorkie standing in front of them. 'Payne,' he shouted, 'what the bloody hell is this? You resigned from the HAC because you couldn't kill someone and you want to join the SAS? What is going through your little f****** head?! Come this way, the O/C needs to see you.' They told Eddie he needed to think long and hard about what he was doing in the SAS. He was a good soldier, they liked him and, from what they saw, he would do well in the SAS. But if he wasn't prepared to kill someone, well, he was no good in the SAS.

By this time, Eddie had shown he could handle weapons and would get through Continuation, and on everything we had seen up to that point, he would comfortably pass Battle Camp and then the beret would be his. He could have told the O/C that he was now prepared to do what needed to be done in the SAS, complete his training, get his beret and then leave. But that night Eddie thought deeply about what he should do and the next day he resigned from the SAS. He knew the Regiment was investing time and money to take him through the various stages of training and if he wasn't going to be in a position to serve in the field, then he was wasting people's time. So he did the honourable thing, but that was Eddie — a very principled man. Going through the SAS training, you have plenty of time to consider what it might be like to serve in the Regiment and whether in the course of duty you would be prepared to take another man's life. My feeling was that if it was in defence of my country or of a comrade, I could kill somebody. I would do it and it was something to which I didn't give a second thought.

James Maxwell was probably the recruit to whom I became closest. He was a remarkable person, small in stature, wiry, but immensely strong. James would never have stood out in a crowd but the Regiment liked that. His parents were both Royal Navy: his dad was an officer; his mum a nursing sister – pretty much the same background as mine. He loved the outdoors and growing up on the edge of Dartmoor in the West Country, he had served in the Devonshire and Dorset Regiment of the Territorial Army. When he moved to London, he joined A Squadron 21 SAS and would show up on those Pre-Selection evenings with his dog, a boxer called Taz. In no time we all got to know Taz, who would jump out of the car, kiss and lick everyone before returning to the car and sleeping soundly until training ended and James returned.

James and I became friends and eventually part of our personal training for Selection included trips down to Devon, where his parents lived, and long runs on Dartmoor with bergens on our backs and Taz at our side. One of the tasks during Continuation was the building of an Observation Post (OP), which was child's play for James, who could have installed plumbing, electricity, laid a floor and connected up water if that had been needed. But James's quality shone through when we were assigned to an OP, looking through a pair of high-powered binoculars, four hours on, four hours rest, four hours on.

It is hard for a layperson to understand the concentration necessary for this kind of intelligence gathering. You keep your binoculars trained on a building and the road in front of it. For two hours, nothing happens and, thinking it is safe to take a momentary breather, you then miss the only thing that does happen. James was one of the best. He never slacked and would diligently write down everything that happened: 'One Toyota Hilux drove past OP at 19h23, moving in a southern direction with two soldiers sitting in front and three on the back . . . At 22h35, five soldiers patrolling along the fence in an east/west direction, carrying AK47s. They were unshaven and talking amongst themselves.' This kind of detail offers insight into the strength and morale of the enemy and James was a meticulous observer and recorder. He got through all the stages of SAS training, earned his beret and then subsequently joined MI5, who recruited furiously after 9/11.

He would have had an outstanding career but two years later, following a relatively short battle with stomach cancer, James died at the age of thirty-three. Words cannot describe the unfairness of one so young being struck down and it was hard to make sense of it. It was a terrible tragedy, especially for his wife Diane and their new child. Having spent a couple of Christmases with his family, I knew James's parents very well and they were obviously devastated by the loss of their son.

During his illness, he did not want any of us from 21 SAS to visit him in hospital, preferring us to remember him as he was. I could see the point but it was hard. There were times when I was in the Arctic training, and I thought of James battling with his illness and strongly felt the need to speak with him. But he wouldn't take our calls. Again I respected his reasons but I found it so damn difficult. Diane asked me to scatter his ashes on his favourite place in the Brecon Beacons. That was easy to pinpoint because he loved VW Valley, perhaps because he knew he would be the last man on earth to withdraw voluntarily.

My favourite memory was of charging down into the valley, about five metres behind James, who was shouting, 'Keep up with me, big guy,' and I didn't need to see his face at that moment to know it was lit up by a smirk. Perhaps he was right about not wanting us to visit him at the end because that's how I remember him, flying down into VW Valley, totally in his element. Diane and I walked together to VW Valley. It was a typical day on the Brecon Beacons with plenty of wind and rain and when I opened the little box ashes blew everywhere. We emptied the box into the stream and they flowed down into VW Valley as James had done so often in life.

Always having to tell lies or, at best, avoid telling the truth is hard and it was one of the tougher challenges of being in the SAS. I had a job in the City, a lovely girlfriend and it seemed that half of the time I was ducking and diving, finding ways of explaining my disappearance for weekends in a way that couldn't involve telling the truth. At Ince & Co, it was easier not to meet colleagues after work because that would have involved more deceit. The evening when I left the jacket of my suit on the back of my office chair, indicating I was still working when I was actually slipping out the back door, was the kind of situation I detested.

My frequent absences caused difficulties with my girlfriend, Anna. I explained my absences by admitting I'd joined the Territorial Army for a bit of excitement. I couldn't tell her that I was actually training for the SAS, partly because Anna was of the view that Britain had been drawn into a conflict in Yugoslavia that it didn't fully understand. Anna loved to chat with her friends and if I'd told her what I was really doing, it might have slipped out at some point. If you don't tell somebody something, they can't accidentally tell someone else. But more important than the secret were the absences and the fact that when I returned from a weekend in Wales late on Sunday afternoon all I wanted to do was curl up in bed and recapture the lost hours of sleep. Anna was patient for a while but, after I moved up to Cambridge and then had to combine serious study with my SAS training, we drifted apart.

Two weeks after getting through Test Week, I was one of sixteen recruits beginning Continuation, which involved training in the use of weaponry. You learned everything about a weapon – how to clean it, how to load it, how to fire it – but it wasn't just weapons. We were shown how to construct and camouflage an observation post, how to move across enemy territory at night, how to set up an ambush, how to avoid being ambushed, how to guide and guard an RAF plane into a Tactical Landing Zone (TLZ). Though you know Continuation is another rigorous part of the training, and that some recruits will not get through, after surviving Test Week you think you've been through the worst. Did that induce just the slightest complacency in my thinking? No. Of the sixteen who started Continuation, two of us had no experience in the use of weaponry. There was nothing I could do about it, but it was a very significant disadvantage and one that I only fully appreciated once the course had begun.

Luckily for me, another recruit, Johnny Benson, had plenty of Army experience and took me under his wing. We had to work in teams of four and within that, Johnny and I worked together brilliantly. In the SAS, somebody must always be on guard or 'on stag' as we called it. After an exercise, Johnny would start cooking while I guarded our position. He would feed me, then himself, clean up and then we would exchange positions. I cleaned up my stuff while he guarded. He would clean his weapon while I was on stag, then I cleaned my weapon and he would guard. It was good for me, as I was learning lots of new skills. What I didn't appreciate was that my progress was too slow.

Our instructor, a tough, unforgiving guy called Matthew Mansfield, was watching me more closely than I realized and he wasn't impressed. Matthew had an incredible memory. If he told you something early on and you made the same mistake a while later, he never failed to make the connection. When he checked your equipment, it was a serious moment. If you didn't have everything in order, you went into his little black book. 'Pugh, show me your compass, and your spare compass in case the first one breaks.'

Matthew was the kind of hard, pernickety character that some of the recruits didn't like, but I liked him and respected his unwavering commitment to the highest standards. When the time came for me to lead teams to Antarctica and the North Pole, it was Matthew's standards I applied when dealing with my team. Nothing was taken for granted, as every member of the team had to show me that he was properly prepared. Double-checking became standard practice and it saved us on a number of occasions.

One weekend we did a training exercise with live ammunition in which I was patrol commander of a four-man team walking along a mountainside. We saw the 'enemy', shot at them and separated into pairs: one pair fired to force the enemy to keep their heads down and the other pair darted forward. We then switched roles. Once close enough, we lobbed a grenade at the enemy position and, all the time, we were going forward. In the background, Matthew Mansfield watched like a hawk, monitoring how quickly we moved across the ground, how easily we dived into position, how natural we were in the use of our weapons, how slick we were in changing magazines, whether we had the presence of mind to have our safety catches on when we moved. Through every weekend of Continuation, I wish I had been given the opportunity to do a basic infantry course beforehand. On the second weekend, Matthew pulled me aside and warned me that I was going to have to improve substantially to get through. Working really hard, I did improve but on that training exercise I was still learning in a situation where I needed to be the finished product. Matthew saw my performance for what it was.

At the end of the training exercise, he addressed me. 'Pugh,' he said, 'come over here. Hand me your weapon please.' The moment was crushing. When your weapon is taken away, you know what it means. When a Tour de France rider is forced to abandon, race officials formally remove the race number from his jersey and he experiences the same feeling of being disrobed. It wasn't just the weapon Matthew was taking away but my career in the SAS. He took the magazine off, unloaded the weapon and then gave it to me straight. 'I am sorry, Pugh. It would not be safe to send you on to Battle Camp [the final element in the SAS training]. You haven't sufficient experience in the use of weaponry and you would be a danger to yourself and to other people.' Then he added the final blow. 'And I will be honest with you, I am not sure you will ever make it through this course.'

If you fail Continuation, you can reapply, but if the chief instructor believes you're not suited, there is a good chance you will not be allowed to try again. They don't like wasting time on those they believe are not going to make it. I had a sense that Matthew had been watching me all the time, waiting for the right moment to bin me, and that thought didn't make me feel any better. An officer, driving me to the train station, sensed my devastation. 'See if you can get yourself on a basic infantry course,' he said. 'Recruits who had no infantry experience always used to get sent on the course, but for some reason they're not any more. You just need more time. The rest of the recruits have more experience. You were trying to learn in a few weeks what they learned over a number of years, and some have even learned it on the battlefield.'

To have argued or complained would have been pointless and also wrong. Whether I liked it or not – and I didn't like it – I wasn't good enough. Matthew Mansfield didn't pick on me for personal reasons. When the officer driving me to the station suggested I get myself onto a basic infantry course, he wasn't saying I had been harshly dealt with. But it hurt and

I was again faced with the possibility of a temporary disappointment becoming long-term failure. I hadn't done an
infantry training course but I had recently started a new job
at the law firm Stephenson Harwood, and extra holiday time
wasn't a possibility. That new job actually turned out well, as
I worked for a partner, Tony Concagh, who couldn't have
been kinder in welcoming me into the company and then
involved me in all kinds of interesting cases. After settling
back to work, I mulled over the SAS conundrum for a few
weeks and then went to the HQ in London and asked if they
could put me on a basic infantry course. They didn't exactly
jump with excitement, but instead mentioned Matthew
Mansfield's doubts about my suitability. I asked again, more
passionately, and they agreed. As soon as I'd worked enough
to merit two weeks of holidays, I went up to Catterick in
Yorkshire for my infantry course.

Our instructors were from the Royal Irish Regiment and
they were good fun. Knowing I had passed Selection in the
SAS, they were extra helpful to me. After the ultra-
competitive experience of Continuation, the course in
Catterick was a fresh breeze. It was also one that I could
handle and, as a result, I thoroughly enjoyed it. Admittedly,
things were done at a slower pace. It was not like in the SAS,
where you were handed any weapon and expected to be able
to use it ten minutes later.

Failing at Continuation forced me to look at myself and I
drew from the experience two of the best lessons of my life.
First, you must never allow anyone else's estimation of your
worth to become your estimation. One of the factors against
continuing was Matthew Mansfield's feeling that I 'would
never make it'. I don't mean any disrespect to Matthew in
saying this but what kind of life would I have if he and others
were allowed to determine the limits to which I could go?
Certainly not the kind of life I wanted. That was the first

thing: I would allow no one the right to set limits on my behalf.

Secondly, I had to perform to the very best of my ability. This is not the same as being 'the best', or 'top of the class', or 'first over the line'; it is doing something as well as you possibly can. Sport is a good example: someone wins a race or a team wins a match and they talk about having given it 100 per cent. Often they give just 95 per cent but because their rivals give even less, they still win. I wanted to be 100 per cent – the absolute best I could be.

So when we ran at Catterick, it wasn't enough for me to finish the run before every other recruit; I had to win by as wide a margin as possible. Once my weapon was cleaned, I went and helped other recruits clean theirs. It wasn't enough to be the fastest or the quickest at completing a task if you could have done better. When your attitude is right, good things follow. A young Lieutenant in the Royal Irish Regiment took me under his wing during a live firing exercise and showed me how to lie in a comfortable position, how to hold my weapon without allowing it to quiver, how to aim it, how to control my breathing and finally how to squeeze the trigger without causing any movement. My accuracy improved astonishingly.

'Lewis,' he said, 'I want you to say to yourself, "I am the best sniper in the British Army". Now look at the target, focus on the bull's-eye, don't snatch at the trigger, squeeze smoothly. Now watch the bullet all the way into the target. That's it. Good bloody shot, Pugh.' Catterick couldn't have gone better.

On my first day back on Continuation, Matthew Mansfield walked into the changing room and said, 'Pugh, I hope you won first prize on that infantry course?' There was a smile on his face, as if he were half-joking. We both knew he wasn't.

'Yes, Staff, I got the prize for best recruit.' It was the least he expected of a recruit aspiring to be in the SAS.

This time I was a different person: more confident and practised in the use of weapons but, far more importantly, I was stronger because my attitude was far better. Previously the aim had been to get through but now it was to perform to the very best of my ability. Matthew quickly noticed the difference and soon after that he was on someone else's case.

My new instructor on second Continuation was Nick Peterson, who went on to become a very good friend. In civilian life, Nick was a barrister and perhaps it was his court-room skills that allowed him to argue with Matthew because no one else dared to. Nick was also a brilliant instructor who could explain difficult concepts in the simplest of terms and never, ever, make you feel your question was stupid. With Nick's help, I passed all the Continuation weekends the second time round and again had that intoxicating feeling that perhaps I was going to wear that sandy beret after all.

Battle Camp is the final leg in the SAS journey. You have proven your physical stamina and your ability to cope with hardship; you have learned to navigate through mountains, to work effectively in the dead of night; you know how to use a weapon, build an observation post, gather intelligence and move like a leopard through long grass; and you know how to get behind enemy lines. For two weeks at Fort David on the west coast of Wales, Battle Camp challenged us to apply what we had learned in conditions that recreated a battle zone. It was hard soldiering.

We did an OP, during which I spent three days gathering intelligence, alternating between four hours on and four hours resting. It wasn't the most stimulating work, as not much happened, but you had to be alive to everything that did and then to record it accurately. Worse than the demand on concentration was the wet and cold from which there was no escape. Fires were not permitted as they would attract the attention of the enemy and, though I was wearing every layer of clothing I had, it didn't stop me shivering most of the time. Your body grows weary of the constant battle to keep you warm but you dare not cave in. Miss something on your watch and that's it; there wasn't going to be the chance to miss anything else.

At the end of three days at the OP, we had to attack the enemy position. At that point, you are feeding off adrenalin because that is all you've got left. All our training was designed to make us the best soldiers we could be: tough, clear thinking and extraordinarily well trained. We were schooled to look after ourselves, get the job done and then get out of the battle zone. Of course not every mission pans out exactly as it is planned and the SAS has to gauge how its soldiers will react to being captured and then interrogated. This was certainly not the type of thing you'd want to undertake very often and two recruits failed at this penultimate hurdle.

We were then taken to Cardigan Beach in West Wales for our final exercise: guiding an RAF Hercules safely onto the beach. It was a dull, wet day, as the previous days had been, but as the Hercules approached, the rain stopped and the sun found an opening in the clouds. The sea was wild and beautiful but even the sound of the waves crashing onto the beach couldn't live with the thunderous noise of the Hercules. After it landed, the door opened and out came the Commanding Officer of 22 SAS, the regular unit. It was a total surprise to us, as we had not been told he was coming. Then the engines stopped and everything went quiet. He stood in front of the seven recruits from 21 SAS who had made it. 'Guys, you have been through a lot; some more than others. I want to congratulate all of you. And I wanted to come here today to give you your berets personally. This is the most coveted beret in the British Army. There are very few of us in the SAS. Our predecessors fought in the desert of North Africa, in Normandy, in Argentina, in the Falklands, in the Gulf and many other places. Colonel David Sterling, our founder, believed that small teams of highly motivated and trained men could completely change the outcome of wars. He was right. We have done that many times and will continue to do so. Wear this beret with pride. You deserve it.'

He shook my hand and handed me my beret. I will never forget holding the sandy-coloured beret for the first time. It seemed surreal. I put it on my head. And pressed it down and tried to make it fit comfortably. I was finally in. I had got there. And it felt right that the beret was presented on this deserted beach in Wales, for it had been in this small country that we had been tested like never before and here that we found reserves of physical and mental strength we didn't know we possessed.

To me it was perfect that the presentation of the berets was done with little ceremony or fanfare, far from the admiration and applause of our families and friends. Only those who had gone through the course from Pre-Selection to Battle Camp could know what it had been like. Each SAS soldier who stood beside me on that beach with a beret now on his head had sacrificed so much to be where he was: one lost his job, another lost his girlfriend, another flunked his university career, one would later be divorced. Of approximately 200 recruits from A Squadron 21 SAS whom I had been with at Selection on my three efforts to progress, only three of us got berets: Steve Brown, James Maxwell and me.

Among the men I met and grew close to during my SAS training, there was a bond that words cannot describe. It took me over three years to get the beret and the most enriching part of the experience was getting to know men for whom you would have given your life on the battlefield. It is a big thing to say there are people who are not your family for whom you would give up your life. But that is how close we became. There were personal benefits in that I achieved a goal that many considered beyond me and, along the way, I discovered an inner strength that would power the rest of my life. And it is ironic that I gave everything I had to become a member of the SAS and, having done so, still felt that it was I who owed the Regiment.

I served another eighteen months in the regiment. They were tough but exhilarating. I found leaving one of the hardest decisions of my life. I remember handing in my weapon and my kit and walking in civilian clothes to the train station to catch a train home with tears streaming down my face. The Special Air Service had been a huge part of my life, but it was now time to move on.

9

INTO THE UNKNOWN

Sometimes events happen that seem calamitous at the time but later take on a different significance. In mid-2001, when in the throes of my third attempt at earning my SAS beret, my employers at Stephenson Harwood asked if I'd be prepared to work in their Singapore office. There had been a slowdown in the maritime industry in London but their Singapore office was thriving. As I was unmarried and not as tied to London as others in the company, it was logical to offer me Singapore. The only problem was that my SAS dream remained unfinished business. If I said yes to Singapore, I would have to say no to the SAS. None of the partners at Stephenson Harwood knew about the SAS and from their point of view there was no obvious reason for me not to accept the offer. 'I'm sorry,' I said to the head of our department, 'I really don't want to go to Singapore.' My refusal didn't go down well and, fearful for my job, I spoke with the partner most likely to keep a secret.

'The reason I can't go to Singapore is that I am committed to finishing SAS training, which has become a big part of my life.'

'But, Lewis, if I can't tell the Head of Department, it isn't going to help,' he said.

'I would prefer it if you didn't,' I said, feeling that once one or two people knew, everyone would soon find out.

'Lewis, he can only act on the information he's got and if he doesn't know . . .'

Things worsened after the terrible tragedy of 9/11, when al-Qaeda struck down the Twin Towers in New York, causing nearly 3,000 people to lose their lives. Further acts of terror were expected and corporations braced themselves for the ripples through the commercial world. Months later I was called to a meeting with the Head of Department, the partner with whom I had spoken and the Head of Human Resources. 'I'm sorry, Lewis,' the Head of Department said, 'a number of lawyers in our area are going to be made redundant and you are one of them. This is the package we are offering you,' and with that he pushed an envelope across the table. I felt sick. Not knowing what to do or say, I picked up the envelope and tried to remain dignified; at the same time I wanted to make sure they felt my disgust.

'You guys are cruel,' I said, and walked out.

Only when your job is taken away do you realize how much your self-esteem depended upon it. Take away the livelihood and self-confidence soon disappears. That day I left the offices of Stephenson Harwood, and walked past St Paul's Cathedral feeling alone and without a future. What in God's name was I going to do? The next morning I woke and wanted to put on my suit, go to work and forget the previous day had happened. Instead I had to begin another journey.

It took time, but I came round. First I had to put a stop to the endless search for answers. The questions had been so destructive: was it because they saw me as South African and felt it easier to get rid of their overseas lawyers? The only other non-English guy in our department was Croatian and he, too, was made redundant. More likely, I told myself, it was because of my refusal to go to Singapore. Perhaps they saw that as a lack of commitment to the company and that I had turned down a good offer. No matter how mentally strong you might be, being made redundant leads to a certain amount of self-doubt: maybe I just wasn't a good enough lawyer. And in the post-9/11 world, there weren't many companies out there screaming for new lawyers.

Not too long afterwards, an old Stephenson Harwood client, Guy Lether, called to say thanks for the work I'd done on his case. He also said he gave a lot of work to a company called Clyde & Co and was friendly with one of the partners there. Would I mind if he recommended me to them? Guy's support encouraged me to think more positively and my £35,000 redundancy payment allowed me time to think about what I would do.

My first decision was to take a cycling holiday, on my own, in Norway. There were many reasons for it. Getting away from London's corporate urban jungle was one of them. I'd also heard about Norway's beauty from so many people that I wanted to see those deep fjords and the towering mountains behind them with their snowcaps. But the greatest reason for wanting a bicycling holiday was to do something that would stretch me physically and allow me to become super-fit. All my life, I have found that my self-esteem is partly affected by my physical fitness: when I am in really good shape physically, I'm generally in pretty good shape mentally. So my bike was fitted with panniers, the panniers were packed with a small tent, the minimum amount of clothes and a wash bag, and one inexpensive flight later I was on my way to Bergen in the south-west of Norway.

It was a brilliant holiday, cycling all day, mostly over the mountains that were the starting point of the huge glaciers that inched their way downwards, swept everything before them and dragged forward much of what was underneath so that, millions of years later, we have the most spectacular fjord coastline on earth. It was a struggle riding uphill, as my physique is not what you'd look for in a Tour de France rider, but I loved every minute of it.

Summertime in Norway is extraordinary, as daylight stretches to eleven o'clock at night and re-emerges at about 3.30 in the morning. That was in the south-west of the country; as I rolled north, the days lengthened even more until there were twenty-two hours of daylight. If the cycling was physically tough, it was also spiritually energizing. Everywhere you looked, the view gave you a picture of nature's wondrous beauty. Someone once said you can't eat scenery, and that's true, but beauty nourishes the soul. London, with its rat-race hustle and threats of terrorist attacks, was a million miles away. On the climbs, I gasped for breath; on the descents, I filled my lungs – always with the thought that air didn't come any purer. At the northern port of Ålesund, I walked up the ramp of the coastal steamer, the *Hurtigruten*, and we sailed across the Arctic Circle to the Lofoten Islands. Travel writers claim these are among the most beautiful islands in the world and that's not an exaggeration. They are so peaceful, so quiet and so unspoiled. I was lucky to have come to this part of the world. In my gratitude I contemplated writing a thank-you card to my former Head of Department at Stephenson Harwood but, unsure he would get the point, I resisted the temptation.

On my last day, a long cycle towards the tiny Narvik Airport, I stopped at a beach to test the coldness of the water. The sand was golden, the sky was a clear blue and the jagged peaks of the surrounding mountains stood out against the uniform blueness of the sky. A few years had passed since

I'd swum and the thought of the cold water didn't get my enthusiasm racing to fever pitch. Still, ten seconds would be exhilarating so, casting off everything except my cycling shorts, I waded in. Ooh, it was cold. Hot and sweating from the bike ride, my body didn't care for the assault, but after the first flush of stinging coldness subsided, there was the realization that it was bearable, at least for a few seconds. The water was about six degrees. My ten seconds became two minutes and, back on sand, there was a difficult-to-explain yearning to get straight back in for another taste of Arctic coldness. This time I swam crawl for about three minutes, as fast as possible, and for a moment it was like old times. Feeling exhilarated afterwards, I sent texts to a number of friends back in London: 'Just swam in Arctic Ocean – cold but cool!'

Far from looking forward to getting back to England, I reached the airport with a heavy heart and feeling nothing but sadness. Two weeks was all it had been – one of the shorter holiday romances – and though the romance was with a country rather than a woman, the passion was no less. Getting in the water got me thinking. Not far from where I'd swum was the North Cape, the northernmost point in Continental Europe. As I was the only person to have swum around the southernmost point in Africa, the idea of swimming around the most northern point in Europe excited me. As far as I knew, no one had done it and the thought of coming back to Norway was very appealing.

Having spent so much time living in England and South Africa, it seemed to me that the Norwegians had created a more equitable society than either. They didn't have the gulf between rich and poor that is, for example, so evident and so demoralizing in South Africa and they were more egalitarian than the UK, where the class system continues to be a part of society and where educational opportunity for the well-off is very different to the opportunities for those who attend state schools in the toughest areas.

I went to Norway to clear my head of debris and, having done that in next to no time, I came back with lots of new ideas. For the first time I was considering the possibility of a life beyond a law office, and a future more interesting. Time, effort and expense had been poured into my education, especially the law degrees at the University of Cape Town and Cambridge. According to society's conventions, I was now expected to work as a lawyer. Norway gave me a glimpse of an outdoor life and I loved it, but there was still a need to earn money to pay the rent and buy the groceries.

After Guy Lether's suggestion to his friend at Clyde & Co, I was interviewed and immediately offered a job. I started working there soon after my return. It was a fresh start but only in name. It was just another law office, a continuation of a way of life that ultimately didn't appeal to me, and I had the sense of settling for less. But you do, don't you? The idea of not having a job scared me; it took away my 'respectability' and I wasn't ready to leap into something so unknown and uncertain.

If I jump forward a bit, to the end of 2003, there was an evening when the future appeared clearer and the dilemma of what I should do with my life resolved itself. This little epiphany happened on holiday in New Zealand, which is a very beautiful country and somewhere I'd always wanted to see. It's not surprising that the fog of uncertainty lifted on New Year's Eve, because that is a special time of the year and an annual opportunity for reflection.

On that final evening of 2003, I was at a party in a hotel near Mount Cook (3,754 metres) on the South Island, where the music was ridiculously loud and everything else was dull. By 11.30, I'd had enough and wanted somewhere quieter to think about the passing of the old year and the possibilities for 2004. It was dark outside but there was a bright moon and soon I was at the statue of Sir Edmund Hillary, the Kiwi who was the first man to reach the summit of Mount Everest. The statue depicted the young Hillary, rucksack on his back, about to climb Mount Cook, and on his face you could see a zest for life. I knew something about Hillary. He had climbed Mount Cook before setting his sights on Everest and he went on to achieve great things in his life after the summit climb in 1953. As well as becoming a charismatic and deeply respected figure in the world of mountaineering, he was appointed New Zealand's High Commissioner to India. He also devoted much time and energy to Nepal, where he built schools and worked tirelessly on behalf of the Nepalese people.

The night was beautifully clear and, as it was the middle of the New Zealand summer, it was also warm. On the grass beside the statue, I lay down and tried to take everything in. Mount Cook's outline was clear against a sky full of stars. The moon looked so far away, yet men had flown there and walked on its surface. Four days it had taken Neil Armstrong and his colleagues to get there – the ultimate long-haul flight. I thought about Hillary and Armstrong and those who achieve great things in their lives. What differentiated them from others? The key, it seemed to me, was they took on the challenge that excited them. They weren't scared by their dreams. As for me, the thought that hit home that night was straightforward: you don't see statues of corporate lawyers. A yearning to do what I was passionate about became stronger than ever.

Some time before this I had sat down with David Becker, who has been a best friend since our university days in Cape Town and who has long been a confidant. There isn't much I won't discuss with David and he picked up on my restlessness. 'You know, Lewis,' he said, 'for about a year now you haven't been passionate about law. You've got to follow your passion. Life is too short to do anything else.' I was coming to the same conclusion. To be truly happy I would have to be the person I had dreamed of being. I wanted to fulfil the hopes of the teenager who had looked out across the ocean from the high-up classroom at Camps Bay High School and imagined himself on a ship bound for Antarctica.

Before I could get to faraway places, I first had to make the short but key journey from the office of the highly qualified lawyer into the great unknown, where there were no offices or regular pay-cheques. It was taking time but I was getting there. That evening in the company of Hillary's statue simply accelerated the process. Now there would be no turning back.

Dreams of a life beyond a law office weren't killed off by my experience at Clyde & Co. As a relatively junior new recruit, I was assigned to work with Russell Ridley, a senior lawyer who had recently joined the firm, and his assistant, Lisa Molyneaux. Most of the work was in the oil and gas sector, which wasn't particularly interesting. At the end of my six months' probation, Russell called me and said the company wasn't extending my contract. Another partner at the company had just given me a very good review, so I asked Russell why I was being let go. He didn't have a clear answer but shortly afterwards he, too, left the company.

Old questions and new self-doubt followed. In search of space and tranquillity, I headed off to North Cape at the tip of northern Norway. The cycle ride along the northern coast had given me a sense of the landscape at the North Cape – the ruggedness of the coastline, the towering cliffs, the unspoiled nature of the place – and I longed to get back there. The short swim I'd had in the Arctic Ocean on that biking holiday created a yearning to go back and swim round

the North Cape as well. While enjoying the peace of northern Norway, I would explore the possibility of doing that
swim. So, in the spring of 2003, I flew from London to Oslo,
on to Tromsø, and then on a smaller plane to Hammerfest.
The final leg was another short hop to Honningsvåg, which
is the town closest to the North Cape. It was a day spent on
airplanes but I loved it, especially the three internal
Norwegian flights. On the Tromsø to Hammerfest leg, the
sudden disappearance of trees told us we had passed into the
Norwegian Arctic and the views from the sky were spectacular. Honningsvåg is a small town of around 2,500
inhabitants, although it was officially declared a city in 1996,
and claims to be the northernmost city in the world. My
hotel overlooked the harbour. After settling in and finding
the local tourist office, I enquired if there was anyone who
might take me on a boat ride round the North Cape.

Hugo Salamonsen was the man to see. He ran a small
diving operation, owned two Zodiacs and, with his cropped
hair and earrings in both ears, he looked like a pirate, but it
was the heartiness of his laugh that struck you. One of the
things we'd learned during SAS training was the need to
make good judgements about people quickly. I wanted to see
the area where, at some point, I would come back and swim;
it was also important to decide if Hugo would be involved in
the project. 'Do you think it's possible to swim round the
North Cape?' I asked, as interested in how he answered as
the answer itself.

'I don't know how good a swimmer you are, but you definitely need the right day.'

I liked that. He was neither dismissive of the plan nor was
he blasé about it.

We then spent the day on his Zodiac reconnoitring the
North Cape. Seen from the sea, the cliffs at the North Cape
and the strength of the ocean as it smashes against the rock

face are formidable, but it is better to stand on the cliff and look out to sea. About 1,000 kilometres north is the island of Spitsbergen and, roughly the same distance further north, is the North Pole. Close to the cliff edge, you see and hear the waves as they swell and crash, and the birdlife all around is extraordinary. If you turn and look in any direction other than north, you will see the reindeer that have long been a way of life for the Sami people indigenous to this area. Having lived in South Africa and grown to love the coastline in the Western Cape, I thought nothing could surpass the beauty of the Cape of Good Hope. That was before laying eyes on the North Cape. On the Zodiac with Hugo, I talked of my plan to swim around the North Cape and he saw my enthusiasm and determination.'No one's ever done it,' he said, 'that's for sure. I want to help you.'

More than ever, I wanted to become the first man to do a long-distance swim in these waters. I also knew that Nick Peterson, my old instructor and friend from the SAS, was the person to work with me on what was a step into the unknown. Like everyone in the Regiment, Nick understood the paramount importance of safety and he sensed danger before most people. With him, I would feel safe in the water and that counted more than anything. Besides that, he was fun to be around and would make sure the trip was enjoyable. Physically impressive, he was naturally confident and had a way with people, especially good-looking women. When not serving in the Regiment, Nick was a barrister in criminal law and, while his life was hectic, he could, with a little advance notice, take some time off. I paid for his flight as well as mine, booked us a hotel in Honningsvåg and set the date for August.

As this would be the first challenge I was going to undertake in dangerously cold water, I prepared as well as I could. Through the last couple of months at Clyde & Co, I'd started twice-weekly trips to Dover on the south-east coast. From London, it's not the easiest place to get to and, remarkably, the bus service from Victoria Coach Station was often quicker than the train. After finishing work, I travelled across the city from Clyde & Co's offices at Tower Bridge to Victoria and got on a National Express bus around 7 p.m., arriving in Dover some time between 9.30 and 10 p.m. Generally, the bus catered for migrant workers and back-packers and I tried to get a seat in the back and sleep. I stayed in a B&B near Dover harbour and, after dropping off my stuff there, I would swim up and down in a section of the harbour where Channel swimmers train, which was lit up by nearby street lights. This was during April and May. Air tem-peratures were often low and the water wasn't too warm either but, for an hour and a half or so, I was in the water and back in my element. Living in London, engaged in the quest to get into the SAS, I hadn't swum for five years. It was like falling in love with a girl you had known and loved in your youth. It would often be midnight when I climbed out of the water and 12.30 when I got to sleep, 4.30 when the alarm sounded and around 5 a.m. when I boarded the bus bound for London to get to my desk by 9.00 to start work. It was challenging but necessary.

Nick and I arrived at our hotel in Norway one evening in early August. The receptionist was a middle-aged lady who casually asked why I'd come to Honningsvåg.

'To try to swim around North Cape,' I said.

Startled, she looked to see if she had heard correctly. 'Does your mother know what you are doing? North Cape is one of the most dangerous capes on earth.'

'Yes,' I replied, trying to be polite but at the same time let-ting her know that the warning was falling on deaf ears.

'You sound like Captain Scott,' she said, and I sensed her

condescension – here was another Briton biting off more than he can chew. Though Norwegians are the loveliest people, they know the history of polar exploration and they're all very proud of the fact that Amundsen beat Scott to the South Pole. Her denigration of Scott infuriated me because five men, including Scott, perished on that expedition and, to my mind, theirs was an heroic attempt that ended tragically – not something to be lauded over. How dare she? Still, it was grist to the motivational mill and I savoured it.

Norwegian TV arrived and wanted to know if it was true that I was proposing to do a long swim round North Cape. They spoke with Hugo Salamonsen's uncle, who was well known locally for kayaking around the coast, and asked him about the wisdom of swimming North Cape's waters. 'He is obviously a tough guy to even try this,' said Hugo's uncle, 'but this is not the English Channel. These waters are cold. Fishermen who fall overboard around here die quickly and I'm not sure he's going to be able to stay in there as long as he thinks.' He, too, didn't believe.

The irony was that this scepticism helped. It added to my determination because I kept thinking, 'Do you want that receptionist to be able to say to her friends afterwards that she knew I couldn't do it, that she'd even told me in person?' As it suited my purposes, I imagined half of all Norwegians were laughing at my British arrogance and it became a battle: me against them and I wasn't going to give in.

A meteorologist at the Norwegian Meteorological Institute in Oslo advised me that the typical water temperature off North Cape in August would usually be seven or eight degrees but might well drop to four or five. Eight degrees should be possible because there had been a few days when it was nine degrees off Clifton Beach in Cape Town, but four – that was something else. At four degrees I wouldn't make it.

An important decision had to be made in relation to distance: what constituted a long-distance swim? Geography encouraged me to say five kilometres because two and a half kilometres on either side of the tip of North Cape there were easily identifiable bays from which it would be possible to start and finish. So, five kilometres it was.

Though Nick was an SAS-qualified medic, we didn't know enough about the precise effects of being in very cold water. The danger was that you could be hypothermic before you realized there was a problem, so we came up with a series of questions that Nick would ask me every 15 or 20 minutes. What are your middle names? William and Gordon. What is your postal code? E1W 3QZ. What was the name of your headmaster at primary school in England? Mr Wortham. If I failed to answer any of these questions or if I took too much time to answer, Nick would immediately get me out of the water. To make sure he understood the assault on the body inflicted by extremely cold water, he volunteered to jump off a very high bridge near Honningsvåg and swim about 100 metres to where I was waiting for him. So he jumped from the top of the bridge and, being a very fit and athletic individual, we expected he would easily complete the short swim. Well, he did but it was far from comfortable. The cold water affected him badly and, as he was getting towards the end, it was clear he was struggling so I swam towards him and got him out of there quickly. Nothing I could have said would have had the same effect on Nick.

On the day before the swim, Hugo Salamonsen and I went slowly over our five-kilometre course in his Zodiac, as I wanted to take in every detail of the coastline to ensure I would know where I was on the course. There is nothing as deflating as thinking you are further into the swim than you are and I paid particular attention to the little landmarks through the second half of the route, so that I would know how close I was to Hornvikka, the little bay where I would finish.

On the big day, 6 August, the weather was with us. There was hardly a breeze and the water was millpond still. But the water was also brutally cold and the prospect of an hour-long swim scared me. True to the tradition of long-distance swimming, I wore just a cap, goggles and small Speedo swimming trunks. In the time just before starting a challenging swim I'm sharply aware of everything around me; what people say tends to have an exaggerated impact and is likely to stay with me during the swim. 'Lewis,' Hugo said just before I got in the water, 'I'm very proud of you and what you are attempting to do.' It was all I needed to hear.

Hugo and Nick were in one Zodiac; the press were in another. It was reassuring for me to have Nick in such close proximity. The boat was never more than a metre or two away from me. As he had spent hours on duty at observation posts in the SAS, I knew he would not lose concentration.

Swimming from west to east and naturally turning to my right for air, I was able to enjoy the sight of North Cape's extraordinary 300-metre cliff face. In your head, there is a battle between the almost spiritual beauty of the landscape and the physical discomfort of the cold water. One attracts your attention; the other demands it. Though you want to dwell on the splendour of the cliff, it's not possible because the cold eventually grips you, vice-like, and just when you've convinced yourself it is only pain and nothing to worry about, there is a reminder that it's more than pain. In my case, it was searing pain in a calf muscle that was the forerunner to cramp.

Getting the balance right was important because if I kicked too hard in an effort to move fast and stay warm, I brought on cramp, but if I moved too slowly, I would definitely get hypothermia. In the end, I went a shade too fast, my left calf cramped up and I had to float on my back and stretch my calf to reduce the cramp. That was bad too because I got much colder. The cramp eased but was still present. After beginning to swim again, I kicked gently and progressed more deliberately. It was painful but the only way to manage the situation. Through the tough parts of the swim, I thought of my dad and that made me dig deeper; I thought also of the receptionist who had dismissed my chances and spoken so disrespectfully of the British team who had lost their lives in Antarctica.

Kim, a medic from Honningsvåg who'd agreed to help us, got to the bay in Hornvikka well before I was due to finish and started the bonfire that would warm me up. He used driftwood and I could see the fire from some distance away. Anticipation of its heat pulled me to the finish. The swim took 65 minutes. On my arrival, I stumbled on the slippery rocks when I was getting out of the water and needed Nick and Kim to come and grab me. They had to hold me upright. My speech was slurred, and it was clear to them that I was showing the early signs of hypothermia, but the heart-rate monitor told them I was fine and would quickly come round. I stood before the blazing bonfire, a few metres closer than either Nick or Kim could bear. Though they told me to stand back, that I would get burned, I was still freezing and wanted to get closer. Nick produced a mug of hot chocolate and it tasted delicious. A Sami herder passed me a cup of cold reindeer blood, which, at that moment, I wasn't exactly desperate to drink. Out of courtesy, I took one sip and passed on the rest.

Once I'd warmed up, Nick and I walked to the top of the enormous cliff that overlooked the bay. On the mountain we planted the British and Norwegian flags and that evening we went to a local hotel where we were fed reindeer steaks with the most beautiful berry sauce, potatoes and fresh vegetables.

Everyone was so pleased the swim was successful. After eating, we had a few beers and then went out to party. The parties went on for three days and everyone continued to be wonderfully hospitable, especially the Norwegian girls, who were particularly stunning. We never wanted to leave Honningsvåg but eventually we had to.

After arriving at Heathrow, we were struck by the impersonality, the urbanity, the pollution and the noise as we travelled on the Tube to central London. 'This is Leicester Square, mind the gap.' Outside everything was grey and crowded, and I felt lost.

After swimming North Cape in August 2003 and spending New Year's Eve in the company of Edmund Hillary's statue four and a half months later, I was ready for my life's equivalent of the Everest ascent. Was I prepared to risk everything to follow my dreams, especially as that meant disappointing those who would say, 'But, Lewis, you have spent seven years studying law, how can you give that up?' I was concerned that my mother would worry about my future and, for a long time, I was caught up in the desire to be the person I imagined my dad wanted me to be.

In the end, it actually doesn't matter what your parents want; it doesn't matter what your friends want; it certainly doesn't matter that you've gone to Cambridge and then spent years working in law firms if you're not happy doing what you're doing. The decision was made easier when David Becker spoke to me again. 'Lewis,' he said, 'if you don't follow your own dreams, you will be following someone else's. And imagine getting to the end of your life only to realize that you have followed someone else's dreams. Nothing could be sadder.'

Ultimately I wanted to be a pioneer swimmer, a distant descendant of Scott, Amundsen and Hillary, except that I would be an explorer of the water. I wanted to be the best. I wanted to be the greatest pioneer swimmer in history and, at last, I resolved to follow my dream. I wanted to push every boundary. I wanted to swim further than anyone else. I wanted to cross seas and round capes that no one had dreamed of swimming before. And I wanted to swim in waters that were so cold no one thought it possible to survive in them. And though it promised to make me poor and would take away the security provided by a career in law, that didn't worry me.

About a month after returning to England, I wanted to get back to Norway. Honningsvåg was my destination and I got a job as a tourist guide taking English-speaking visitors to North Cape. They came on the coastal steamer *Hurtigruten* and arrived at Honningsvåg, where six coaches awaited them: two for English-speakers, two for German-speakers, one for French-speakers and one for Norwegians. Remuneration was decidedly modest, career prospects were zero and the tourist season lasted just three months but, for me, it was the job from heaven.

I stayed in a blue wooden house close to the harbour, woke at 8 a.m., went for a run to the top of a nearby mountain and loved the crispness of the Arctic air. At eleven o'clock the *Hurtigruten*'s horn announcing the steamer's arrival into the harbour and I would quickly make my way down to the ship. 'Welcome to North Cape,' I'd say with a smile, and it wasn't forced because they had come to see one of the most beautiful places in the world and it was my privilege to guide them. On the 90-minute coach journey to North Cape, we stopped at a Sami camp and the tourists got a close-up view of a reindeer herd and met with Sami herders. The reindeer is a fine example of an animal perfectly adapted to its environment, as its thick fur coat protects it from wind and cold; if you stroke it, you can feel softness just

My parents.

My sister Caroline, my father and me in Cornwall.

I have always loved water!

Dad looking very smart for the Queen's Silver Jubilee in 1977.

My first headmaster, Tony Wortham.

Otto Thaning and me – exhausted and burnt after completing the first swim across Lake Malawi.

About to swim across the English Channel in 1992.

Fourteen hours and fifty minutes later.

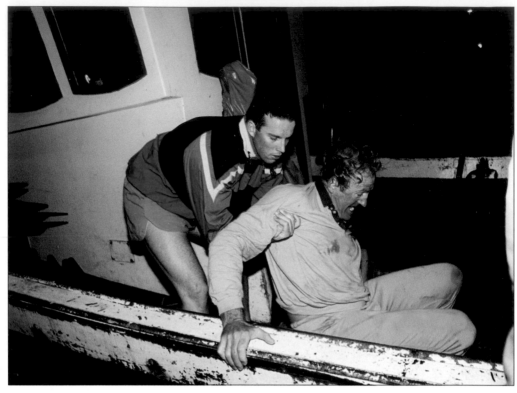

Picking up Otto Thaning after his failed Channel crossing.

Riding in Spioenkop Nature Reserve in South Africa.

Graduating from Cambridge University in 2000.

The day I finally got my SAS beret.

Checking parachute in the hangar at RAF Brize Norton.

Nick Peterson helping me out of the sea after swimming around North Cape, Norway.

Passing Chapman's Peak on my 100km swim around the Cape Peninsula, South Africa.

A wonderful reception at the end of my Cape Peninsula swim.

Training in an ice pool at I&J's fish factory in Cape Town.

Swimming in front
of the huge Monaco
Glacier, Spitsbergen.

About to dive into
the sea off Antarctica.

Swimming past the
Houses of Parliament
on my swim down
the River Thames in
2006.

Stopping off at No 10 to discuss the UK's position on climate change with the Prime Minister.

Celebrating with James Mayhew after completing the first swim down the River Thames.

Above: Training in the Namibian Desert for my North Pole swim.

Left: The final training venue – the icy waters of Nigards Glacier Lake, Norway.

Below: My North Pole team (left to right – Chris Lotz, Tobi van Heerden, me, David Becker, Professor Tim Noakes and Jørgen Amundsen).

The photo that was on the front page of countless newspapers around the world. Diving into the sea at North Pole.

Swimming across the North Pole with agony written all over my face. The IB *Yamal* is in the background.

About to go on Jay Leno's
Show in 2007.

Describing the North Pole
swim to Prince Charles and
Field Marshall Sir
John Chapple.

Training on the River Thames for my Arctic kayak in 2008.

Robbie Hegedüs and I, leaving the Island of Spitsbergen en route north.

It gets cold paddling in the Arctic Ocean!

Addressing a group of bankers in London on protecting the environment.

Planting the flags of the world on the Arctic sea ice for a photo shoot.

The happiest day of my life – coming out of St Peter the Fisherman's Church in Hout Bay with Antoinette.

beneath the surface. Its hollow hair follicles hold in air, which allows the reindeer to stay warm during the coldest Arctic weather.

At North Cape, we spent two hours doing the customary tourist things: watching a short film of the area, going through the visitor centre and just taking in the extraordinary North Cape landscape. Sometimes it got so windy we had to insist that everyone stayed inside the centre. On one such day, an elderly gentleman wandered outside, was literally picked up by the wind and was blown towards the edge of the cliff. It all happened in a matter of a few seconds and the man didn't have time to think what he should do. Running outside, I got to him seconds before he was smashed against the railings and I had a hell of a job getting him back inside. He was like a child, scared and helpless, but full of gratitude to me for having 'saved his life'. Though the work of the tourist guide involves much repetition, I never tired of introducing people to North Cape and singing the praises of a landscape and a way of life that inspired me. And I enjoyed the challenge of entertaining a coachload of tourists every day.

Three months of poorly paid work, no matter how enjoyable, could not sustain me for long and the future was resolved by an interesting job offer from a Norwegian P & I (Protection and Indemnity) company. They wanted a maritime lawyer trained in English law. As they were one of the best P & I clubs in the world, the offer was one that forced my hand. If I accepted, I would move to Arendal, one of the prettiest towns on the south coast of Norway, and that wasn't an unattractive proposition. Arendal has a beautiful feel to it. It has the sea alongside and mountains not far away, and the wellbeing of the town, both economic and spiritual, is something you sense from the well-maintained and brightly painted wooden houses that are everywhere. Speaking to people from the town, it seems half of their time is spent out on their boats, the other half cross-country skiing in winter. Everyone at the company spoke English and there would be no pressure on me to speak Norwegian but, in time, that was something I would want to do. The job, the lifestyle, the possibility of getting married, settling down and raising a family in this small beautiful town appealed to me.

At the same time, it wasn't enough. If I accepted the Arendal option, my life would be predetermined until I retired at sixty-five. The dreams of doing great things, of swimming in places no one had swum, would have to be forgotten and the desire to take on big challenges would be unfulfilled. Then one morning in beautiful Arendal, when my mind was a small battleground for so many conflicting thoughts, I bought the local newspaper and was charmed by a front-page story of what to do about pigeons defecating on an important monument in the centre of town. Whether they fully appreciated it or not, Arendal's citizens didn't have that much to worry about if the pigeons were so much of a problem. World poverty, international terrorism, the terrible consequences of climate change – they all seemed such a long way from the peace of Arendal, but it was the peace and tranquillity of this small Norwegian town that scared me. Ultimately, it wouldn't be what I wanted and I turned down the job offer. Instead I opened up my big *Times Atlas of the World* and began to look again at places I might swim. The simple act of looking at major seas and rivers, and wondering about temperatures and currents and distances and predators, convinced me I had made the right decision.

Once I'd said no to Arendal, I wasn't going to say yes to any other offer of work in maritime law. It was time to get on with my new life as a pioneer swimmer. With its cold waters off Camps Bay, its warmer waters in nearby False Bay, its multitude of swimmers and its excellent coaches, South Africa was the logical place for me to begin. In moving back to my second country, I was mindful of the high level of violence that was undermining progress there but I was also aware of the country's great potential. South Africa was on the edge but, in a curious way, that was part of the attraction.

I had a notion to swim the entire Cape Peninsula from the Victoria & Alfred Waterfront on the one side to Muizenberg on the other, a 100-kilometre journey through some of the roughest and most predator-populated seas in the world and one that could be completed only in stages of around ten kilometres each day. Soon after arriving back in Cape Town, I bounced the idea off a few experienced swimmers. 'Do you reckon it's possible?' I asked. Optimists said it was unlikely; the rest thought it impossible. Without meaning to be dismissive of the swimmers' views, they didn't put me off. They had all done Robben Island to Three Anchor Bay, a ten-kilometre swim that would have left them in no mood for another long effort in the water the following day. But if a person prepared properly, why not?

One person whose view interested me greatly was Professor Tim Noakes, a world-famous exercise physiologist who ran the Sports Science and Sports Medicine Research Unit at the University of Cape Town. Although we had once shared a walk on Table Mountain with a mutual friend, Alan Danker, I didn't really know Professor Noakes. After making an appointment, I showed up at his office at the Sports Science building fearing he might be about to end my Cape Peninsula project. My feeling was that Professor Noakes knew what was and wasn't possible physiologically; if he said it wasn't possible, I doubt I would have tried it.

'Professor Noakes,' I said, 'I'm here because I want to swim round the Cape Peninsula – ten swims of ten kilometres on ten consecutive days: the V&A Waterfront to Sea Point, to

Llandudno, Hout Bay, around the Cape of Good Hope, around Cape Point, on past Simon's Town and into Muizenberg. Nobody has done it before. The water temperature, as you know, will be cold and on some days it may get to nine or ten degrees; on other days the wind will make the sea rough and progress will be slow. So, can my body handle it?'

He looked at me and without hesitation said, 'Yes.' Just one word – 'Yes.' That was good enough for me. At the time Professor Noakes knew nothing about my SAS training nor did he know a lot about my past exploits in the waters around the Cape but he did know that I made it round Cape Point in big seas fourteen years earlier. It was only five kilometres but he knew how brutal that was on a bad day and that convinced him I had the mental strength to cope with a 10- or 12-day challenge around the Cape Peninsula. His view was that if you had the mind, the body would follow and that made him believe in me.

Once Professor Noakes said yes, he then laid down the law: 'Right, Lewis, if you're going to do this, we'll need to put you on a really good training programme. I want you to come here to the Sports Science Institute and work very closely with Stephan du Toit, who is an excellent physical trainer. He will make sure you are where you need to be physically. To monitor your progress, I will do lots of tests when you're here and you'll be able to work with your swim coach, Gary Freeling.'

I could never bring myself to call Professor Noakes 'Tim' and settled on 'Prof', which was my attempt to be informal and at the same time recognize his standing as one of the world's most respected exercise physiologists. Working with him inspired me to train assiduously and I began to achieve new levels of fitness. All the while, I stayed relatively quiet about what I was doing because if it was widely known that I was training to become the first person to swim around the

Cape Peninsula, someone might decide they were going to dive in before me. After all, Roald Amundsen took on the challenge of the South Pole because he knew Captain Scott and his team were about to begin their journey to the same destination. At the time many felt that Amundsen had acted dishonourably but that didn't change history – he got to the South Pole first.

The decision to do the 100-kilometre Cape Peninsula swim led me to the door of Daantjie Truter. He was a remarkable man, or at least to me he was remarkable. A fisherman from Table View, a well-named suburb of Cape Town, he was into the last season of his life when we met and he knew it. He had cancer of the throat and, judging from his generally emaciated appearance, it had probably spread. But Daantjie came from an era when people didn't make a fuss and if illness came they accepted it without complaint. What seemed important to Daantjie was that he wasn't a burden to anyone and that the dignity with which he lived his life was present all the way to the end. Cancer of the throat is one of the tougher crosses to bear but you wouldn't have known that from Daantjie. Though few members of the medical profession would have approved, he found relief and even good times in brandy and Coke. If you knew him, you certainly didn't begrudge him his escape. I look back now and smile at the memories.

He owned an old fishing boat, the *Cavalier*, and liked nothing better than to fish for tuna off the Cape of Good Hope. But a lone fisherman couldn't compete with the big fleets from Taiwan and Japan. Daantjie had to find new ways to supplement his old livelihood, so for extra cash he escorted swimmers from Robben Island back to the mainland. He knew what was involved, had a nice personality, did the job well and among the long-distance swimming community was known as a trustworthy skipper.

He agreed to escort me on the swim knowing it would last ten to twelve days. Because the swim was raising awareness for David Becker's Aids charity, Starfish, I was able to attract enough sponsorship to pay for the hire of Daantjie and his boat. What I liked about Daantjie was his reliability. He preferred to get up early in the morning and get things done before the day got too hot. What I loved about him was his positive attitude. From the first day he empathized with the difficulty of what I was attempting and supported me wholeheartedly. It became *our* challenge rather than just mine.

Our days started with the same phone conversation every morning. At 6 a.m., I called him.

'Morning, Daantjie.'

'Morning, Meneer.' ('Morning, Mister.')

'Daantjie, are we going to swim today?'

'Hold on, Meneer, let me have a look.' He would then put the phone down, I would hear the front door of his house open, and a minute later he would return. 'Jaaaa,' he would say, drawing it out as if still considering the situation as he spoke, 'looks okay today. Meet me at seven o'clock and then we swim.'

A lifetime as a fisherman had taught him to read the skies and the winds. One long look at the clouds over Table Mountain and he knew what the weather would do for the following six hours. He never needed to listen to a forecast and he was never wrong. I would get my stuff ready – Speedo swimming trunks, goggles, cap, suntan lotion, food and drinks for the day – and would go to whatever sailing club or pier we were using to launch the boat that day. Daantjie would arrive in a pick-up truck, pulling the boat on a trailer, and would reverse the boat down the slipway and into the water. You could tell he had once been a big man but illness had taken its toll and he was now quite frail. All the heavy lifting, which would have once been bread and butter to him, he left to me. His fits of coughing were a reminder of what he was dealing with but he wouldn't let it affect his moods. Often he talked about how good his life had been and how lucky he had been to earn his living at sea because he loved the ocean. Occasionally he spoke about knowing he would soon die, not in a morbid or fearful way, just matter-of-factly and with an acceptance that, on balance, life didn't owe him anything.

I decided to swim from Muizenberg to the V&A Waterfront in Cape Town because the beautiful waterfront was the perfect stage for the finale of a 100-kilometre marathon. A second and probably more powerful reason for wanting to begin at Muizenberg and swim in a clockwise direction around the Cape was that when I turned right to breathe, which is the more comfortable side for me, I would be looking towards the coastline and enjoying one of nature's most magnificent landscapes, much as I had in Norway.

On the first morning we drove down to Muizenberg and were greeted with a howling southeaster. When the wind blows from the south-east on the Cape Peninsula, it is hard to describe just how violent it can be. Water is whipped off the surface of the ocean and sprayed in every direction. As I was due to swim in a southerly direction, there wouldn't have been much progress. Otto Thaning, who had come to see me off that morning, shook his head in a way that said, 'Don't even think about it.' Though I was desperate to get started, I knew enough about the Cape waters not to take on a southeaster. We had to call it off that day. The next morning the same southeaster was blowing. When it was blowing again for a third consecutive morning, there had to be a decision. We had plenty of interest from the local media but three false starts were draining their enthusiasm for the story. Typical of the local weather patterns, the conditions on the western side of the Cape had been fine on those three mornings and I was well aware that if I'd started from the V&A Waterfront in the first place there wouldn't have been a problem.

After the third false start, I surrendered to the southeaster and headed for the V&A. It was 28 April 2004 when my first marathon 'staged' swim began. That first day I did eight kilometres down the Atlantic seaboard and finished at Clifton Beach, where I had been a life-saver through my university years. A number of Camps Bay High School pupils were there to wish me well. Their teacher, Henry Robbins, had once been my teacher and it was lovely to see him there and to chat about old times.

The Cape Peninsula swim was tough – unrelentingly tough. That first day, I'd been sensible and settled for eight kilometres, knowing there were another 92 kilometres to go. On the second day a strong current hindered my progress but I was determined to do a good swim and stayed in the water for five hours and twenty minutes, which was too long in those conditions. A difficult day was made worse by the huge waves breaking onto the beach at Llandudno. However, it has never taken much to raise my mood: I just needed a warm shower, some good food and a good night's sleep. When I called Daantjie the next morning, we started again with renewed enthusiasm.

It was just as well because the third leg from Llandudno took us up to Duiker Island, which is also called Seal Island for the simple reason that it is home to hundreds, if not thousands, of Cape Fur Seals. Where there are seals on the Cape Peninsula, there are Great White Sharks in search of their next meal. Three weeks earlier a young boy, J. P. Andrews, lost a leg after being attacked by a Great White at Muizenberg and that played on my mind. An anti-shark device had been invented a few years before: it was a small black box that could be tied to the outside of the support boat and would emit an electronic pulse that frightened sharks and kept them away from the boat. Its existence was key but it worked only if you swam within ten metres of the boat; often it is impossible for swimmer and boat to remain consistently that close if the sea is rough. It was also key to make sure that the batteries powering the device didn't go flat. They say that most Great Whites aren't interested in eating humans and attack only because they mistake the person for a seal. That's fine, but it doesn't help if you're unlucky and your black Speedos confuse the poor shark.

A friend, Ryan Stramrood, swam with me on the Llandudno–Duiker Island leg and paced me for much of the way. Unfortunately, Ryan got sick about 45 minutes before I was due to stop and, as a result, I was on my own as Duiker Island loomed before me.

'Daantjie,' I shouted, 'that battery still working?'

'Ja,' he said, and I stayed as close to the boat as I could.

But the sea was lumpy that afternoon and, inevitably, the boat intermittently moved away from me. Coming up to Duiker I had a choice: I could swim the narrow channel between the island and the mainland, but that was full of seals and the most likely place for a rendezvous with a Great White, or I could swim far out to sea to avoid Duiker, but I would also have to go around a reef called Dungeons, which is notorious for big waves, but that would make the detour even longer. At the end of a tiring day, the thought of a long detour was too much. 'Look,' I told myself, 'the engine of the boat will frighten the sharks away, the device does work, the sharks have a whole colony of seals, humans are not their natural prey and, finally, I'll be lucky.' I was tired and cold.

'Daantjie,' I shouted again, 'we're going the shortest route.'

'Ja, Meneer,' he said, 'let's go!'

It's funny how the thought of a shark surging from underneath banishes tiredness and makes you forget how cold you are. Without consciously deciding to accelerate, I was sprinting. When the wind picked up and carried the boat away from me, I had no trouble in finding the energy to alert my partner. 'Daantjie, Daantjie, for God's sake, closer, closer!' All around me seals swam and dived and occasionally one would pass with his mouth open and teeth showing. They were so many and so close, I actually saw a few defecate in front of me and momentarily hoped that a shark would repay them for such indecency.

About 500 metres past Duiker, the fear lessened and the adrenalin drained away, leaving exhaustion and cold. 'That's it, Daantjie,' I shouted, and jumped into the boat. You knew how scared you'd been once you felt safe again. We marked our position with the GPS and headed for Hout Bay, where Daantjie and I went to the yacht club, ordered the best food they had and a couple of beers, and laughed about those seals and the way they jumped to attention and swam around me. Sometimes they came up on me so fast, there was a fleeting sense that it was a Great White and, now, over a lovely meal, we could afford to laugh about it. But it was an experience you didn't want to have too often in your life because it was too nerve-shredding, too dependent upon luck. You may imagine I'm exaggerating the danger but a short time later an elderly woman was taken by a Great White at Fish Hoek, which was on my route. People watched in horror as she was killed, unable to do a thing about it.

I loved being with Daantjie at the end of the day like that, especially that afternoon in the yacht club at Hout Bay. Everyone knew him and liked him. Even though I was sitting there beside him, they would say, 'Ah, Daantjie, how's your swimmer getting on?'

'*Ja*, *ja*, good, good,' he would say. 'And how are you?'

'*Ja*, good too.'

Later I remembered the following morning's start would

still be pretty close to Duiker Island. 'Daantjie, I wish I'd gone a bit further away from the island today.'

'*Ja, Lewis, moenie worry nie* [Yeah, Lewis, don't worry], tomorrow will be another day.'

It was, and we got there in the end, but it was a tougher swim than I'd anticipated. There were days when the south-easter blew and I spent two hours fighting it, travelling just one kilometre in that time, and felt demoralized. And there were days when the wind was so unfavourable we couldn't even get in the water. Once we got round Cape Point and into False Bay, the water temperature rose significantly and that was a great help. On the eleventh day, which took us from Cape Point Nature Reserve to Simon's Town, where my father is buried, weather conditions were good and men-tally I felt very strong. I knocked out 13 kilometres in 3 hours and 40 minutes. On the twelfth and penultimate day, my friend Nic Marshall swam with me and, for whatever reason, we raced the entire way. Nic does that to me, and I think I do it to him. It was just as well we were moving quickly because a number of Great Whites had been seen in the vicinity in the previous weeks. I know it's a sad way to think but it was reassuring to have Nic nearby. 'There's a fifty–fifty chance,' I thought, 'that the Great White will take Nic before me.' We could have made it to Muizenberg that day but we GPS'd our position 1.5 kilometres from the end and the following day about thirty friends joined me for the last leg of the swim. It was lovely to share the moment with so many.

After the swim we had a get-together at Tony Sellmeyer's house for all the people who had helped. I made a short speech thanking everyone: the members of CLDSA who had given up their time to verify the swim, friends who had swum with me and, of course, Daantjie. I spoke about how nice it was for me in the water when the sea was calm and not too cold and we weren't thinking about Great Whites. I might glance up then and see Daantjie sipping a brandy and Coke and it always made me smile, no matter how I felt. Before the Cape swim and in the years that followed, there would be many men who skippered my supporting boat but there was no one quite like Daantjie with his quiet, uncomplaining way, his reliability and his total belief that we could get round the whole peninsula.

That day at Tony's, everyone wanted him to speak and with a few brandies under his belt, he stood up and spoke from his heart. 'I had never been involved in a swim like this,' he said, 'and I haven't been involved with anyone like Lewis. It is normal for swimmers sometimes to get cross with the guy in charge of the boat: "Slow down, you're going too fast," or "Go the other side of me, the fumes of the boat are in my mouth." People's personalities change when they're under pressure and I suppose it's natural. But, Lewis, you weren't like that, you never stopped being a gentleman and these have been thirteen of the happiest days of my life.'

Hearing Daantjie say that, knowing what he was dealing with, made the long swim all the more worthwhile. Every metre of the 100 kilometres was worth it if it added something to Daantjie's life. Afterwards I did a couple of training swims in the Cape with Daantjie at the wheel of the *Cavalier*. A year or so after that, he passed away and, though I knew it was coming, his death was a great sadness. Whenever I am in Cape Town next to the coast I marvel at the vast expanse of sea that Dantjie and I crossed together. Every bay, every jutting piece of headland, every little island means something to me and, in my memories, Daantjie is always there, on the boat, always seeing the good side of life. After his passing, I never felt any great desire to swim in the waters off Cape Town. I had my memories of swimming around the Cape Peninsula with Daantjie and they were enough.

10

KING OF THE FJORDS

With the fitness accrued from the 100-kilometre swim around the Cape, there came a strong desire to push the boundaries further. Why not be the first human to swim across the North Sea from the Shetland Islands to Norway – 300 kilometres of pretty cold water? It would be the most ambitious long-distance swim ever undertaken and it was the severity of the challenge that attracted me: I would swim 15 kilometres each day, GPS the point at which I stopped, sleep on the boat that accompanied me and begin again the following morning. Twenty days it would take, if everything went well. That kind of time at sea costs money – hiring a boat, the support team, food, expenses, etc. – and it was money that I didn't have. After returning to Cape Town from London, I moved back to my mother's place to save on rent and her understanding of what I was trying to do was a huge help – but then she has always been a very generous person. Even she couldn't pay for a 20-day expedition from the Shetlands to Norway though, so off I went to Bergen in Norway in search of sponsorship.

North Cape had introduced me to Norwegians and got

me a reputation as someone with pluck and a genuinely pio-
neering spirit. Perhaps naively, I thought that would translate
into financial backing. From Billy to Jack I went but got
nowhere. After a good visit to the Mayor of Bergen, there
was hope. He rang influential people he knew but didn't find
any sponsors. People thought it was a bad idea: they felt
swimming from the Shetland Islands to Norway was too
much and not something they wanted to support. Stranded
in Bergen, I wanted to cry. Why couldn't they see this was
an epic challenge, starting off in waters as cold as seven
degrees and braving elements that would often be brutally
tough? But they were right. With the benefit of hindsight, I
thank the Lord that no one sponsored me, because if there's
a more horrendous long-distance swim than the Shetland
Islands to Norway, I can't think of it. Out there in the North
Sea, swimming past the oil rigs, some days in the roughest
water, trying to live with the cold and the reality of twenty
consecutive nights aboard an old Norwegian fishing boat – I
shudder now at what I'd planned to do.

Then Helen Siverstol, a lovely Norwegian girl who was
the marketing manager for the country's fjord region, turned
up. After speaking with her, I went to have a look at some of
the country's biggest fjords. Their beauty overwhelmed me.
Turquoise-blue water was overhung by cliffs that in places
were 1,000 metres high. As you moved down the fjord
towards the North Sea, little villages and occasional towns sat
at the end of valleys, with houses painted red or yellow or
white, their little gardens lovingly tended. I thought this had
to be one of the most exquisite places on the planet – nature
at its extraordinary best and hardly touched by man.

Why didn't I try to swim the longest fjord in the world?
That would have been difficult, as it is in Greenland and
much of it is covered by a glacier, but the world's longest
unfrozen fjord is Sognefjord in Norway, 204 kilometres from

the outstretched tongue of Jostedal Glacier in the centre of Scandinavia to the North Sea. I made up my mind. I would swim the length of this breathtaking stretch of water. Norwegians refer to Sognefjord as the 'King of the Fjords' and that's certainly right. Nothing comes close to it. Two hundred and four kilometres was going to take over two weeks and that would cost more money than I had. But, for this venture, I had Helen fighting my corner and that made the vital difference.

She didn't have access to the high-powered and couldn't make one phone call and get things taken care of, but she was resourceful and charming. She looked at a map, noted the towns dotted along the bank of the Sognefjord, found the number for the best hotel in each town and called them. 'A British swimmer is going to try to swim the entire length of the fjord. Would you please accommodate him and two support people for one night?' One after another they agreed and, in next to no time, accommodation and meals were taken care of. National Geographic said they would film the swim and that helped our cause no end.

Ideally, I needed two people to help: one to kayak alongside me as I swam; the other to drive the car to the point at which we would end each day's swim and take us to our hotel. After his help at North Cape, I was keen for Nick Peterson to come again. Long days in the fjord would be slow-moving and I knew from our SAS training and all the hours manning an OP how well Nick dealt with potential boredom and the need to maintain concentration through hours in which nothing much happened. I also invited Dave Richter from Durban, who was a good kayaker. Both were willing to help provided I could pay their airfares to Bergen.

Once the seed of an idea is planted in my mind, it grows quickly. Two hundred and four kilometres – I could handle that. Up to twenty consecutive days in the water – that wasn't a problem. Doubt is the enemy and I have learned to keep it at arm's length. You know it's there, knocking at the door, but you don't let it in. I had done 100 km – all I had to do was double it.

National Geographic film-makers spoke to different people about the feasibility of swimming the full length of Sognefjord and nearly everyone scoffed at the idea. They didn't think it was possible; their sense of the difficulty was heightened by the fact that so few local people saw the fjord as a place to swim. Living on the edge of the world's most spectacular and most natural swimming pool, they had unwittingly turned their backs on it. Everyone knew about the two German tourists who had attempted to swim across the fjord at one of the easier points. It was a five-kilometre swim but neither made it to the other side. One body was recovered; the other was never found. They talked of a mysterious maelstrom in the middle of the fjord that sucked swimmers to their deaths. When children did swim in the fjord, they were told not to stray too far out. It was local mythology, I decided; in good old SAS style, I binned it. Maybe when you have swum in water with its fair share of Great Whites, the possibility of malevolent currents that could spiral you to the bottom doesn't faze you.

To attract attention to our Sognefjord adventure, I agreed to swim in Nigards Glacier Lake at the foot of Jostedal Glacier a few days before the start. A huge glacier, like a giant slab of ice, descended from the top of a mountain; at the bottom, water gushed from the belly of the glacier and plunged into a pool that became Nigards Glacier Lake with water temperatures of around two or three degrees. I had never swum in water so cold but I wasn't concerned as this was going to be a short little dip. As a publicity stunt, it worked, but I was thankful that the Sognefjord water wouldn't be as cold – the lowest temperatures would be about six degrees and that was low enough. I couldn't have lasted more than a couple of minutes in the two degrees of Nigards Glacier Lake.

Dave Richter arrived from Durban the day before we were to begin and was exhausted from the series of flights that got him into Bergen. He asked if it was okay for him to drive the car rather than paddle the kayak for the first few days. Nick didn't have a problem with that; he would kayak. The next morning we got to the point of our departure and, as Nick was easing the thin kayak into the water, I said, 'Nick, you have kayaked before, right?'

He looked at me matter-of-factly. 'Not in something like this, I haven't – but what could possibly go wrong?'

'Nothing,' I said.

That was why I always wanted Nick on the team: nothing ruffled him. He was fit, strong and confident. The water was like a millpond. He looked at it and thought, 'The only way this could capsize is if I unbalance it and I'm not going to do that.' He set up an iPod in the kayak, with speakers strapped to the stern, and announced that we would have the company of good music. Dressed in a black wetsuit and dark glasses, he so looked the part. Norwegians who came to see us off stared at the James Bond-like figure and must have thought, 'These guys know what they're doing.' Nick's coolness gave me confidence.

Beginning a journey that will last longer than your mind wishes to consider, the best thing is to concentrate on getting through the first leg. Break the swim down into little chunks – 204 kilometres didn't bear thinking about. As I eased into the water, I said to myself, 'Just take this easy; it's not a race. Focus on making nice long strokes, stretch your arms as far as they will go and glide through the water. Let's take care of day one before considering anything beyond that.'

From overhead I could hear the buzz of the helicopter used by Norwegian television to film the beginning of my odyssey. 'Lewis,' I said to myself, 'this is the first time a helicopter has been used to film one of your swims. People are beginning to notice.' The attention was welcome because the water was cold, bitterly cold, and it would remain so until I got far away from all that glacial water plunging into the fjord. Physically, I was in great shape and even if I hadn't experienced water this cold, I had prepared for it mentally and that has always been vitally important. Consider how you feel as you prepare to walk into relatively cold water. For me, the only way is to accept there will be a shock to your system and get straight in – no hanging around. Sure, it was bitingly cold but there was so much adrenalin coursing through my veins that the icy water couldn't penetrate.

I watched Nick in the kayak take his first strokes: careful, tentative but sure. He was feeling his way in the water, learning quickly and still managing to look über-cool. After a while, warmer water made conditions less hostile and I giggled across at Nick, who was feeling confident enough in the kayak to lean back and talk with the ease of the seasoned kayaker. 'Ah, Pugh,' he said, 'it's just another glorious f*****g day in the fjord.'

Indeed, it was glorious. The press had gone; the surface of the fjord had a glass-like stillness, the cliffs on three sides stretched high towards the sky and there wasn't another boat or human to be seen. Of course, such peace couldn't last and Nick got the iPod going, playing among other stuff a song by Hoobastank, a hard-rock American band. A line in the song ran 'I'm not a perfect person', and as it played, Nick would say, 'Lewis, that is your theme tune', and we laughed. We knocked out twelve kilometres that first day, which was a good effort in waters that started off very cold. Though they warmed up a little, they stayed on the cool side all day. At the end I was exhausted but encouraged. It had been a good start to what would be three of the best weeks of my life.

Terje Eggum, a Norwegian journalist, played an important part in the trip, as he became the medium through which the Norwegian people learned about what we were doing. When he first emailed me, he identified himself as being from *Sogn Avis* and I thought he was an answer to my request for a sponsored rental car, but *Sogn Avis* is a local newspaper in his region of Norway and not the car rental company. Friendly, enthusiastic and energetic, Terje wrote features for different Norwegian newspapers and, as our journey progressed, he skilfully wove stories about the little towns where we stayed into the narrative of the swim. He used the swim to write about the history and people of the fjord and reawakened his readers' appreciation for a resource they had perhaps taken for granted.

From my point of view he was invaluable in publicizing what I was doing and occasionally he was able to help with the day-to-day operation of the swim. A perfect example came early in the second week. Originally, I had thought it possible to swim the entire fjord in two weeks and that was fine for Nick, who was able to get two weeks off work. Closer to the time, it became obvious the swim would take three weeks and Nick made the decision to be part of the team for the first and third weeks. That left Dave Richter and me with a big problem: Dave would accompany me in the kayak but we still had to get the car to the finishing point of each individual leg. To do that, I drove the car to a predetermined point and then hitch-hiked back to the starting point where David was waiting for me with the Kayak. But a 35-year-old man dressed in shorts and a T-shirt doesn't get rides so easily. After standing at the roadside for an hour or so on the first two days, I spoke to Terje about this and he did a radio interview in which he explained the difficulty I was having getting back to the point where I needed to begin that day's swim. The next morning I was picked up straight away and thereafter lifts weren't a problem. Local people would pick me up and want to talk about my great adventure in the fjord.

Through Terje's writing and radio work, people along the fjord knew when to expect us in their towns and villages and each sought to give us a better welcome than the village before. The local band would be ready and waiting to play, the mayor would be there and our efforts were fuelled by their enthusiasm. If I mentioned in an interview with Terje that six hours in cold water tended to leave my feet feeling frozen afterwards, some kind lady would knit me a pair of woollen socks and be waiting at the side of the fjord that evening.

When Helen Siverstol began to help me, the potential payback for her was good publicity for Sognefjord and the region for which she worked. But as the swim progressed, something else began to happen, more important in my view than the promotion of Norway's fjord region as a tourist destination. This was the effect the swim had on the local people who had been sceptical about my chances of swimming from the source of the fjord to the North Sea but whose attitude changed as the swim progressed. As we passed villages, local children began to jump in the water and swim alongside. I encouraged them, as it was company for me and it was helping them to love their fjord. My feeling was that too many of those living on the banks of the fjord had turned their backs to its possibilities because of the mistaken view that the fjord's waters were really unsuitable for swimming. They hadn't been availing themselves of a magnificent resource on their doorstep. In Leikanger, the biggest town on the Sognefjord, the locals were particularly enthusiastic and many of them swam with me.

Late in the second week, when Nick was back in London and it was just Dave and me, James Mayhew came to

Norway to help. We had met on a parachuting course during our time in the British Army. Educated at Eton and later at Brown University in the United States, James was a first-class officer and had done tours of duty in Bosnia. After moving on to civilian life, he joined the Territorial Army and served in the airborne section of the Army Medical Corps. I told him Sognefjord was calm and that he would enjoy kayaking alongside me. He joined us when I was at Balestrand, a town favoured by Kaiser Wilhelm of Germany as his holiday destination and a spectacularly pretty place.

Balestrand was 100 kilometres into our 204-kilometre journey and, as is the case with most journeys, there is a feel-good factor once you reach halfway. Certainly there was a perceptible shift in attitude among local people as the swim progressed to and beyond the halfway point: 'Maybe this mad British swimmer is going to make it after all.' But the further we went, the more the fjord meandered. At a few places we needed to cross from the north bank to the south or vice versa to take the shortest route. Near Balestrand there was a bend in the fjord and, if I followed the meander, I would have added two or three kilometres to my journey. But by aiming to cut across the bend and head for the south side of the fjord, you had to run the gauntlet of currents that local people, especially the skippers of various ferries in the area, had warned us about. Another consideration was the weather because it was clear the further west we travelled, the more the wind tended to blow and cause the water to get choppy. This was particularly so in the afternoons. Norwegians call it the 'Sun Wind' and it made the water so difficult at that time of day that we started to do night-time swims to avoid it.

James arrived on the day when I'd planned a night-time swim to take a shorter route across the fjord. It wasn't easy for him to land in Norway and within hours to be kayaking across the country's biggest fjord in darkness. Dave drove the car ahead to the south bank, parked it in a place where it would be visible to us and, flashing the headlights, he vectored us in. It was like an army manoeuvre in which the Special Operations guys would guide you in and it all happened without mishap. Now we were on the south bank of the fjord but another bend meant we needed to re-cross it and get back to the north bank. On the other side, close to the north bank, a strong current ran from east to west that would take us away from our destination but I guarded against that by telling James to aim his kayak well to the right of where we wanted to end up.

In the morning when we set out I kept James on my right and repeatedly told him to aim further right but it was hard. As it reached mid-morning, the wind picked up and within a short period a serious storm developed. We had to stop for some food; James threw me some juice and, as he did, the wind drove the kayak towards me. It caught me in the neck and instinctively I pushed it away, but a bit too strongly, and it flipped over on its side. James was still in position but his head was beneath the water. If he fell out of the kayak, it would fill with water and probably sink. All our equipment, including the GPS, would go down with it. I reached for the kayak, grabbed it and tried to force it back into an upright position. Without anywhere to anchor my legs and get some leverage, I shouldn't have been able to get James and the kayak upright but, almost panic-stricken, the usual limitations didn't exist and I twisted the boat until it and James were back in their normal positions. You have heard of the man who lifted the wheel of a car off his child, finding a strength he didn't know he had: for a second, that was me. The experience shook us up but we still had to get to the other side in terrible conditions. We'd been in the water for over two hours at this point. About half a kilometre from the north bank, we struggled against the current. We were being taken too far west but there was nothing we could do about it. The bank seemed so close but we were rushing away from it in the current. After three and a half hours in the water, we didn't have the strength to fight any more and resigned ourselves to the fact that we were not going to get to the north side. The current drove us fast down the fjord, and spat us out on the south bank not far from where we had started earlier in the day. It was near midday when we clambered out at Vik and the experience left us in a state of shock. For almost two weeks, everything had gone swimmingly and the dangers seemed minimal. Then, in the matter of a few hours, we were reminded of how difficult and unpredictable the fjord can be. It is always like that when you're in the water. You must never forget that conditions can change in a flash.

After the storm came the calm of Norwegian hospitality. Terje Eggum found us in our shaken and bedraggled state and the story of our near disaster made the front page of *Sogn Avis*. Terje happened to know a farmer nearby who offered to give us food and shelter until we were ready to carry on. We went to his farmhouse, enjoyed an excellent dinner and, still feeling shattered, we went to bed around ten, setting our alarms for 3 a.m. as that was the time to cross the fjord when the water would be calmer and the current less powerful. It was important to get back in the saddle straight away. Dave drove round to the north bank and parked the car in a good place; his flashing headlights gave us a target that we did not let out of our sights.

As we neared the shore, I could hear Dave's voice. 'Here I am,' he shouted as he came through bushes. 'Are you out there?'

'We're here,' I said, more than a little relieved to be back on the north bank.

It was 5 a.m. The six-kilometre swim across the fjord had taken two hours but we were back on track.

Swims at night became so enjoyable that I was quick to schedule them if the conditions were in favour. Night-time calmness is different, more tranquil, and the stars seem more brilliant when seen from the water. But there was another element to the attraction: those night-time swims took me back to my SAS days, trekking through the mountains in moonlight, the sense of being invisible as you progressed and, perhaps most of all, the feeling of having the world all to yourself. But the closer we got to the North Sea, the greater the volume of shipping on the fjord. At one point, a big Russian freighter that had run aground lay directly in our path on the north bank. My first thought was the best thing would be to walk on the shore past the freighter, but that would have meant I hadn't swum the entire fjord and I binned that idea. There was a tugboat further out in the fjord that was attempting to tow the freighter back into deeper waters and the authorities conducting this salvage operation didn't want me anywhere near the tow ropes for fear they would snap. They told me not to swim round the freighter but there wasn't a choice and that's what I had to do. On the way, I wondered whether the freighter's skipper had been asleep or drunk or both!

Jellyfish made the last days of the swim torturous, as if they had lain in wait, pounced and said, 'You didn't think you were getting through this so easily, did you?' They were there, as big as frying pans, floating on the surface, almost stalking me. I was certain to be stung if I somehow came into contact with their underbelly because that's where they keep their poison. Swimming at night meant I was among them before I realized they were there and, at one point, I found myself in the middle of a shoal of jellyfish. There were so many that when I lifted my head out of the water, I carried one upwards on the top of my head. It might sound funny and Nick, who was with me again and in the kayak alongside, tried not to giggle. Apparently, with the jellyfish doubling up as a headpiece, I looked like an orthodox Jew with curls and yarmulke. In those last two days, we had to cover 50 kilometres and I did that with white gunge oozing out of the multitudinous stings on my body.

We were still on the north side and had to make one last crossing of the fjord to finish the swim. As the fjord was wide open at this point, the water was choppy, potentially dangerous and not that suitable for kayaking. Mindful of what had almost come to pass at Balestrand, I decided it would be wise to have a local guide in a proper fishing boat accompany me on this last leg. Geir Ivar Ramsli, a fisherman who knew the waters like the back of his hand, agreed to help. He asked if it was okay to bring two friends and I told him that was fine. Geir himself was about forty-five; his friends were elderly gentlemen. Nick travelled with them in the boat, while Dave drove the car around and would be waiting for us on the other side.

'You are military guys?' Geir asked, looking Nick and me up and down.

'We are,' said Nick.

'Okay, I want you to meet this guy,' and he called the eldest gentleman towards us.

The old man had brought some photographs. 'These are photos I took in 1945,' he said, 'when I was a young man and the British SAS freed my town, Høyanger. They were sent because there were still pockets of German resistance and I will never forget how quickly the SAS got to work and gave us back our town. We had so many parties afterwards and everyone loved the British.' The old man then showed us photographs of him and his friends with members of the SAS, shirts off, sitting in the sun, splashing around in the fjord with a few Norwegian girls. It was the summer of 1945. As you looked at the photos, the joys of freedom regained and a war just ended were obvious and real. Geir and his two buddies were patriots and they had a big Norwegian flag pinned to a pole on the boat and, in a lovely way, I found that appropriate. Three weeks of hospitality had endeared Norway to me and to make the last leg of the Sognefjord journey alongside a boat flying a big Norwegian flag was just right. We made that final crossing of the fjord at night and there were plenty of shooting stars falling from a brightly lit sky. It was a spectacular way to end three glorious weeks.

The next morning when I swam into Eivindvik there was a huge armada of boats and hundreds of people turned out to greet us. Tourism people from Lusterfjord, where we had begun our three-week adventure, hired a boat and drove the 204 kilometres to be with us at the finish. Along the way, they picked up people and I was touched by the warmth and appreciation so evident in the local people. At one point during our interviews Terje asked me if the finances of the trip had worked out and I told him that, as the budget had overrun, there was a £5,000 deficit. I wasn't asking for help because this was my responsibility but word got out and the head of the local tourism board presented me with a £5,000 cheque, thanking me for opening everyone's eyes to the possibilities of the Sognefjord. That was typical of the generosity of Norwegian people. I was overwhelmed.

One of the locals who swam with me in Leikanger was Sarah Jane Hails, an English girl who had come to this area and fallen in love with Terje Eggum. She could swim but didn't have any experience of doing long distances.

'Do you think I could swim across the fjord?' she asked.

'Yes, I believe you could. If you want, I'll come and help you to do it. I am in Norway for a week and I can come back to help you. And if any of your friends would like to try it, they can come as well.'

So the week after finishing my swim I went to Leikanger

and helped to organize and officiate a swim across the fjord for Sarah Jane Hails and four of her friends. 'This is what I want you to do,' I said before they set out, 'you relax and swim at your ease. It is not a race and you do whatever stroke you are most comfortable with – breaststroke, crawl, whatever is easiest for you.'

Each person had a kayak next to them, and we had two support boats travelling with the swimmers, so there was plenty of help if anyone got into trouble. A couple wore wetsuits, the others were in ordinary swimsuits, but it didn't bother me how they dressed. This wasn't about adhering to English Channel Swimming Association rules but helping people to go further than they thought possible. It was also about helping them to enjoy the Sognefjord better, showing them how they could see it and experience it like never before. All except one made it across and the story of their crossing of the fjord was front-page news in *Sogn Avis*.

So successful had the swim been that we decided to turn it into an annual event, the Sognefjord Challenge. The following year we had twenty people do it, then thirty the year after, and the Fjord Swimming Club came into existence. Swimmers from Britain and Russia came to the Challenge and in the years after my swim I returned each summer to participate in the swim across the fjord.

One example of how the Sognefjord Challenge inspired local people was Sonnove Cirotzki, who was a very good pool swimmer who hadn't done much in open water until participating in the Challenge. After that she set her sights on swimming the English Channel and in her small village, Sogndal, people were impressed but slightly fearful. 'Surely you need a little more experience to attempt something as great as the English Channel,' they said. I felt she was strong enough and, unless conditions were absolutely foul, she would make it. Having encouraged Sonnove, it was my responsibility to help her and, when the big day arrived, I swam sections of it with her. She made it in 14 hours and 43 minutes, which was a heck of an achievement because conditions weren't nice and it was a battle. Terje Eggum was on the support boat and he wrote a piece for his local newspaper. Sonnove's achievement was celebrated back in her part of Norway. I was very proud of what she had done and didn't at all mind my Norwegian friends ribbing me about the fact that Sonnove's time for the Channel swim was a few minutes faster than mine.

Sognefjord promised me a huge physical challenge and it was that. Apart from the sheer distance, the currents, the frequent choppiness of the water and the jellyfish, there were the terrible changes in water temperature caused by glacial waters pouring into the fjord at different points. One minute you were gliding along in water that was a comfortable fourteen degrees and suddenly you were trying to race through stingingly cold water that was as low as six degrees. We could have swum further out into the fjord, away from where the valley water entered it but, even though I was sceptical about the stories of swimmers disappearing into some maelstrom in the middle of the fjord, I didn't want to put their maelstrom theory to the test for six or seven hours every day. So I endured those changes in water temperature and swam close to the shore.

As well as being hugely enjoyable, the swim was worthwhile. As part of the Sognefjord Challenge, we got about 100 little kids to swim not in the main race across the fjord but in their own gala in the fjord. They raced up and down the marina in front of the impressive Kvikne Hotel. What pleased me most of all was the acceptance from their parents that the fjord was now a safe place for their children to swim.

On a personal level, the end of the Sognefjord swim meant the breaking up of the team. Nick Peterson and James

Mayhew would go back to London and Dave Richter to South Africa. Because there had been such a good rapport between us, there was sadness as well as a sense of satisfaction when the expedition came to an end. I remember Nick getting on the ferry that would take him to the airport and feeling alone and unsure. After three weeks in the King of the Fjords, you would have thought I'd have had enough but I didn't want it to end.

11

HEADING NORTH

Sognefjord gave me a sense of what it was like to swim in cold waters, as North Cape had, and it was satisfying to come through both. Though the quick dip in Nigards Glacier Lake was nothing compared to the other two, the fact that the water temperature was just two degrees made it significant. It was a feeling I wanted again and, after the reaffirming experience of Sognefjord, I wanted to carry on and push the boundaries even more. That meant going further north and swimming in a sea colder than either Sognefjord or North Cape. I settled on Spitsbergen, part of the group of Norwegian islands called Svalbard. At its northern tip Spitsbergen is 80 degrees north and, given that the Arctic Circle begins at 66 degrees, the water there would be seriously cold – less than four degrees, I reckoned. Obviously, no human had ever attempted a long-distance swim in waters so far north.

It was time to speak again with Professor Tim Noakes. We met as we had previously at his office in the Sports Science Institute in Cape Town. I'm not sure Tim understood at this point how much his opinion meant but having outlined how far north Spitsbergen was and how cold the water would be there, I asked, 'Can I do it?'

He paused for a little bit and then said, 'Yes.'

And that was it for me: Spitsbergen was now the plan. A closer look at the map showed Verlegenhuken was the most northern point on the island and, translated, its Dutch name means 'Corner of Desolation'. Around that point of desolation was where I intended to swim. After receiving Professor Noakes's go-ahead, I called the Norwegian Meteorological Institute and asked about water temperatures around Spitsbergen. They could tell me that in winter the surface of the sea around the island was frozen solid and that in summer the sea ice melts but the temperature ranges from four degrees down to minus 1.7°C. It would depend upon the precise time of year and the particular part of the island. Verlegenhuken was likely to be where the water would be coldest.

Then I began to think about my team. I wanted Nick Peterson back on board; I wanted David Becker as both my best friend and my mind coach; and, as I was going into waters much colder than I'd previously experienced, it was imperative to have a doctor. Otto Thaning, my sparring partner on Lake Malawi and for the English Channel, was the obvious choice. I didn't consider Professor Noakes because I presumed he would be too busy to accompany me on a swim deep inside the Arctic. But of the three people I asked, only David Becker was free to travel. Neither Nick nor Otto could arrange the necessary time off work and Otto wasn't sure about the wisdom of attempting a long swim in water close to freezing. I don't remember where exactly the conversation took place but he told me, 'Lewis, as a close friend of yours and as a heart surgeon, I believe that if you try to swim one kilometre in zero-degree water, you could possibly kill yourself.'

When someone you respect deeply says you may be

putting your life at risk, it makes you think. But my experience at Nigards Glacier Lake and in the coldest stretches in Sognefjord convinced me I could survive at temperatures close to freezing. And, I suppose, there was part of me that wanted to find out how I would do in really cold water. Otto doesn't recall advising me against going to Spitsbergen but that's how I heard it.

Concerned about the danger, I called round to Professor Noakes again and explained. He could see that I had deep reservations about going to Spitsbergen without scientific and medical back-up. 'Look,' he said, 'it so happens that at the time you are planning to do this, I am giving a lecture in Norway. Why don't I extend my trip to Norway by a little and go with you to Spitsbergen?'

'That would be brilliant!' I said. 'You can be my doctor as well as the scientist.'

'Fine,' he said, 'but you may have to work on Marilyn [his wife] because I would really not want to be there without her.'

The Prof and Marilyn: you can't have one without the other – not that you would want to. Through his work, Professor Noakes had travelled to many overseas destinations and discovered that he didn't like being away from his wife. After one cricket tour to India, he came home and announced that he wouldn't ever again travel out of the country for a long period without her. He said it was my job to convince Marilyn that the trip to Spitsbergen would be fun. Naturally enough, I wasn't going to start by translating Verlegenhuken from the Dutch; instead I researched the Arctic's extraordinary flora because I knew that Marilyn loved to paint flowers. As it turned out, the Arctic is rich in flowers. When I spoke with Marilyn, I didn't have to lie or exaggerate and she was soon sold on the trip.

Tim Noakes has the most wonderful smile of any person

I know. He can make the most perceptive observation or the most straightforward statement and, almost always, it comes with his trademark smile. It is boyish and expresses his love of life and conversation and simply interacting with other people. But there is another side to the Prof, one that doesn't banish the smile but does express his intelligence and his desire to see things done correctly. It was his view that I could do a one-kilometre swim in extremely cold water, but if he were going to be involved, then I would have to prepare thoroughly, and by that he meant cold-water training.

As soon as Professor Tim Noakes agreed to travel to Spitsbergen with us, the project moved to a different level. No longer was its purpose simply to see whether it was possible to do a long-distance swim in hostile conditions. The Prof is a scientist who has devoted much time to researching the physiological responses to performance under extreme conditions. He has done groundbreaking work on the effects of heat on the athlete and what constitutes the optimum intake of fluids for those in marathons and other long-distance events. His conclusions have challenged and exposed the flaws of conventional thinking, much of it inspired by studies financed by soft-drinks companies. Professor Noakes has demonstrated the dangers of over-hydration and pointed out that fatalities in marathons are more likely to be caused by over-hydration than dehydration. Once he agreed to join our expedition, the Prof was always going to want to study the physiological effects of swimming in extremely cold water. It was a bonus for me that some worthwhile scientific analysis would be applied to what I was doing.

There was no comprehensive research available to those wanting information on how long humans could survive in very cold water. Among the medical experiments carried out by the Nazis at their various concentration camps was one designed to see the effects of immersion in icy water. Although the notorious Dr Josef Mengele was the central coordinator for the medical experiments, two of his underlings, Professor Ernst Holzlohner and Dr Sigmund Rascher, supervised the cold-water research. The immersion experiment took place at Dachau and involved using prisoners in experiments that led to the deaths of many of the participants. It was one more atrocity inflicted on Jews and other groups during the years of Nazi terror. As a result of the means used to gather the information, no one has wanted to refer to the Dachau research as anything other than the grotesque and obscene abuse of human beings that it was.

From the Prof's point of view, my swims were an opportunity to advance his understanding of physiology. He would be working with an extreme athlete who wanted to be in cold water and who had prepared for the challenge. Research had been done on swimmers in the English Channel but that was at medium to low temperatures – 18 to 14 degrees. No legitimate testing had been done on humans in extremely cold water. Partly because of the Dachau experience, the Prof had to get permission from the Ethics Committee at the University of Cape Town, which was granted. Knowing the Prof would be both supervising my swims and doing what could be important research was a huge boost for me. My reasoning was simple: if the Prof could explain to me precisely what was happening to my body when I was submerged in extremely cold water, it would enable me to maximize my performance. To every serious athlete, I would say, 'Embrace science', because it is key. When someone like Professor Tim Noakes, who has run over sixty marathons, says: 'This is how you must prepare for a cold-water swim', you listen carefully.

The Prof is a 'big picture' man whose keen intellect is insulted by having to deal with life's smaller details. I should have known better than to ask him to bring the K–Y jelly before we left South Africa – it was like asking Pavarotti to make sure the microphone was working. But K–Y jelly was needed and badly.

In terms of ensuring my safety while swimming in cold water, it was vital for the Prof to know my core body temperature at all times. Our core temperature doesn't vary as much as might be imagined: 37.2°C is normal; anything above 39 is too high and needs to be lowered. Anything below 35 is considered hypothermic. At 32 degrees you will get cardiac arrhythmias and at 28 you will be departing this life. From the moment I entered the water, the Prof had to know my core temperature and if it dropped below a certain point, he would pull me out of the water. He monitored my temperature through a plastic thermometer, which had been inserted in my rectum and which was strapped to antennae that relayed temperature readings to the Prof's laptop. It was something we'd used in my training and I'd learned the value of K–Y jelly. Without it, that plastic thermometer is not your friend.

'Don't forget the K–Y jelly,' I said to the Prof before we left Cape Town.

'Yes, don't worry,' he replied. 'How could I forget the K–Y jelly?'

We arrived in Longyearbyen, the main town on the island of Spitsbergen. Now a disciple of the SAS way, I decided to check the equipment. Everything was in place except the – K–Y jelly. I asked the Prof about its whereabouts but knew without needing to hear the answer. He had forgotten it and thought it all very funny. The rest of the team also saw the funny side – all except the poor guy who would have the plastic thermometer inserted where, to be polite, the sun doesn't often shine.

David Becker, Terje Eggum and I went to the town's main

store in search of K-Y jelly. Two young and beautiful Norwegian girls were behind the counter, and because David had laughed a little too enthusiastically at the Prof's lack of remorse, I made him ask one of the girls for the K-Y jelly. Though she spoke perfect English, she had never heard of 'K-Y jelly'. David and I were puzzled as we thought K-Y jelly was a global brand. It wasn't, because Terje, whose English is perfect, hadn't come across it. 'What is it?' he asked us. David explained it is a product often used as a lubricant in lovemaking, especially if the man is using a condom. 'Ah,' said Terje, 'you mean glidecreme. That's what it's called in Norwegian and it means "gliding cream". If you ask for "glidecreme", they will know exactly what you mean.'

David and I were reluctant to do the asking. We were two strangers in Longyearbyen, a town of 2,000 people, and we didn't like to imagine what the girls would think. 'I've already asked for K-Y jelly,' said David, indicating that it was my turn.

'David,' I said, 'I've brought you all the way up here. Can you not do something useful? You're supposed to be the manager on this expedition.'

David was shamed into asking for glidecreme and, though the girls tried to remain businesslike, they glanced over towards Terje and me, then back at David, and it was obvious they were suppressing the urge to giggle. We knew what they were thinking. David came back and said, 'They've run out. There's no glidecreme on the island.'

'David,' I said, 'stop jacking around. They've got to have this stuff.' But it was true, they had run out. They get long and very dark winters in Longyearbyen, which are clearly good for the sale of glidecreme. We were left with Vaseline lip balm, which wasn't exactly what we needed but it was worth it to see the Norwegian girls look at David and tell him he was out of luck.

*

The goal of the trip to Spitsbergen was to do the most northerly long-distance swim in the world. At its northern-most point, the island lies at 80 degrees latitude; the North Pole is about 1,000 kilometres further on. Lynne Cox, the well-known American swimmer, had swum across a section of the Bering Strait between Alaska and the USSR and, though not as far north as Spitsbergen, the waters are simi-larly cold. Lynne's was a significant effort. I would swim more than 2,000 kilometres further north but, because of the effects of the Gulf Stream, the water temperature wouldn't be much different to what Lynne had experienced. For me, it was an important challenge. Swimming at six degrees, as I had done in Sognefjord, is one experience; two degrees lower is another world. Get it wrong in water that cold and you are going to end up hypothermic and then it's a question of how much damage is done.

For this swim I would prepare as never before. As much as I would be putting my life at risk by swimming so far north, the Prof was putting his reputation in my hands. If some-thing calamitous happened while I was swimming in the Arctic Ocean, accusing fingers would be pointed at him.

We thought about how we might prepare. Even if the Cape is a good training location for most swims, it wouldn't be enough for something as arduous as a long-distance swim at temperatures not much above freezing. I needed my own small ice pool – so I threw lots of bags of ice into my friend's swim-ming pool. It felt like a good idea at the time but no sooner did the water and ice mix but the ice melted and the water temperature rose quickly. We needed to think bigger, and came up with the idea of locating my training camp in the I&J factory at the V&A Waterfront in Cape Town. I&J is a big fishing company in South Africa and the one thing they had at their warehouse was tonnes of ice. So we set up an inflatable swimming pool outside the factory, half filled it with water and then had a couple of the I&J workers shovel industrial quantities of ice in around me. Using the ice, we could get the temperature of the water down to three or four degrees. By suspending me in the water through the use of a harness, I was able to 'swim' while remaining in a stationary position. Because of the size of the pool, I had to do a breaststroke and not a crawl.

Through the training programme at I&J, I built up to a 22-minute 'swim' in water that was maintained at around three to four degrees. The fun was in the shovelling, as two I&J workers, both black, came to enjoy the act of tipping all that ice into a pool containing one freezing white body. It was all good humoured as the Prof's colleague, Jonathan Dugas, took temperature readings and gave the nod to the two I&J guys to shovel in more ice. They were laughing so much they hardly could keep their shovels steady and, in their enthusiasm, they would sometimes toss ice over my head. 'The edges,' I would scream, 'shovel it around the edges.' We did our training at 4 p.m. every afternoon, when I&J workers were leaving the factory to catch trains home, but the two guys helping us didn't mind staying behind. In the inflatable pool with all that I&J ice, I trained my body to deal with water so cold that the Arctic no longer seemed beyond the realm of possibility.

That's the point about proper preparation: it changes your sense of what's possible. Two years before, after swimming round North Cape, I had taken a flight to Spitsbergen and hiked around the island for about a week and a half. Translated from Dutch, Spitsbergen means 'Spiky Mountains'. During that holiday, I'd loved the island's Arctic landscape: the mountains, the glaciers, the wild flowers, the birdlife, the desolation and the overwhelming sense of remoteness. I had been there in summer, when daylight is endless, and thought how different it would be in winter when the seas around the island froze over and 24-hour darkness closed in. You try to imagine what it would be like during the dark months and you can't even get close. But people do live on the island and they survive the winters. On my 2003 visit to Spitsbergen I didn't think about what it would be like to swim this far north and, if someone had suggested it, I would have laughed and said it was completely impossible.

Funding the trip was the usual ordeal, lessened on this occasion by the generosity of Spitsbergen Travel, the company that owned the MV *Nordstjern*, a beautiful little coastal steamer with an ice-strengthened hull that took tourists on five-day voyages through the waters around the island. They gave us a couple of free cabins on the *Nordstjern* and that helped because there were six of us: the Prof and his wife Marilyn, David Becker, James Mayhew, the photo-journalist Terje Eggum and me. David, James and I flew from London to Oslo, on to Tromsø and from there to Spitsbergen. The Prof and Marilyn were already in Norway, where he had given a talk, and they made their own way to Spitsbergen. There were some bread-and-butter concerns, as our cabins on the *Nordstjern* were, let's say, 'cosy', which wasn't good for the Prof's claustrophobia. His bed was high up, quite close to the ceiling, and only by taking off the mattress and lying it on the floor did we convert it into a room in which he could sleep.

Even though I'd been there before, I was again blown away by the extraordinary beauty of the place. In encouraging Marilyn to make the trip, I had not played down the unique quality of the Arctic landscape and the abundance of wild flowers that appear, almost miraculously, from otherwise barren terrain. Thankfully, Spitsbergen lived up to my hype and Marilyn loved it. She and the Prof walked round in wondrous amazement. 'Tim,' she would say, 'look what's here, you've got to see this,' after finding a small flower behind a rock. They would take photographs and walk on, hand-in-hand, until they came across the next example of nature's beauty and resilience. Often they seemed to me like a honeymooning couple, even though they have been married for more than thirty years.

We set off in a north-westerly direction, stopping at various points along the way. At the most north-westerly point of the island, we found ourselves in Magdalenefjord, and sailed into its heart until we arrived at the foot of an incredible glacier. It was turquoise blue and its scale was like nothing I had ever seen. At the tip of the tongue of the glacier, blocks of ice broke off and dropped into the sea, causing a massive explosion of water, then the ice blocks resurfaced and sailed off into the sea. Closer to the ice blocks, you could hear the pop of trapped air being released and I was always struck by the antiquity of the ice. How long had that air been in there? Millennia?

A little bay inside the fjord seemed to the Prof the perfect place to do the swim. We talked about whether we should make this the principal swim or use it as a trial run for something longer and more challenging the next day. Magdalenefjord was at 79 degrees latitude but I'd anticipated doing my swim at the most northerly part of Spitsbergen, which was at 80 degrees, a further 110 kilometres north, and wanted Magdalenefjord to be a prep swim rather than the real thing. The others made the point that we didn't know what the conditions would be like further north. If we found they were so bad we couldn't do a swim, what would we do then? I was easily persuaded to do the full distance – one kilometre – in Magdalenefjord to make sure that no matter what we would have one swim safely in the bag. It was a perfect venue with a nice sandy beach. The Prof decided I should do the kilometre in two 500-metre legs – out and

back. He argued that if there were a following current that
made a straight swim less difficult, it would invalidate it. I
agreed. It would have been like running the 100 metres with
a strong tailwind – not that a one-kilometre swim in water
that is three to four degrees would be easy under any circumstances, but after the training at I&J I felt confident I
could handle the assault to my system.

As is true for all the tough swims, it was key to get my
head in the right place for Magdalenefjord and not to see it
as a practice swim. Thankfully, help was offered by a gentleman who had served me at Ing Paulson, a big outdoor store
in Longyearbyen, the previous day.

'What are you guys here for?' he asked.

'I am going to try to swim around Verlegenhuken,' I replied.

'You are doing what?'

'I am going to try to break the record for the most northern long-distance swim,' I said.

'It's impossible for anyone to swim in these waters,' he said.
'You will die.'

Coming from a guy who showed no interest in discovering
my previous experience or how I'd prepared, I was under-
whelmed. His view was: 'I live here, therefore I know.'

Trying to be as polite as possible, I said, 'I'm sorry but
what is your name?'

'Edward,' he said. He didn't think for a second that his
name was important, but I knew then it would be the pass-
word to the motivation I would need for the swim. He was
more interested in pointing out the impossibility of swimming this far north. 'No human will ever survive in this
water,' he said.

'Thank you, Edward,' I said, aware that the memory of the
encounter would spur me on. Without doubt, the best motivation comes from within yourself and the desire to be as
good as you can be. That is a very positive force and, as it

doesn't depend upon external factors, it is reproducible from one performance to another. Taking motivation from the dismissive attitude of other people is, in my opinion, a lesser means to the same end but it can work and it certainly has worked at different points in my career. Over time, I learned to rely more on and put greater trust in the motivation that came from within.

The Prof measured out his 500-metre stretch of water. It took me 21 minutes and 30 seconds to do the kilometre. At one point, when I might have been flagging slightly, David wrote the name 'Edward' on the whiteboard and everything was a little easier after that. Completing the swim gave me the mark for the most northerly long-distance swim and, though the coldness of the water made it extremely unpleasant, I got through it well enough. From the thermometer in my rectum, the heart monitor and his GPS, the Prof was able to know exactly how far I'd gone, what my core temperature was and how my heart was coping with the physical demands. He was fascinated by the results and, as the readings appeared on his computer screen, he passed the details to David Becker, who would write them on the whiteboard for me to see. This was the first time this kind of data was available to me and it was a considerable help. Seeing your core temperature remain normal through a swim is very encouraging. It says, 'Okay, you're surviving here, your body is not letting you down, so keep going.' Always, the trick is to go fast enough to get through the water in reasonable time but not so fast that you use too much energy and destroy your body's defences. There is a perfect speed for hostile water and you've got to find it.

After the swim, I felt a little stiff and had the sense of having done something very physical. Of course, what happens is your body tightens in the cold water and that tensing of the muscles taxes you far more than a normal 21-minute swim would. But my recovery was good and I was keen to do another swim – this time at 80 degrees on the northern tip of Spitsbergen. When the *Nordstjern* turned out of Magdalenefjord and moved off in a north-easterly direction, we left a sheltered fjord for the exposed rocky coast. The wind was suddenly strong and it brought flurries of freezing cold snow. The worsening conditions gave the Prof second thoughts about another swim. 'Lewis,' he said, 'I think you've done enough. I really don't think it's sensible to try to do a second swim twelve or thirteen hours after the first.' I could understand his reluctance. He felt we'd be pushing our luck. But it was in my mind to do a swim at 80 degrees and once the Prof sensed my determination to go ahead with it, he agreed. There was a proviso: 'If I tell you to get out of the water at any time during the swim, you get out. Okay?'

'Prof,' I said, 'that's always the case. Safety comes before everything.'

We spent about twelve hours making the journey to Verlegenhuken, the point on the map of Spitsbergen that I had picked out as the place to do the swim. Verlegenhuken is flat, barren and exposed. Desolate barely begins to describe it. Drizzling rain didn't help and the cold cut right through us. Absent were the glaciers that lent beauty to other parts of the island and the beach was more rocky than sandy. After the *Nordstjern* anchored at Verlegenhuken, we travelled to the beach in two Zodiacs that took us from the steamer to the shore. Getting out of the Zodiacs, the Prof looked around at the awful – some might say spectacular – bleakness and said, 'Lewis, I can't imagine there is a more inappropriate place in the world to do this swim.' Enthusiasm wasn't exactly at fever pitch.

'I know, Prof,' I said. 'I couldn't agree more but we just have to do this thing.'

I will never forget that beach. It was covered in litter – horrible plastic that had been used to package consumer products in the US and Europe and had travelled all the way here on the Gulf Stream. What an eye-opener it was to see at first hand the consequences of abusing the environment. You carelessly discard a piece of plastic in New York, Belfast or Tromsø and it causes a litter problem on an island near the North Pole.

The Prof and I are optimists and we collected as much of the rubbish as we could and made sure that when we started filming the swim, the background shots showed a beach free of litter. But all that litter left an indelible mark on my consciousness and a conviction that unless we seriously change our ways, our planet will struggle to survive the explosion in population that is likely to take place over the next fifty years.

In Magdalenefjord the water temperature had been four degrees; here it was three and that one-degree drop is far more significant than you'd imagine. Routinely, I would get myself dressed and prepared before leaving my cabin on the boat and that had the particular advantage of allowing me to get the thermometer in place in the privacy of my own room. But at Verlegenhuken the sea was too rough and the thought of sitting in the boat bouncing up and down with the thermometer in place was unappealing to say the least. So I had to find a big rock and squat down behind it – an inconvenience preceded by the ritual of the Prof claiming to have again forgotten the Vaseline.

'Come on, Prof,' I said. 'Where is it?' Only then did I begin to realize this wasn't a prank. He was convinced he had left it on the *Nordsjtern* and only discovered it in a small zipped pocket that was the last he searched. Everyone else again thought this was hilarious. Well, behind that rock the air temperature was well below zero, the wind was howling and my bum wasn't very excited by the imminent arrival of the thermometer. Once that was done, I had to have the cord that links the thermometer to the antennae taped to my body and all the while I was getting colder and colder.

Because the conditions were foul, the Prof wanted me to swim four legs of 250 metres so that everything was kept compact and the support team would always be close by. I agreed, because this was going to be a tough and potentially dangerous swim. David Becker helped to prepare me mentally and on this, of all days, it was key that I was properly psyched up for the swim. The thought that motivated me more than any other was the fact that this swim was at 80 degrees north and it had always been my aim to do a long-distance swim at this point. 'This will be an unbreakable record,' I told myself. 'No one will do a swim further north than this.' Little did I know that, two years later, I would be the one to smash this 'unbreakable record'.

Towards the end of the third leg, almost 750 metres into the one-kilometre swim, I slowed down quite noticeably because I was so cold. The Prof and David thought something serious might be happening, though my core temperature was still fine. As they were deciding whether to pull me out, my stroke improved again and I completed the kilometre. If my temperature had dropped below 35, they would have pulled me out, but it didn't. What happens in water that cold is that the veins and capillaries close to the skin constrict and push blood towards the core to protect the vital organs – heart, lungs, liver. Arms and legs are important but not vital, so you can imagine how cold the arms and legs get. Out of the water, my limbs were rigid and that made it impossible to dress me, so they just wrapped a big blanket around me, got me into a Zodiac and whizzed me back to the *Nordstjern*. As we boarded, all the passengers were on deck wanting to congratulate me. I waved at them, they clapped and cheered and I ran into a hot shower.

After a while, my blood began its return journey to the extremities and the reheating of the limbs started. A hot shower accelerated that process. Knowing that two one-kilometre swims in a twelve-hour timeframe in waters so cold was risky, I was ecstatic to have completed the second one without anything going wrong. While I was in the shower, the Prof continued to gauge my core temperature because it continues to fall for a certain time after you're out of the water. At Verlegenhuken it went from 38.4 to 36.5, then 36, down to 35. There was then the nervous wait because anything below 35 is worrisome. I was sitting on a chair in the shower, the blissful hot water fighting the cold of my body, and waiting for the Prof to give me the next reading. 'It's going back up again, 35.5,' and the relief in his voice was music to my ears. He never stopped telling me how valuable this whole exercise was from a scientific point of view. Some of the results fascinated him.

In normal times I might have argued that in all the barren desolation, there was a certain charm about Verlegenhuken, but sitting in the shower that day, I wasn't sad to be on a ship that was putting some distance between me and that place. The Prof's words were still ringing in my ears: 'I can't imagine there is a more inappropriate place in the world to do this swim.'

We had two more days on the *Nordstjern*, which, without the worry of an impending swim, were magical. On the coast of Spitsbergen we went down a fjord and our boat slowed to a stop to allow us to gaze upon Monaco Glacier, a work of nature as awe-inspiring as anything we had seen on the trip. Prince Albert II of Monaco's great-grandfather had visited this part of the world about 100 years before and the glacier was named in memory of that visit. I was persuaded to do a short swim in front of the glacier and it was worth it, as a polar bear watched me from the nearby mountainside. They showed us photographs of the glacier taken at the time of Prince Albert I's visit and it was shocking to see the degree to which the glacier had retreated; the place where I swam had until recently been covered over by the glacier. At every other glacier we saw, guides told how much they had retreated too.

Those two days of sightseeing on the *Nordstjern* could have been six weeks and I wouldn't have complained. It was a time to relax and integrate with fellow passengers. It's interesting to discover the kind of people attracted to the Arctic and Antarctica. In time I would meet the latter and they were different. In Antarctica you encountered people who were often box-tickers: been to the Amazon, tick; been to Paris, tick; been to Antarctica, tick. The North Pole attracted very wealthy Germans and Americans who decided they wanted to go there and had the money. Spitsbergen was very different; it didn't have the glamour of the other two and it attracted people who really wanted to experience the Arctic landscape. They had read and heard about the glaciers; they knew about the possibilities of seeing polar bears; they sensed how different it would be; and they came because they had a passion for nature. Of the tourists I would meet at the three locations, I enjoyed the company of the Spitsbergen tourists the most.

On the final part of the journey back to Longyearbyen, the town that didn't sell K-Y jelly, I picked up a magazine in the lounge of the *Nordstjern* and it had an advertisement for trips to Antarctica. Nudging the Prof, I pointed to the ad without saying a word. He just smiled. We both knew what I was thinking.

12

HEADING SOUTH

Sailing to Antarctica was truly the realization of a childhood dream. Days at Camps Bay High School in Cape Town were spent staring out over the Atlantic Ocean, knowing there was land beyond the horizon and believing that, one day, I would get there. The best dreams play out in the waking hours when you consciously imagine things you want to happen. Without understanding how or when, I somehow knew it would come to pass. The trigger was that advert for voyages to Antarctica I'd noticed in a magazine on the *Nordstjern*. That was in August 2005. Because the trip had to take place at the height of the Antarctic summer, the choice was between doing it four months later or a year after that. It was really no choice because my training at I&J's warehouse had prepared me for water temperatures not much above zero and it would have been silly not to have used that preparation for Antarctica. A 16-month wait would mean losing that fitness and tolerance of cold water only then to have to regain it.

After each major swim, I liked to rest my body and, though it always felt like a luxury, it was necessary. Three weeks was

all it took to have me grouchy and itching for a more energetic lifestyle. It was early October when I got back to
training and began to organize the logistics of the Antarctic
trip. Because you so badly want something to happen, you are
convinced you can make it happen. But expertise in maritime
law and an ability to swim long distances in cold water don't
teach you how to attract sponsorship and raise funds.
Nonetheless I had been on one of those courses where they
teach you that each 'no' is, in fact, one step closer to a 'yes'.

Getting from Cape Town to Antarctica begins with a flight
to Buenos Aires and then an internal flight to the town of
Ushuaia on Tierra del Fuego at the bottom of South
America. Flights were a cost I couldn't do a lot about because
there wasn't anything to offer the airlines. By far the greatest
cost was the berths on the ship from Ushuaia to the Antarctic.
I checked who carried tourists to the Antarctic and concen-
trated on the Norwegian ship-owners because they were
more likely to know of me than their British and US counterparts. A record-breaking swim off Antarctica would be a
big news event and would help to show the beauty of the
area – surely they would see the logic of supporting that. My
first target flatly refused; the second was a company registered
in Canada but owned by a Norwegian, Martin Karlsen. After
sending an email to Martin, I was put in touch with the company's marketing manager, Mary Pilbee, and, unhelpfully,
Mary's one experience with giving free berths in return for
publicity had been a bad one. They had given a few berths
but received nothing in return. She said they would give us a
couple of berths only if they were not sold before the departure of the ship, which was called MV *Polar Star*. Eventually
she agreed to give us a couple of berths, but then shortly
before we were about to leave the offer was withdrawn.

The greatest pressure came from knowing members of my
team had arranged time off from their jobs to accompany

me. How could I then go to them, at the eleventh hour, and say, 'I'm truly sorry but the expedition is off?' In the case of Tim Noakes and his assistant, Jonathan Dugas, they had put so much into preparing me for Antarctica that I felt I couldn't let them down, but for weeks it was on a knife-edge. Without those free berths on the *Polar Star*, I hadn't a hope. There were so many people that I asked for sponsorship and so many times I was refused that it was hard to stay 100 per cent focused on training. Some people can juggle two or three balls in the air and continue to perform – not me. When I concentrate on trying to raise sponsorship, my mind can hardly entertain any other thought.

One day my mother overheard me on the telephone to some new, potential sponsor and knew from my reaction that it was another refusal. She could see I was going through agony. For her, it was so difficult to watch. 'Lewis,' she said, 'your father bought some antiques and he always said if we needed money we were to sell them and not be sentimental. Now is the time. Let us use them to pay for your expedition.' My heart swelled and ached at the same time. My mother has always been an incredibly generous woman. 'She'd sell the family silver to help you,' I would have said and here she was doing just that. It pained me that it had come to this. 'No, Mum,' I said. 'You can't sell your antiques for my expedition. That would be wrong.' Her generosity and her love inspired me: this trip, I decided, must happen. So I wrote another letter to Martin Karlsen and somehow persuaded him to renew his kind offer.

While training at the I&J warehouse in Cape Town, I worked closely with the Prof's assistant, Jonathan Dugas, and his wife Lara, who oversaw my preparation. Even with the financial worries, we prepared well and ended up doing a programme of eight controlled swims, during which we took the water temperature progressively down to one degree above freezing. As well as my cold-water training, I did a lot of cycling to strengthen my legs and began to lose weight quickly. That was fine by me but it concerned Lara, who is a nutrition expert. Her concern was that with a smaller body mass and a lower fat content, I would be less protected in the freezing waters of Antarctica. She sent me an email saying I was to eat as if my life depended upon it, which she believed it did. I liked my thinner, more athletic physique but it had to go. From 85 kilograms my weight was forced up to 104 kilos and it bothered me. It shouldn't have, but it did. I felt obese and probably wasn't far off. The horrible part for me was doing photo-shoots in my Speedo swimming trunks and feeling like a fraud. Because I had done all these swims, the photographers expected an athletic, well-cut type but I was a guy with a gut and a lot of extra pounds. Even though I explained the reason for the rounded shape, they still looked at me as if I were swimming's answer to Eddie the Eagle.

Another issue was national identity: was I British or South African? Because I was better known in their country than in Great Britain, South Africans regarded me as one of theirs. I went to school and university there, most of the training for my swims was done in Cape Town and my support team had many South Africans in it. It wasn't a surprise that they should have presumed I was South African. I did feel South African but I also felt British. My parents were British, I was born in Plymouth in the West Country, I'd lived in Hampshire for a time and, soon after completing my law degree at the University of Cape Town, I'd returned to England. Though I loved South Africa, I felt more British having been in the British Army. It's impossible to serve in the SAS and not feel a deep affinity for Great Britain. Against that, it was to South Africa that I returned following the decision to leave my career in maritime law. So where did that leave me? Was I connected to two countries or lost between the two? Neil

Diamond brilliantly captured that sense of being torn between two places in his song, 'I Am . . . I Said':

Well I'm New York City born and raised,
But nowadays, I'm lost between two shores,
LA's fine, but it ain't home,
New York's home but it ain't mine no more.

In the South African newspapers, I was the South African long-distance swimmer. In the British media, I was referred to as British-born, although it was easy to pick up the sense that the British writers didn't quite know where to place me. The only companies who would sponsor me were in Norway, where I was regarded as British. All of this came to a head when Speedo agreed to back me, for a small amount of money, to wear one of their new swim caps, which carried a large British flag on it. It felt right because I was British and another, lesser motivation was the certainty that being associated with Great Britain would help commercially. Perhaps naively, what I hadn't foreseen was the reaction in South Africa. There was genuine disappointment that, in their eyes, I was switching my allegiance to the UK. They had presented my story as that of a South African swimmer and it was as if I had betrayed them.

John Robbie, a former Irish rugby player who had come to South Africa in the early 1980s and is a popular morning show presenter for the Johannesburg radio station 702, asked me straight out: was I British or South African? I could tell where he was coming from because he'd become a South African citizen though he'd been born and raised in Ireland. It wasn't as clear for me but my difficulty was that I couldn't talk about my time in the British SAS and how that had left its indelible stamp on me.

The question of what nationality you feel yourself to be

is an evolving one and relates to a great degree on where you are living. Having been born and spent my childhood in England, I saw myself as British, though the next fifteen years were spent in South Africa. I then returned to England and spent five years in the SAS, thus strengthening the bond with the country of my birth. But I didn't relinquish my love for South Africa. When there were important moments in my life, I returned to where I have felt most comfortable and that is Cape Town. I am now married to a beautiful Cape Town woman, and as much as one can predict these things, our future is likely to remain split between the two countries.

If ever you travel to the Antarctic, there is a sound that will at once shake you and then thrill you. I was lying on the bunk in my cabin on the MV *Polar Star* when the first violent contact of the ship's hull with packed sea ice made me jump. It is an awful, scrunching noise, a loud and thunderous sound, but it is also a wondrous moment. I immediately looked out the window, saw the most incredible seascape, then bounded up the stairs to the top of the ship and was blown away by what I saw: tabular blocks of ice in the distance, Adélie penguins rushing to get out of the ship's way, leopard seals torpedoing through the water – it was everything I'd dreamed of, magical. Thirty years before my mother had sent me to sleep with the Ladybird book of Scott's expedition to the South Pole and, in that account, the blocks of ice were likened to giant cubes of sugar. That wasn't a bad description. We hit the ice at about 62 degrees south and it forced the *Polar Star* to slow as it wove through a floating obstacle course.

Our journey had begun in Ushuaia, the Argentinean town that is capital of Tierra del Fuego province and the southernmost city in the world. Our team numbered eight:

Professor Tim Noakes and his wife Marilyn, Jonathan Dugas
and his wife Lara, and our cameraman Chris Lotz, who all
came from South Africa; Terje Eggum came from Norway
with his partner Sarah Jane Hails; and me. We had a couple
of days in Ushuaia, which allowed me to train in water that
was five to six degrees and gave Jonathan a chance to test the
scientific equipment. I did a one-kilometre trial swim and
the Prof thought I was so comfortable that the water must
have seemed lukewarm to a body grown used to training in
much colder water. Jonathan worked night and day until he
had everything operating perfectly and his dedication was a
reminder that Antarctica wasn't solely about my breaking the
record for the most southern long-distance swim but was
also to gather scientific data on the ability of a human being
to survive in extremely cold water. In Spitsbergen we learned
what happens when you swim in water that was three to four
degrees; now we would learn about the body's response to a
long swim in zero-degree water. I felt good about doing
something that would contribute to a better understanding
of humans' ability to survive in extremely cold water. The
Prof and Jonathan would later produce a paper based on
what they had learned from the swims in the Arctic and off
Antarctica and that was pleasing, though I couldn't quite get
my head around being described as 'the subject'.

Anyone who has ever left Ushuaia on a ship bound for
Antarctica will know about the Drake Passage, named after
the famous sixteenth-century English sea captain Sir Francis
Drake. This is the body of water between the southern
tip of South America and the Antarctic Peninsula. Because
of fast-flowing southern ocean currents squeezing between
land masses, it has some of the roughest seas anywhere.
Evidence from satellite images shows that a cyclonic low of
hurricane strength passes through Drake Passage once every
few weeks. We picked our moment well, catching one of

those infamous cyclonic lows. Virtually every one of the one hundred or so passengers was sick and for a couple of days the MV *Polar Star* reeked of sickness. Among our group, Jonathan and Lara Dugas were the worst affected and didn't leave their cabins for a few days. There's just no predicting who will be badly affected. Jonathan, for example, had spent a year on a university ship sailing around the world and Lara had done plenty of sailing, yet the only person in our group with natural sea legs and a calm stomach was the Prof. When everyone was dying, or wishing they could die more quickly, the Prof was walking around without a care in the world, that wonderful, goofy smile of his making us all even more sick.

We were about halfway through the Drake Passage when the Ukrainian captain announced that because of an elderly lady's serious illness he would have to return to Cape Horn and ensure the passenger had proper medical care. Perhaps there is one thing worse than a bad Drake Passage crossing and that is turning back when you've almost crossed it. We returned to the southern tip of South America, and the lady was transferred to a smaller boat and taken ashore before being taken by a Chilean Navy helicopter to the nearest hospital. It would be nice to report everyone's sole concern was for the lady but it wasn't. Many were Americans who had paid a lot of money for their trip to Antarctica and were sore about losing a day of their holiday and at the prospect of another bad Drake Passage experience. They complained and talked of their right to compensation but the expedition leader wasn't fazed by the commotion. 'You know,' he said, 'this lady could have been your mother or your wife or your sister. She could have been any one of you. I am sorry about the disappointment but we've done the right thing and there's no need for us to apologize.' I wanted to cheer.

At the same time, I was thinking, 'We lose a day or a day

and a half and we may not get as far south as I'd been
hoping.' At times such as this it's hard to see beyond our own
concerns and think, 'Well, actually, that lady is very unwell
and my problems don't compare.' But the captain did the
right thing, we went back to Cape Horn, the seasick got
sicker, Jonathan and Lara stayed in the prison of their cabin
and I worried they wouldn't be able to do much when we
got to Antarctica. As leader of our team, I couldn't afford to
be seasick and fought it.

The awfulness of so much sickness had its lighter moment.
On the first day, I walked into the dining room and saw
Marilyn Noakes coming towards me on her way out. It was
obvious she was unwell and something in the urgency of her
walk said she wasn't going to make it back to her cabin. To
my left there was a tray of glasses on a counter; they were
biggish glasses and I grabbed one. 'Here, Marilyn,' I said,
'into this.' She quickly filled the glass. I put it back on the
counter and picked up another one. 'Okay, again,' I said. She
filled it again, this time to overflowing and it spilled onto my
hand. I wanted to giggle and make light out of it but
Marilyn looked so sick and felt so embarrassed that I just
nodded and reached for a third glass. Marilyn is classy and
bright but seasickness is a pretty unforgiving enemy.

Once I won my little battle with the elements, I wanted to
train on the deck because three days of doing nothing had
blunted my fitness. The *Polar Star*'s deck was built to accommodate a helicopter and it became my running track. Round
and round I would go, doing push-ups at regular intervals,
and the rolling of the boat meant I had to concentrate to stay
upright. On one occasion a huge wave caused the ship to
lurch violently and sent me flying towards the side. 'You know
what, Lewis,' I thought, 'if you're not careful, the swim is going
to start right here.' From then on, I stuck to doing push-ups
in my cabin.

All the time Tim ambled from cabin to dining room and onto the deck and never took an uncertain step. You could have thrown him into a man-size spin dryer, given him 30 minutes, opened the door and he would have walked out without the slightest readjustment. Our Ukrainian captain said the Drake Passage was a rite of passage before one earned the right to see Antarctica. There were a lot of people on that trip who would have preferred a calmer passage, not least the ship's staff, mostly Filipinos, who spent three days working with mops and buckets and trying not to breathe through their noses. On one point the captain was right: when you first hit sea ice and see how it transforms the seascape, your instinctive response is: 'Yes, it has been worth it.'

A half day after first hearing that scrunching noise of hull on ice, we arrived at Petermann Island, which is one of many islands off the Antarctic Peninsula. It was fairly late at night but this far south we still had enough light to do our swim. Petermann is a degree further south than Lynne Cox's swim at Neko Harbour and allowed me the opportunity to set a new mark for the most southerly long-distance swim. Under pressure from his passengers to stick to the original schedule, the captain insisted that our swim must not interfere with the running of the ship. Passengers got off at Petermann to see the Adélie penguins and that gave us the opportunity to do our swim. But there were worries.

The grey sky did not make the water any colder but a touch of sunlight would have made it seem less severe. In extreme situations, as in most situations, perceptions do matter. You know the story of the middle-aged man with bad health who goes for a check-up and is told by his doctor that he must give up cigarettes, alcohol, rich food and late nights. 'Will you guarantee me that I will live longer?' said the guy. 'It'll seem longer,' replied the doctor. With sunlight, the water would have seemed less icy.

An option was to postpone the swim to the following
morning – but you don't put off until tomorrow what you
can do today, especially in Antarctica. Who was to say the
weather would be any better the following day? My great
concern was that the dull, grey light would adversely affect
the quality of the footage that Chris Lotz was shooting for
TV news. Doing the swim was the priority but we also
wanted to make sure that as well as recording the event, the
footage would show the Antarctic in all its majesty. Chris
assured me the footage would be good enough and that
clinched it. Zero-degree air temperature, zero-degree water:
we were doing it.

On the journey from Ushuaia, I'd introduced myself to the
members of the crew who would ferry the passengers ashore
on Zodiacs because I wanted to have the best. I chose Jørn,
a Norwegian, and a Brit, Damon Stanwell-Smith. Picking
Damon was easy. He had once been attacked by a leopard
seal and would respect the dangers. A year and a half before,
Kirsty Brown, a marine biologist with the British Antarctic
Survey (BAS), had been dragged under and drowned by a
leopard seal close to a British base nearby. Before getting into
the water, I had to know there were no leopard seals about
and so we used BAS's new safety procedure of watching out
for leopard seals for 30 minutes before the swim.

Once Damon says we are good to go, I strip off and focus on
what I am about to do. Everything goes into a kind of slow
motion, as my heightened sensitivity takes me to a strange
but powerful place. I can hear the voices around me: the
Prof, Jonathan and Lara are getting the last details in place.
Though I hear the sounds, they are not registering. This is
where I need to be. Wearing just my usual Speedo
swimming trunks, cap and goggles, I am wired for temperature and heart rate so the Prof will know at all times what

my body is doing. They are here to learn about the human capacity to survive in ultra-cold water but also to protect me. Now I am just vaguely aware of their presence as my mind desperately prepares my body for what is coming.

Zero-degree water is colder than anything I've ever experienced. The music I listen to has been carefully chosen by David Becker. These are songs that have helped me through tough training days and hearing them now reminds me of what I have done to get here. David arranges the songs in a way that mirrors the change in my mood as the minutes pass and the time to begin the swim draws near. There are powerful and moving tracks to begin with – songs that connect with the incredible beauty all around me. Then the songs become more strident and I feel a rush of adrenalin during the theme song from *Rocky*, then finally I am listening to Puff Daddy's 'Come With Me':

> You can't run
> You can't hide
> No surprise
> Close your eyes
> Come with me, yeah.

When I close my eyes, just two or so minutes before entering the water, I am alone with Eminem's 'Lose Yourself':

> Look, if you had one shot, or one opportunity
> To seize everything you ever wanted – One moment
> Would you capture it or just let it slip?

Now I am moving towards the water, slowly, purposefully, because I am full of aggression but I am also controlled and utterly calm. There is no shouting, no final shriek of intent because I am ready and I know it. Evidence of this comes from the desire to quicken my step and dive straight into this hostile water but I know the Prof's scientific paraphernalia would probably be dislodged by diving. I concentrate on easing into the water without showing one moment's hesitation. Wading in, I think, 'Oh my Lord, this is brutal,' and then chase that thought away. I glance towards the Prof in the Zodiac and, lifting his head from the laptop, he gives me the thumbs-up, which means he's getting my body temperature readings. Everything is ready.

The key to a good swim in very cold water is to start positively but sensibly: too fast and your body will lose heat too quickly and near the end hypothermia will destroy you; too slow and you will spend too long in the water and hypothermia will definitely destroy you. I swim fast, but within myself – strong, controlled strokes. To take my mind away from the stinging pain, I look at the bottom of the seabed and, though it is 20 metres down, it is crystal clear and stunningly beautiful. Every now and then an Adélie penguin darts beneath me. I get to the 500-metre turn without incident. At regular intervals, Jonathan writes my body temperature on a whiteboard and holds it up for me to see. As I entered the water, my temperature was 38.4°C – 1.2 degrees higher than my norm – but that's what the adrenalin charge has achieved. Standing almost naked on a zero-degree day in Antarctica, my mind subconsciously persuades my body to increase its core temperature by this amount. Without that increase, I have little chance of completing the one-kilometre swim.

All through my swim I wait for Jonathan to show me what my temperature is doing. It will drop but it must do so slowly and, if things are going well, it will fall very little in the first ten minutes in the water, which should see me at the halfway point. Around the 500-metre mark, it begins to snow and I know this will make it harder to see the figures on Jonathan's whiteboard. The Prof and Jonathan's caps have turned white with snowflakes and I even notice snow on the Prof's eyebrows – the beginning of a Father Christmas. I glance up every so often to check on my temperature but from the 600- and 700-metre points there is no update. Jonathan is bent over, looking at the floor of the Zodiac; the Prof is glancing towards Jonathan. 'Concentrate on your next stroke, Lewis,' I tell myself. Thirty seconds later I look up again – still nothing and it is beginning to get to me. 'What the f***!' I think. Has my core temperature dropped more than it should? Why are Jonathan and the Prof speaking to each other when I need updates? This confusion lasts maybe a minute and a half but it feels like an eternity. I push my head out of the water and screech what I'm thinking. 'WHAT THE F*** is happening!?'

I would never normally speak to the Prof like this but I feel I might be dying and no one is prepared to tell me. Feeling my desperation, the Prof yells back, 'Two-fifty to go, just keeping going!' This is all I need to hear, because if the Prof says to keep going, it is safe to do so. Many times the Prof has told me about Major Jason Zirganos, the Greek Army officer, who was the first from his country to swim the English Channel. In 1959, the 49-year-old Zirganos tried to cross the difficult 23-mile North Channel from Northern Ireland to Scotland. Three miles off the Scottish coast, he lost consciousness and had to be dragged from the water. His heart stopped beating. A doctor in the support boat then decided to make an opening in his chest wall with a borrowed penknife to try to massage his heart back to life. Perhaps unsurprisingly, Zirganos died. 'Lewis,' the Prof would say, 'if things go wrong, I certainly won't do that.' With the Prof monitoring my core temperature, I don't feel in danger. So, towards the end, after the whiteboard messages stop, the Prof's thumbs-up sign is all I need. 'Focus on the rock, that's where you finish. One more stroke, one step nearer.'

I get to the rock and clamber out of the water. Though I know the danger of hypothermia remains real, I am unable to resist screaming in delight. They put a big blanket around me. 'The ship, a hot shower' is all I can say. I can't stop smiling because the job is done: I've completed the most southerly long-distance swim in history. Anticipation of the hot water helps me to climb the ladder onto the *Polar Star* and underneath the streams of liquid heat I am in paradise. There is no joy in the world greater than this.

By now, the team is around me and, though they are smiling too, something is not quite right. 'Lewis,' said the Prof, taking control, 'you didn't have the watch on that monitors your heart rate, and we needed that for our work.' I feel like crying, then screaming and, most of all, I want to crucify the person responsible for not ensuring this was in place. But I keep my mouth shut and just allow the impulsive urge to pass, then I try to be more rational. Who is the leader of this expedition? I am. Who is responsible if something goes wrong? I am. Nothing hurts a team as much as the blame that can follow a mishap. It is divisive and it drains the morale of the group. When it ends, there will be scars. Above all, blame will not fix the problem. I think Lara should have remembered the watch but I hadn't specifically given her that responsibility. She sometimes put it on my wrist for I&J swims in Cape Town but not always. Sometimes I had done it. But critically I had failed to list this as one of her duties.

Nothing would be gained by pointing a finger at her or blaming myself now. Far better to accept that mistakes sometimes happen: Michael Phelps's goggles filled with water during the final of the 200-metre butterfly at the Beijing Olympics; Usain Bolt's shoelace came undone during the 100-metre final at the same Olympics. But they still went on to break world records. These things sometimes happen. It is a time for calm. My principal aim in coming to Antarctica was to beat the record for the most southerly long-distance swim and now I've done that. A secondary aim was to help the Prof, Jonathan and Lara in their scientific work. We intended to do one swim but as we haven't collected all the necessary scientific data, there is only one solution. 'Right, we need to organize another swim,' I say. It is the last thing I want to do but the first thing I need to do.

Much later we talked about what had gone wrong in the second half of the swim, and Jonathan explained how the pen slipped out of his hand onto the floor of the Zodiac. Then the worsening snow wet the whiteboard and made writing impossible. The Prof explained that severe cold gets to him, slows his brain and robs him of his normal razor-like sharpness. He didn't realize that the current had helped me through the first 500 metres, and not knowing that gave him a false impression of how comfortable I was. When Jonathan lost his pen, the Prof hadn't reacted quickly enough because he wasn't tuned in to what was happening. Once he began to shout distances to me, he sharpened up. It was a lesson for all of us, especially me. I could hear my SAS instructors barking the questions at me: 'And what happens, Pugh, if you lose that pen? Where is the replacement?' 'What if it snows, Pugh, and the whiteboard is rendered useless? What's your back-up plan?' They would have binned me if I hadn't come up with answers and I felt as though I'd failed my team. Jonathan and the Prof felt they had let me down but, in my eyes, the fault was mine.

Two days later the MV *Polar Star* pulled into Deception Island, one of the South Shetland Islands and one of the best-known landmarks off Antarctica. Deception is horseshoe in shape and the centre of the island, flooded with water, is a caldera or sunken volcano. There is only one way to access the island and that's through a narrow (230-metre) opening called Neptune's Bellows. Because it is so sheltered, Deception Island has been a refuge from storms for sailors and was a famous whaling station until the early 1900s. Whaling ships pulled into the island and in a cove called Whaler's Bay whale blubber was converted to whale oil. The British, the Argentines, the Chileans and the Spanish have all had scientific stations at Deception but only Argentina and Spain still maintain theirs.

You sail through the Bellows and find yourself in the centre of an active but sunken volcano. Deception erupted in 1967 and then again in '69, and steam rises from the surface of the water. You can dig a big hole in the black volcanic sand, watch it fill up with water and then take a warm bath on a beach in Antarctica. You can enjoy your own outdoor jacuzzi in the midst of one of the world's most impressive colonies of penguins. Sailing into this extraordinary place, I felt like an extra in a James Bond movie, so exotic was the location. Yet if you looked closer, there was grim evidence of man's presence in the old, rusted metal tanks once used for burning whale blubber. Fifty-eight workers were buried in a graveyard at Deception Island but, after the last volcanic eruption, the graveyard disappeared. At first sight, it was a perfect place to do a swim because the steam rising from the water suggested temperatures that would permit a long swim.

'Let's go for a big one,' I said to everyone. 'Ten kilometres, okay?'

This was going to be good; I'd stick by the coast where the water was warmest and enjoy two or three hours in one of the world's biggest spas. Jonathan put the thermometer into the water – the shallower, warmer water. It hovered around two degrees. 'Nooooo,' I shouted. Ten kilometres was quickly reduced to one mile.

Before I was rigged up for the swim, Jonathan and I went

through a checklist of everything we needed and made sure we all knew who was responsible for what. I had written everyone's responsibility down so what happened at Petermann would not happen again. Our course was four legs of 400 metres and, after running 50 metres through very shallow water to get to the starting point, I dived in. Within seconds I could not believe what I was seeing: everywhere there were whalebones. Thousands of them, stacked on top of each other. They rose from the seabed almost to the surface of the water. They were big, big bones. I could make out many of them: rib bones, jawbones, vertebrae. In some places they were piled so high that when I took a stroke my hands touched them. I thought of all the beautiful whales I'd seen around the coast of South Africa and Norway that add so much to the area. How many whales were hunted and brought to this island before having their carcasses burned for oil and their bones dumped in this way? It disgusted me to such an extent that I considered stopping the swim to move it elsewhere, but I decided I had to press on.

It was a tougher swim than I'd anticipated and, towards the end, I got very tired. The Prof noticed a big change in my stroke and physical appearance at the 1,500-metre mark, and worried. My core temperature was fine but he was sure something was wrong, though unsure exactly what. I could no longer feel my arms but didn't understand why. They were going through the swimming motion but independent of any discernible effort on my part. The Prof started shouting, 'One hundred to go Lewis . . . ninety metres to go, keep going . . . eighty metres left, you're almost there.' I was still swimming, still moving towards the end but the Prof felt sure I was no longer with it.

The swim off Petermann Island two days before had taken its toll and I struggled through that last 100 metres. During the previous swims, the Prof realized that in concentrating so much attention on my core temperature, he had ignored what was happening to the rest of my body. After finishing the swim at Petermann Island, he wanted to insert a thermometer into my leg to gauge my muscular temperature. Freezing and exhausted then, I said no, but I couldn't refuse again. I lay down on a towel while the Prof crouched beside me, held me with one arm and rammed the sharpened thermometer into the centre of my leg with the other. The pain was excruciating. With this thing still stuck in my leg, the walk to the Zodiac was torture and there I curled up in the fetal position with a blanket wrapped around me. Each rung of the ladder to the deck of the *Polar Star* was a twist of the thermometer in my flesh and, by the time I got to the shower, I was physically and mentally gone. The Prof was telling me to stay awake, but I just wanted to close my eyes and forget.

'Lewis, stay awake, stay awake.'

'I'm fine,' I mumbled.

Hot water revived me but I could tell the Prof was concerned by the relatively sudden drop in my temperature. It was 36 when I got out of the water; now it was 34 and falling.

Hypothermia is official when the core temperature drops to 35 degrees. Mine went down to 33.3 and, though he remained calm, the Prof looked concerned. Any lower and there might soon have been a loss of consciousness but the hot water continued to do its work and the slide was reversed. Once that happened, the Prof took more interest in the stake he had speared into my leg. It told him that my muscle temperature was 31 but he wasn't too concerned about that. Later when the Prof and Jonathan sat down to analyse all the data, it was the muscle temperature that fascinated them because it stayed at 31 for an hour and a half after the swim ended, despite the fact that I was still in a boiling hot shower.

They worked out that the body's initial response is to protect the core and, in doing so, it neglects the peripheries. Without much blood going their way, muscle temperature at the peripheries falls quickly and continues to fall. But at a certain point, extremely low temperatures in the arms and legs begin to affect the core, as returning blood, which is cooled by being in the extremities, can quickly lower the core temperature. What the Prof found was that this process began at a particular point, and estimated that for me the danger point came when I had been in the freezing water for approximately 25 minutes. Deception Island was a 30-minute swim, hence the difficulty of the last 100 metres. He also believed that if I'd stayed in the water much longer, I would have had a very serious problem.

My strongest memory of the aftermath of that swim was coughing about 30 minutes after entering the hot shower. Instinctively, I put my hand to my mouth and was startled to feel the coldness of the air exhaled from my lungs. Even on the coldest days, our breath is warm. Now, with all the extremities warm, I was breathing out freezing cold air.

Taking the Prof's hand, I said, 'Feel this,' and coughed some very cold air into the palm of his hand.

'Oh my Lord,' he said.

He wondered aloud if I was using my lungs to exhale cold. He thought about it and came back with a name for what he thought might be taking place. Respiratory Expulsion of Cold he called it, or REC for short. His argument was that as we use our lungs to radiate out heat when we are running as a means of cooling, equally maybe we use our lungs to radiate out cold. To me that sounded logical but, not knowing the science, I told him that the name was perfect. I was a REC.

13

THE HOLY GRAIL AND BEYOND

In early summer 2006 I was back in England when my friend James Mayhew invited me to join him on a visit to his mother's home in Yorkshire. At the time James was dating Clare Kerr, daughter of the former Conservative Party chairman Michael Ancram, and he brought Clare to Yorkshire that weekend. Barely six months had passed since the expedition to Antarctica and less than a year since I had been to Spitsbergen in the Arctic. Over the weekend, James, his mother and Clare plied me with questions about those expeditions. As well as telling them what I saw and speaking about the extraordinary beauty of both places, I confessed to missing the Arctic and yearning to go back there. We spoke also about how climate change was having a serious impact on the Arctic: sea ice was melting earlier in the summer and freezing later in the autumn than it had in the past and glaciers were retreating. It was clear that, unless we all changed our ways, there would be a terrible price to pay in the not-too-distant future. Having seen polar bears in the Arctic and marvelled at the colonies of penguins and seals off Antarctica, I couldn't believe the threats to their environments weren't being taken more seriously. Everyone was pretty much in agreement.

On a walk through the Yorkshire Dales, James, Clare and I were discussing my plan to swim the River Thames, all 350 kilometres of it, later in the summer. James had agreed to kayak alongside me for the entire journey and we joked about the strange things I might swim past down the Thames. 'Nothing,' I said, 'would be more shocking than what I saw on the seabed inside Deception Island off Antarctica,' and I proceeded to tell them about the mountain of whalebones that lay at the bottom of the sea there. Because the water is close to zero all year round, the bones are in the same condition as they were the day the whales were killed almost 100 years before. 'This,' I said, 'is what man has done to the environment and is continuing to do. Whales were almost hunted out of existence, and now the Arctic and Antarctica are in great peril because of man-induced changes to our climate.' I knew little then of Clare's passion for the environment or about her work as an ambassador for the World Wide Fund for Nature (WWF), the biggest conservation group in the world.

'Why don't you swim the Thames for the WWF?' said Clare.

'What do you mean, "for the WWF?"' I asked.

'I mean do it in conjunction with the WWF. You've been talking about the Arctic and what climate change is doing to that region. Well, you need to stand up for the Arctic and this is one way of doing that.'

'How can I when I know nothing about the science of climate change? I'm a maritime lawyer and a swimmer, not a scientist.'

'Lewis, you've got this wrong. You don't have to be a scientist to talk about climate change; you just have to be passionate and genuine in your concern for the environment. You can be a voice for the Arctic. And if you feel climate change is the greatest threat to the environment, you couldn't have picked a better time to swim the Thames. You know they have started rationing water in London. This is the worst drought we've had in living memory in Britain and there will be floods in the future because climate change is causing these extremes.'

Hearing the clink of a penny dropping, I didn't immediately commit to Clare's suggestion. 'If I'm going to do this,' I said, 'I need to know far more about climate change than I do and I'd like a little time to think about it.' But, at that moment, I knew. Clare touched the nerve that had been central to almost everything I'd felt and done in my life.

Jacques Cousteau once said we will only truly protect those things that we love. Without aligning myself to any group or organization, I had become an environmentalist. It wasn't something I spoke about because I wasn't conscious of what was happening. 'I'm a pioneer swimmer,' I said to people who wanted to know. 'I have given up my career as a maritime lawyer to be a pioneer swimmer. It is a dream for me and I'm determined to follow it.'

But so much of my life had been shaped by my relationship with the environment. I remember my parents taking me to Kruger National Park in South Africa's eastern provinces of Limpopo and Mpumalanga and to Addo Elephant National Park near Port Elizabeth and being enthralled watching wildlife in its natural habitat. I was in my early teens when those trips took place and in my early twenties when oil from a sunken ship destroyed the beach and wildlife at Clifton where I worked as a lifeguard. That same oil wreaked havoc on the penguin colonies off Robben Island and the damage made me so angry.

My teenage daydreams had been of the Atlantic Ocean that I'd watched endlessly from a classroom at Camps Bay High School. Every plan involved swimming in that ocean or sailing beyond it. Then, later in my life, to see and feel the places that stirred my imagination, I became a swimmer and found reasons and challenges that gave each swim a meaning: Otto Thaning and I were the first to swim across one of the great African lakes, Lake Malawi, and I was the first man to swim the length of Norway's majestic Sognefjord. Later I would set the record for the most northerly long-distance swim, then the most southerly. Though it was important to achieve whatever target I'd set myself, the ultimate motivation wasn't a time or a distance but to see these extraordinary places.

I had swum in the Arctic Ocean at Norway's North Cape, which is one of the most spectacular landscapes on the planet. It was the beauty of North Cape as much as the challenge of swimming five kilometres in chillingly cold waters that drew me. After that, I decided to do the 100-kilometre swim around Cape Peninsula in South Africa and, though the thought of a Great White mistaking me for a tasty seal was a constant, the Cape's majesty depends upon the presence of the sharks and the seals, the dolphins and the whales. I thought of North Cape and Cape Peninsula as tough physical challenges, which they were, without understanding that I loved these places. With that love came a yearning to protect: you don't want what you love to change and it scares you to think it might be in danger.

Sitting with the Sami people at North Cape, amid herds of reindeer, I marvelled at the simplicity of the herders' lifestyle and how they seemed to blend in with the landscape. They weren't building factories or polluting the sea; they were just doing what their ancestors had done forever. You cannot stand on a mountain at North Cape, watch a Sami reindeer herder go about his work and not feel how special the relationship between man and his environment can be. I felt equally comfortable in the company of Daantjie

Truter and fed off his enduring love for the sea. Fishing had
been a way of life for Daantjie; the sea was all he knew, all he
had wanted and, though I paid him to chaperone me on my
two-week swim around the Cape, he gave the impression he
would have done it for the price of the fuel for *Cavalier*, his
fishing boat. The Sami and Daantjie had an innate understanding of nature's beauty, just as Stuart Grant, the wonderful
man I'd met on my visit to Lake Malawi, appreciated the
privilege of living and working close to a lake so vast and so
startlingly set in the heart of Africa that it seemed a freak of
nature.

Virtually everything about Norway I loved. There was just
one point of dissension and that was whether it was right to
hunt whales. Many Norwegians believe it is their right and
argue it is something their fishermen have done for centuries. I tell them I have lived much of my life in South
Africa, where the beautiful Southern Right Whale all but
disappeared because of man's thoughtless exploitation of the
oceans but changes in the law have restored the Southern
Right to South African waters. On a winter's morning on
the vast South African coastline, you can sit on a cliff anywhere between Cape Town and Durban and expect to see a
Southern Right surge vertically out of the water. It is one of
the wonders of the sea and long may it remain so.

In too many places man has left a trail of destruction.
Literally, you could see that in the litter discarded in the US
and Europe and washed up on a beach at Verlegenhuken on
the island of Spitsbergen in the Arctic. I told James and Clare
how sickened I'd been by all the whalebones at Deception
Island because I had imagined Antarctica to be utterly
unspoiled. But the most depressing moments had been spent
listening to guides in Spitsbergen point to glaciers and tell us
how they had retreated over the last century. Then I saw
photographs of glaciers taken in the 1900s and compared

them with the same glaciers today, and it was obvious that things were happening that would heavily impact the rest of the world. Though I saw the consequences of climate change and felt the dangers, I had somehow cast myself as a cold-water swimmer, somehow detached from a problem that threatens man's very future on this planet. Clare's challenge to 'do it for the WWF' was like a grenade tossed into the bunker of my existence as an extreme swimmer and I just had to do something.

I went away and read a lot of books and other material about climate change. It wasn't that I had found my calling, because it was there all the time, but, at last, I had recognized it.

Yet it would be wrong to diminish or downplay the part that swimming had played in my life and would continue to play. Prior to Antarctica I had changed coaches, switching from Gary Freeling to Brian Button, and that was an important change. I'd worked with Gary for about a year but he had lots of swimmers who participated in Masters Swimming galas for fun and to keep in shape and occasionally the mood was too relaxed for me. Brian, I had been told, ran a tighter ship and his swimmers came to work. We met at the pool in the Sports Science Institute at the University of Cape Town, where he ran his classes. He was probably seventy-five years old at the time but still swam twenty kilometres per week.

'Brian,' I said, 'I would like to please come and train with you.'

'I've heard about you; you're really special. Please jump into lane six.' If Brian had taken out a stepladder and asked me to stand on the top rung, he couldn't have made me feel taller. 'You're really special.' Those three words encouraged me to see myself in a different light. Once I did, Brian was then in a position to push me. By matching me up with swimmers who were better than I was, he helped me to stretch beyond what

I had considered my natural limits. Brian was an excellent teacher of technique. I can still hear his voice: 'Lewis, stretch those arms straight out in front of you; don't allow them to come across your face.' But in his understanding of how people should be treated, Brian was even better. He didn't play at being respectful, that was just the way he operated. As well as that, he gave you belief because his belief in you was constant. Because he didn't doubt me, I didn't doubt myself.

Late in 2005 a journalist called and asked if I was aware I'd done long-distance swims in the Arctic, Atlantic and Indian Oceans and was just about to head off to Antarctica where I would do one in the Southern Ocean. 'You can become the first person in the world to do long-distance swims in all five oceans. This is the swimmer's Seven Summits and you can do it.' The Seven Summits are the highest mountains of the seven continents and it is quite an achievement for the climber to do all seven. I hadn't seen the possibility and it excited me. Why not? Friends of mine said it would become the Holy Grail of long-distance swimming because of the difficulty of doing a long-distance swim in the freezing waters of the Arctic and Southern oceans and, with three of the swims done and one about to be completed, it seemed crazy not to want to complete the set. After Antarctica I had second thoughts about my Indian Ocean swim, which was around Cape Agulhas, the southernmost point in Africa. That swim was, in fact, half Atlantic Ocean and half Indian Ocean and I didn't feel it could safely be called a long-distance swim in the Indian Ocean.

Instead, I set off in January 2006 for that little part of South Africa where my father's ancestors on his mother's side had landed with fellow settlers in 1820. They had come from Northamptonshire in England and arrived in Algoa Bay, near Port Elizabeth, in the Eastern Cape; it has been renamed Nelson Mandela Bay. As it was a link between the South

Africa of my father's people and the new South Africa, it was the place I wished to do my Indian Ocean swim. Still in good shape from my training for Antarctica, I knocked out a 15-kilometre swim in choppy seas in just under five hours. Somehow it didn't feel right to be doing a swim just as a stepping stone to the final Pacific Ocean swim. Instead of savouring my 15 kilometres in Nelson Mandela Bay, and enjoying the moment, I was looking to the next swim and wondering whether I should go to Sydney or San Francisco.

Sydney won that battle because Australians love swimming so much and, as far as I knew, nobody had swum from Manly Beach through the Heads to the Sydney Opera House. Most people who visit Sydney end up taking the 30-minute ferry crossing from Circular Quay in the centre to Inner Manly because it is one of the best ways to appreciate the beauty of the city. It was a 15-kilometre swim and going round the jutting headland would make it tough because of the currents. As well as that, there would be plenty of ferry traffic and I wanted my old sparring partner from the SAS, Nick Peterson, in a boat alongside for the swim. In love with life and easily lured to far-away places, Nick immediately agreed. After arriving in Sydney, I hitched up with an Aussie long-distance swimmer, Ben McGuire, who agreed to swim the 15 kilometres with me.

Ben's girlfriend had done a swim from Bondi Beach to the Sydney Opera House and said we would have to get per-mission from the harbour master for our swim. I decided to pop down to the harbour master's office for what I imagined would be a formality – big mistake.

'Hi, I'm Lewis Pugh. I'm a long-distance swimmer and I'd like to swim from Manly through the Heads to the Opera House. Is that okay?'

'G'day, Lewis. I'd like to say yes but first you've got to have insurance before I can let you do it. There are so many ships using that stretch of water and if one of them has an accident trying to avoid you, then there will be a world of trouble. So you must get insurance to protect you in the event of anyone suing you.'

'How much might this cost?'

'I don't know how much but you need two to three million dollars' worth of protection.'

'Ah, thank you very much,' I said, and walked out of his office.

You didn't need to be an insurance broker to work out that the premium for this insurance was going to be counted in thousands and that was money I didn't have. Seeing him was a mistake because it alerted him to my intentions and meant I couldn't plead ignorance. Nick and I were SAS trained and someone saying no didn't completely deter us. Luckily Ben McGuire, who worked for Sir Richard Branson, was cut from similar cloth and we rendezvoused at Manly very early the next morning. During the Nelson Mandela Bay swim a few weeks before, a shark had come too close for my comfort and I wanted an anti-shark pod attached to the Zodiac that Nick would drive alongside us. Ben McGuire knew Sydney's waters and brought the anti-shark device we would need.

Nick, who had learned to make every knot in the SAS, fixed the anti-shark pod to his boat with a granny knot, which is about the least reliable of all the knots. While driving through the waves at Manly Beach, he caught one particularly big one. The force ripped the anti-shark device off the boat and it was never seen again. I could have strung Nick up – and it wouldn't have been with a granny knot – but I settled instead for sticking close to Ben in the water. That way if a shark showed up and decided to have one of us for breakfast, I would have my usual 50–50 odds.

The day was wonderfully warm, the sky was a bright blue, the water crystal clear and, for most of the journey, everything

went smoothly. Towards the end of the swim, a chopper
seemed to come from nowhere and hovered over us. 'The
flipping harbour master,' I thought, so I was relieved to see a
man hanging out the door and pointing a camera at us.
Channel Nine were filming for their news bulletins and,
cheered by that, I soon had the magnificent Opera House in
my sights and Bruce Fordyce in my thoughts. Bruce is the
greatest ultra-marathoner South Africa has produced and is a
nine-time winner of the world-famous Comrades Marathon
between Durban and Pietermaritzberg. 'Lewis,' he said, 'you
must always savour the moment of arrival into the stadium or
towards the finish line. Look around, don't rush it, appreciate
the privilege it has been to do what you have done.' Yachts
and ferries were moving to and fro, under a clear sky the roof
of the Opera House glistened and Ben was setting a nice pace.

It would be nice to say that it was a smooth ride all the
way to our destination but tiredness had been creeping up
on me and the closer I got to the end, the more exhausted
I felt. At the Royal Australian Navy base an exclusion zone
meant a significant detour around the ships and, too
exhausted even to contemplate the extra 500 metres, we just
swam straight on. There comes a time when you're simply
too wasted to care. After getting through the exclusion
zone, a diver surfaced alongside us and, this time, I was sure
it was the Navy or someone sent by the harbour master but
it was another Channel Nine cameraman who, naturally,
could double up as a diver. He stretched a hand above the
water and invited me to high-five him. I barely had the
energy.

'Can you slow down a bit, mate, so I can get good footage?' he asked.

'Now you're speaking my language.'

He did his filming and I continued to inch my way
towards the Opera House. The harbour master, or at least his

representative, did show up in the shape of a Port of Sydney boat. Channel Nine's coverage was a two-edged sword. 'Those gentlemen do not have permission to be in that water,' the guy said to Nick, who, as a barrister, was perfectly capable of arguing our case.

'Under what law is it forbidden for a member of the public to swim in this sea?'

So the tennis match began, over and back, each returning as well as the other. Nick knew that by the time they had got to the third set, Ben McGuire and I would be at the Opera House. I was aware they were arguing but was too tired to bother – no one was dragging me out of the water at this point. If we hadn't reached the finish, Nick would still be at it with this guy. There are moments in your life when you don't ask for permission, only forgiveness.

With as much enthusiasm as I could muster, I enjoyed the very last bit of the swim and Nick was there with a bottle of champagne. It wasn't quite the same as the gentleman with the white jacket and the tray of tea on the shores of Lake Malawi but we enjoyed our drink. 'But tell me, Nick,' I said, 'what were you thinking when you made that granny knot? I mean – a granny knot! If you had to abseil off a cliff, would you have done that?'

He laughed and just said, 'Ah, Lewis, whatever.'

Back in London after the Sydney swim, there was little time to hang around because I had agreed to swim at the World Winter Swimming Championships at Oulu in northern Finland. After returning from Antarctica, I'd received a phone call from one of the Oulu organizers who wanted to know if I would be prepared to compete at their championships, which would take place in water close to freezing point. This, they told me, wasn't like the Olympics because there was as much emphasis on everyone having a good time as there was on the actual competition. There would be Finns, Swedes, Germans, Norwegians, Latvians, Russians – lots of Russians – Brits, Irish and many other nationalities. Not having a clue what to expect added to the sense of adventure.

It was extraordinary. Oulu is a city of 137,000 people, with the average temperature in February varying from minus 7°C to minus 14. In the evenings, when some of the swims took place, the temperature dropped to minus 20. But it was still wonderful. I arrived there to find the local organizers using big chainsaws to cut slabs of ice from the frozen River Oulu estuary until they were left with a neat 25-metre swimming pool. They then put in lane ropes and set up little sprays to maintain some movement in the water and to prevent their pool from freezing over.

Of the many Russian swimmers present, the most famous was Colonel Vladimir Lutov. Lutov was a cold-water swimmer with a very good track record; it was said that he would be the guy to beat. I had no details about the competition. What was the distance? Would my rivals be allowed to wear wetsuits that would insulate them against the cold and enhance their buoyancy? Soon after arriving in Oulu I was told the distance of the race is 25 metres and each competitor *must* do breaststroke. I moved my head from side to side, indicating not a snowball's chance in hell, and then went to find the chief organizer, Mariia Yrjö-Koskinen.

'Mariia,' I said, 'twenty-five metres is not a race. I haven't come here for something so insignificant. And I will not be swimming breaststroke.'

'But the water is just above zero; you can't survive in that for too long.'

'I am ready for a two-kilometre race.'

Because they saw my presence as a boost to their championships, I was in a strong position and didn't hesitate to use that. Other forces were also at work. An American TV station had contacted me before I'd left England and said they were doing a piece on the championships for HBO and they were particularly interested in my ability to raise my core temperature prior to swimming in very cold water. 'You know,' he said in a southern drawl, 'we're real interested in that anticipatory thermo-genesis stuff.'

Suspecting that perhaps I could interest him in another aspect of the story, I said, 'I'm going there to beat the Russians. They believe they're the best cold-water swimmers in the world; I believe I'm better.'

Though we were speaking on the phone, I could sense his ears prick up and his imagination go into overdrive. *British guy against the Ruskies, East v West, Cold War in Cold Water.* Suddenly we had a race. To drum up further interest I drafted a press release for the official Russian news agency TASS, which said that Lewis Pugh was in Oulu because he wanted to beat the best Russian cold-water swimmers. In Russia, hard men swim in the coldest water and my promises insulted their manhood. Two days later a bus arrived from nearby St Petersburg with a small battalion of Russian journalists who had come for the fight.

This was all a bit of a circus because the beauty of the World Winter Swimming Championships is that they are a fun event. There are over 1,000 competitors but no one is there solely for the competition. It is an achievement just to get in that freezing cold water and complete your race. In fact, you could argue that the ones who finish fifth or sixth in their races are deserving of at least the same praise as the winner because they have had to survive in the water for longer. The spirit of this event was reflected in the organizers' reaction to complaints from swimming's world governing body, FINA, about the use of the term 'World Championships' in relation their event. 'You need our permission before you can do this,' FINA's people told them. After squabbling for a bit, they told

FINA to jump in a lake – presumably of freezing cold water.

Still, I was intent on stirring things up and wanted to meet Comrade Lutov. In Oulu, it's not difficult to find anyone. 'Hello, Mr Lutov, my name is Lewis Gordon Pugh. I hear you are one of Russia's greatest cold-water swimmers. I would like to have a long-distance race, just you and me, *mano-a-mano*. Are you ready for this?' Hardly had I said it when there were misgivings. Vladimir Lutov was a little older than me and had commanded an elite Russian unit. He was silver-haired, immaculately turned out, very distinguished and I had the impression that he came to the Winter Swimming Championships for nothing other than a quick race in cold water and a little fun as well. He could understand me fairly well but didn't speak English that fluently.

'Me think about this,' he said.

I collared him the following day. 'Well, Colonel, are you going to race me or not?'

'No, me not race you; another Russian will race you.'

That unnerved me. Who was the other Russian? I wondered if my brashness was offending them and if they were coming up with someone who would put me in my place. Later I caught Colonel Lutov speaking to a number of younger and very athletic-looking Russians. They were standing with their arms folded, listening intently to what he was saying. Everywhere I went, the Russians in Oulu looked at me oddly, as if they were trying to figure me out. Colonel Lutov came back to me and said he had two men who would race me, and he wanted to know the distance. 'Two kilometres,' I said, much like a Dhaka street trader asking for a price he knows he cannot get. Lutov played for time and all the while the American TV station lapped up the jockeying for advantage. The Russians came back, said they'd agree to 500 metres and the race was fixed for the following Friday evening. On that Thursday evening, a few Russians were standing in the corridor of the hotel where we were staying and I could feel their eyes on me as I walked to my room. Inside the room I wanted to jam the bedside table against the door to give me a little more security because I had convinced myself that something could happen. That night I made love with my paranoia. The next morning lots of people were talking about the race. Al Petrie, an actor, and his wife were with the British contingent. 'You've got to beat them, Lewis – just got to!' In the evening I walked into the swim area and the people cheered as if I were a prizefighter coming to the ring.

Colonel Lutov approached me. 'The Russians will race you one on each side.'

They are now playing with my head. Why one on either side? What were they up to? Were they going to close in on me? I have never enjoyed races because, for me, they drain the joy from swimming. Here it's like I've walked into an ambush; I can't go back, I can't go forward and it's only a matter of time before they pick me off.

At the start a young Russian girl, who was an official translator, came over to me and I said, 'They're going to play fair, right?' She just smiled back.

I was wearing a Speedo cap with the British flag emblazoned on it; they had ones with the Russian Federation emblem. Bernie, the guy fronting the American TV piece on these championships, sidled up to me discreetly and whispered, 'Stuff these Russians up.' They announced our names on the public address system in Finnish and in English. One of the Russians was Alexander Brylin. I recognized the name and, judging by the rapturous response, most people in the crowd knew Alexander. He stepped forward like they do in the Olympics and raised both arms in the air.

Just before the race I watched Alexander take what looked

like a six- or seven-year-old boy to the 25-metre pool and almost coerce the child into swimming a length. This water was zero degrees, the kid's slight physique offered him no insulation against the cold and he looked terrified. The Brits in the crowd sitting with me thought this was barbaric. Because I knew Alexander was one of my rivals, I used his treatment of the kid as fuel to motivate me. 'What kind of man would do that to a child?' But I was clutching at every available straw. I saw Alexander pull the boy out at the other end and wrap a towel around him; the fear had gone from the kid's face and been replaced by the excitement of having done something way out of the ordinary. Later I would learn the child was his son Danil. As we tut-tutted in our seats, we didn't ask ourselves what we did with our children in the West. We didn't say, 'Hold on, maybe Alexander's way is better than buying a PlayStation for our children and allowing them to disappear into that world for the rest of their childhood?'

Both Russians were wearing wetsuit shorts that, when pulled up, covered quite an expanse of their midriff. I was standing there in my swimming trunks looking and feeling totally exposed. But fear also acts as a spur: I really didn't want to lose to one of those guys and anticipation of what was to come took over.

A group of Finnish scientists, intrigued by the evidence that I can increase my core temperature before getting into the water, had been examining me and taking urine samples at different points. They sent me an email after I had returned home saying that on the evening of the race I had the highest levels of noradrenalin they had ever seen. Their findings didn't surprise me, as I was desperate not to lose and got myself into a fiercely aggressive state. My plan was to begin this race as if it were a 50-metre freestyle sprint and to see exactly what these guys had.

*

'Take your marks, get set . . .' and then a great horn sounds and off I go as fast as I can. A glance to each side shows me the Russians are doing brilliantly quick breaststrokes but, however efficient, their breaststroke can't compete with crawl. As well as that, their heads are out of the water, whereas mine is submerged, which gives me another significant advantage. A gap opens. It encourages me and I pile on more pressure. The gap widens and I go faster again. There is constant cheering from the crowd but I am listening only to the internal voice that urges me to dig deeper, push harder, make that gap wider. I swim like a man fleeing a burning house because my fear is that the Russians have a plan to switch to the crawl for the second half of the race and to reel me in as I tire. But they only ever do breaststroke in these brutally cold waters and their heads remain firmly above the water.

I win the 500-metre by a wide margin: about 100 metres ahead of Alexander and 150 metres clear of his compatriot, Nefatov Vladmir. Once I touch the ice-wall for the last time, the coldness of the water becomes almost unbearable. It is customary at the end of a swimming race to wait in the water for your rival to finish but here it would mean an extra few minutes in the freezing water. The cold forces me to get out quickly but, as the air temperature is minus 20, it's still pretty nippy by the side of the pool. Colonel Lutov immediately walks towards me, stretches out his hand and says, 'You very well done.' In offering his congratulations, he shows the same class and the same nobility he had demonstrated before the race.

Though the cold has gone right to my core, I stand by the side of the pool until my rivals finish. Alexander is first, and when he levers himself out of the water something special happens. I stretch out my hand but he just puts his arms around me and we hug each other. Of course he is disappointed to have been beaten but, in that moment, he acknowledges something greater than winning and losing. He can't speak English and I don't have a word of Russian, yet we understand each other perfectly. Alexander takes off his Russian Federation cap and hands it to me and I give him my cap with the British flag. Then Nefatov finishes and we also embrace. We are no longer enemies or rivals; the barrier between East and West has disappeared and what matters is that we share a willingness – I was going to say desire – to swim in very cold water.

Beside our swimming pool in Oulu there is a bus that has had its insides stripped out and replaced by a sauna. Each competitor, on finishing his or her race, is invited to head immediately for the sauna and heat up in a relatively luxurious setting. All through my swimming life I have resisted the sauna, believing it would seduce and soften me. Even on freezing days, I take cold showers and my body has grown accustomed to that. But now, with my two Russian friends nodding towards the bus, I decide to treat myself to a sauna.

Inside, there was the wondrous sight of sixteen young women reheating after the final of the 4 x 25-metre relay final. The Russians, British, Norwegians and Finns were all still in their swimsuits. If the heat of the sauna was good for our bodies, the sixteen young women were great for our senses. What a way, I thought, to end a remarkable evening. Except that the evening didn't end there. There was a big party and Alexander was by far the best dancer in the banquet hall. Every woman wanted to dance with him.

I learned more about him: he was from eastern Russia, on the Chinese border, and never mind the journey to Oulu, it took him two days just to get to Moscow. We remained friends, and met up again at the Sognefjord Challenge in Norway a year later and again in London. More recently he invited me to join him in a 1,000-kilometre relay swim down the Amur River from Blagoveshchensk to Khabarovsk in eastern Russia. They were doing the swim because pollution from Chinese factories has damaged ecosystems in the area and they wanted the river restored to what it once was. At the time, I was committed to environmental work in South Africa but some day I would love to go to Alexander's home town and spend some time with him.

As it turned out, the World Winter Swimming Championships were never the same again. The organizers agreed that every race need not be 25 metres and they also introduced freestyle to the programme. Before I competed, the perceived wisdom was that in zero-degree water you had to swim with your head out of the water. My preference has always been for keeping my head in the water; whenever I swam with my head above the water, it was no easier and no less painful. Now they have longer races at the World Winter Swimming Championships, many of the competitors do crawl and plenty swim with their heads submerged.

After Antarctica and the race against the Russians, a BBC producer telephoned me and explained that they wanted to make a documentary about me for their scientific programme *Horizon*. They, too, were interested in the process of anticipatory thermo-genesis and wanted to see how my core temperature could actually rise in the minutes before my cold-water swims. They asked if I would be prepared to organize a swim so they could see this process at work first-hand. I agreed and suggested a long-distance swim at Nigards Glacier Lake in Norway, where the water was guaranteed to be zero degrees. We would arrange the swim for the moment in spring when the ice melted. I contacted my friend Peder Kjærvik, who ran the Glacier Museum near Nigards Glacier and would know exactly when the lake would unfreeze.

Television people, though, are notoriously unreliable. They did some of the pre-Nigards Glacier Lake filming for the documentary only to pull out at the eleventh hour because some account executive or higher up decided they did not have the budget. I was irritated, to put it mildly. The whole thing had been put on for them, and I had needlessly trained in freezing water for weeks for their programme.

With the training done and preparations made, I opted to carry on without the *Horizon* programme and brought a small but select team to Norway – there was no point in wasting all the hard work. Jonathan Dugas came to do the scientific work. Martin Jenkins was there to make sure that, when I entered the freezing water, my head was in a good place, and I asked Major General Tim Toyne Sewell to come along because he had long been one of my favourite people. Director of Goodenough College in London, where I had first stayed upon returning from South Africa, the General is a man that I would be happy to follow – anywhere.

But Peder's prediction that the lake would be melted when we arrived proved a little premature. There was a small unfrozen section near where the glacial water entered the lake and, although it was possible to do the swim there, it left us with the problem of how to get me out immediately afterwards. Given the temperature of the water (zero degrees) and the distance of the intended swim (1,200 metres), I would be very close to hypothermic on finishing. To get to the car, we had to negotiate a 700-metre rocky path and, if I was still alive after that, there was a two-kilometre car trip to the Glacier Museum for a hot shower. That route wasn't a possibility.

'General,' I said, 'let's build a fire because that's how I reheated at North Cape.'

'Lewis, I don't like the idea of a fire. What happens if there is serious rain? This place is notorious for rain. The fire won't survive. And I don't like the possibility of you losing consciousness and being so far away from a hot shower and proper medical help.'

'So what do we do?'

'Lewis, you do the swim; leave the rest to me. We must cut a 700-metre path through the ice, wide enough to take a small boat, and that's how you'll get to the car park.'

This man was sixty-five years of age and, at that moment, I believed he had lost his marbles. 'Yeah, right!' I said.

He drew his plan on the gravel. 'Here's the car park, here's where you'll finish and this is the little channel we will cut through the ice.'

'General, this is 700 metres you're talking about. We have measured the thickness of the ice; it is about 30 centimetres or one foot thick. It's not possible, General.'

'Lewis, please don't argue with me. Could someone find me an ice pick and I will show you what I mean do?'

Jonathan and Martin both looked at me and their expressions said the General was bonkers. Leaning towards me, Jonathan whispered, 'Tell me he's not serious.'

'He is dead serious,' Martin said, out of the General's hearing.

A small river runs down from the mountain past the car park; next to the car park there is a small red plastic boat, about the size of two big armchairs. The General pulls the boat towards the small river, gets in and motions towards Jonathan to follow him. Laughing at the madness, Jonathan does what he's told. He picks up the two oars. 'Okay,' says the General, 'one, two, three, row.' They get the boat to the edge of the ice. The General stands up, ice pick in his hand, and starts hacking. Jonathan is on the other side of the boat doing the same job with an oar. A nearby Norwegian, standing idly by, is press-ganged into service by the General's charisma.

I'm doing a *BBC News* interview at the time, and looking over the interviewer's shoulder at three men flailing away at one-foot-thick ice. 'Lord,' I say, 'if you're looking down on this scene, you must be having the most enjoyable day of your life.' I expect one of them to clobber the other accidentally but it never happens; instead they begin to create a pathway through the ice.

I watched the General with mixed feelings. I was annoyed with myself for not making sure the ice was unfrozen when we arrived and yet full of admiration for the General's spirit. How many 65-year-old men would attempt to cut a 700-metre channel through thick ice? Once I invited him to come with us to Nigards Glacier, he became the leader of our team – not because he was the oldest and wisest, which he was, and not because he wanted to be the leader. No, he led because he was born to lead and I've never met anyone with his leadership skills. What the General has shown me is that great leaders are always great team players, men who can just as easily take orders as give them and who never do it for their own personal glory. Before the end of the day, he had blisters on both hands but he also had his 700-metre canal. We called it 'the General's Channel'.

Now it was Martin's turn to work. Martin is a mind coach and has an extraordinary ability to get inside your head and empower you – at least he could do that for me. Martin would tune into my emotions and then deliver messages that were guaranteed to elicit positive responses. For example, he would recreate the feeling of preparing to parachute from a Hercules, knowing that I could only make the jump if my adrenalin was rushing and my aggression was boiling over. He would mention my dad and how much it meant to me not to let him down. Nigards Glacier Lake should have been murderous for me because I hadn't prepared particularly well. Before Martin finished, though, I felt I could do anything, absolutely anything. That day at Nigards Glacier Lake, he took me to a place where the swim in icy water seemed like child's play.

This will seem hard to believe but it is true. I stood there on a cold spring day in Norway, dressed in nothing more than my Speedos, and I was sweating. My heart raced. There were still a few minutes to go but I wanted to plunge straight in. 'Martin,' I said, 'slow down, that's enough. I'm overheating.'

All the Norwegian press were there, and Reuters and *BBC News* had their cameras rolling. As I walked towards the water, it was as if I were on another planet – one where I was invincible and nothing could touch me. The water was brutally cold. So intense was the sensation that it was hard to breathe and I could feel the cold penetrate through to my core. But I was able to deal with that, because even though I felt fiercely aggressive, it was controlled aggression. My swimming stroke was measured: strong but not so fast that it would cause my body heat to drop too suddenly. At the end, however, I was exhausted, having covered 1,200 metres of freshwater at zero degrees. Unstable getting out of the water, I sailed the 700 metres through the General's Channel to the car park, and was then driven by the man himself to the Glacier Museum for a restorative shower. It took me 23 minutes 50 seconds but it gave me the record for the longest swim in freezing freshwater. When I look back on that swim at Nigards Glacier Lake, it is not the swim itself that is my fondest memory but what preceded it.

Antarctica, Nelson Mandela Bay, Manly Beach to the Sydney Opera House and Nigards Glacier Lake all happened in a seven-month period from November 2005 to the following May. In very different ways, they had been great experiences and had come at the end of three years in which cold-water swimming was my life. I was thirty-six years of age. I didn't own a house, didn't own a car and didn't have any money in the bank. In fact, all my possessions fit into two rucksacks: one was for cold-weather gear;the second was for a suit and all my other possessions. I was rich in experience, but penniless. Though I had no ambition to be wealthy, I wasn't against being able to buy new clothes or take a girlfriend away for a weekend or even plan a holiday. For years I had travelled light – no wife, no children, no mortgage – but that wasn't how I saw my future. The thought of settling down and starting a family appealed to me. I had a long talk with David Becker and told him about feeling like I was at a crossroads and didn't know the right way forward. My three years of full-time swimming had been vastly more rewarding than the years I'd worked in maritime law but it was hard to justify a life that wasn't a living.

David is a sports lawyer who has worked with high-profile professional athletes. Once they reached a certain level, he said, they were able to make a living from endorsements and public speaking. He felt I wasn't far away from that point. I wasn't sure. Each swim was individual and interesting but, if you do enough of them, you might begin to feel you are just ticking boxes: done the Sognefjord, done Antarctica, done the five oceans. In reality, the box-ticking feeling came only with the swims in Nelson Mandela Bay and Sydney Harbour, as I sought to become the first person to do long-distance swims in the five oceans. Every other swim was undertaken because I had seen a place on the map that I wanted to visit.

That changed when James Mayhew invited me to spend a weekend at his mother's place in Yorkshire, and I met Clare Kerr and began to understand what it was that I cared about. Agreeing to swim the entire length of the River Thames became meaningful once I agreed to do it for the World

Wide Fund for Nature. It was just as well, because the three-week, 350-kilometre marathon attracted significant media attention and there were constant questions about what I was hoping to achieve by subjecting my body to such a lengthy ordeal. I hoped my swim would draw attention to the fact that our climate has changed and encourage people to look around them to see what was happening to their environment. I had swum in the Arctic and in Antarctica and seen the retreating glaciers and the melting sea ice but you didn't have to go that far.

As Clare said, I had picked a good time to swim the Thames. It had been a long, dry summer in the south of England and London was on its knees, praying for rain. We hired a long, narrow riverboat that the General agreed to skipper. It became our claustrophobic home for three weeks. Nic Marshall, a young friend from South Africa, agreed to swim with me for as much of the journey as he could and James Mayhew would paddle a kayak alongside – my bodyguard on the river.

People like to talk about the weather, especially when their front lawns are burned and they are forbidden to water them. Every newspaper, radio station and television channel wanted a way into this story and my Thames swim offered them that. I did breakfast television, morning radio shows, evening news shows; a journalist from the *Sunday Times* swam with me and did his interview in the water, another from the *Daily Telegraph* did the same; CNN did pieces, Japanese television ran the story, the *Daily Mail* and most of the British newspapers covered it. Such was the impact that the then Prime Minister Tony Blair agreed to see me at 10 Downing Street when my journey down the Thames reached Westminster Bridge.

If the media interest was welcome and an opportunity to discuss climate change, the swim itself was murderously difficult. Seven weeks before we started, Nic Marshall and I drove west from London to do some reconnaissance on the river, as we needed to know where we would start swimming and how fast the river flowed. We got to the source, identified where we could start and then dropped sticks into the water and recorded how long it took them to travel 100 metres. We calculated that the river flow was three kilometres per hour. That would help, as would the fact that the last 60 miles of the Thames was tidal and, by catching the outgoing tide, we would fly through that final section. Ten days, we concluded, would be enough to get this job done; if things went wrong through sickness or exhaustion, it could rise to thirteen or fourteen days.

As was customary, I spent too much time trying to find a sponsor, doing media interviews and organizing the logistics of the swim and far, far too little time doing the hard yards of proper training for what was a significant physical challenge. All I could afford was three training sessions of 45 minutes three times a week – hardly enough when I had to swim the equivalent of half an English Channel every day. Right from the start, it was clear I had bitten off more than I imagined myself having to chew.

According to most experts, the source of the Thames is just outside the village of Kemble, near the town of Cirencester in the Cotwolds. A headstone under a tree marks the spot. The inscription just says: 'Here Starts The River Thames'. We followed the signs to the headstone but this was 17 July, about midway through one of England's hottest and driest summers. Around that headstone, there was parched grass but no water. 'Lewis,' the General said, 'your plan was to swim the Thames from its source to the sea. If it's not possible to swim any part of the river, I think you must run that section.' With an old friend from the SAS, Alex Wales, we ran from Kemble along the Thames route, first finding a small but impossible-to-swim-in stream and then following that until we had a small river deep enough for a swim. We ran for 25 miles in 35-degree heat before we got to that point. Alex collapsed from heat exhaustion when he finished and I wasn't that much better. There were dozens of journalists waiting for me and I did a series of interviews before diving into the river. Though the coolness of the water was such a pleasure after the heat of the run, what struck me was its stillness.

Seven weeks before, the water flow at this very point had been three kilometres per hour but that was now replaced by a millpond-like stillness. No rain for weeks on end meant precious little water was feeding into the river and, without that, there was no flow. Right there, I knew we hadn't a hope of meeting our ten-day target and, far from being carried along by the river, this was going to be one long, hard slog. It was also a wonderfully enjoyable three weeks because the Thames is a beautiful river that passes through some quite stunning countryside and the journey was enriched by people who became family for those three weeks. The General was our leader: kindly, cajoling, funny and always able to see the bigger picture. Nic Marshall swam with me, James Mayhew kayaked beside me and our long, narrow riverboat, the *Thames Crusader*, attracted and accommodated a collection of family and friends who joined us for bits of the journey.

The boat was especially crowded in the first week and, unable to deal with the extra traffic, the toilet got badly blocked up. People moaned, it looked ghastly, it was unhealthy and it was the General who rolled up his sleeves, got down on his knees and stretched his long arms into the mess. Using his hands as sewage rods, he unblocked it and I just thought, 'I will never meet another man like this one.' He was by far the oldest person on the boat and was the last

person who should have had to do what was a very unpleasant job but, before we looked for a volunteer, he had gone
and done it. 'When you kids use the lavatory, I want you to
flush it properly,' he said. 'I really don't want to have to do
this again.' We were all very careful about the toilet from
that point on because none of us wanted to do what the
General had just done. But that was the way he led: he
never asked anyone to do something he was not prepared to
do himself.

Swimming through Oxford, I began to feel unwell. That
evening the vomiting and the retching started and my body
felt as if it had been drained of everything. Alert to how bad
I was, the General put me in a car and drove me to the John
Radcliffe Hospital in Oxford. David Becker came along as
well. As we walked towards casualty, I was still vomiting and
my face was an ashen shade of pale. One look from a nurse
and the next second I was wheeled away to a ward and given
a warm bed and urgent medication. It was an outstanding
performance by the hospital and it made me very proud of
our National Health Service. Those who complain have not
sought free medical care in other countries. I spent the night
in the hospital and the combination of a good night's sleep
and the drugs allowed me to return to the boat early the next
morning. Still very weak, I hadn't much enthusiasm for a
swim that day. 'Come on, Lewis,' the General said, 'every
day is a swimming day.' To the General, I couldn't say no
and, though dying on my feet, I swam one kilometre before
getting back on the boat too exhausted to carry on.

We had some wonderful moments on what turned out to
be a three-week odyssey. Early on we were invited to the
home of comedian Rory Bremner in the Cotswolds. Rory's
house backs on to the Thames and we had tea in the garden
and Rory swam with us. As we progressed, hundreds of
people came out to support us and there was a sense from

those who cheered us on that what we were doing was worthwhile, but the water remained still and the swimming tough. I broke the day into three parts: swimming for two hours in the morning, followed by rest, then another two hours in the early afternoon and a final two hours in the evening. I looked forward to getting to London and the tide helping me through the last 100 kilometres, but there was a worry that we would not be allowed to finish our swim.

At the planning stage, we wondered what to do about the legal requirement to get permission before swimming in that part of the Thames controlled by the Port of London Authority (PLA). That begins at Teddington in West London and, based on my experience in Sydney, my gut instinct was to play dumb and just keep swimming. The General didn't think that was the right way.

'General,' I said, 'there are times when you're better off not asking for permission.'

'You've been in the southern hemisphere for too long. Think of all the publicity the swim is going to get; you'll have to get permission.'

'Take it from me, we're better off not alerting them.'

'No, Lewis, let me handle this.'

The General knows how to get things done; he's got authority, charisma and great contacts. He rang the harbour master, Christopher Mendoza, and came up against a stone wall – a 40-foot thick wall. 'Under no circumstances can Lewis swim beyond Teddington. This is a busy harbour and he would be a risk to himself and to boats using the river. He doesn't realize how dangerous the Thames currents are and, anyway, if we allowed Lewis to swim, it would encourage others who are not as strong as he is.'

For once, the General didn't have an answer. I went to see Mendoza and tried to explain to him that I had swum in the Arctic and off Antarctica and that I knew what I was doing.

He was unimpressed and unprepared to budge. His obstinate nature got to me.

'Imagine if Captain Scott had to deal with this type of red tape; we would never be the nation we are today.'

'Listen, Lewis, you are no Captain Scott and, anyway, Captain Scott was a failure.'

So spoke the great Christopher Mendoza and I left his office determined that I would swim from Teddington, through the heart of London and all the way until the Thames entered the sea at Southend. He could threaten me with arrest – I would push on. Less eager to break the law, the General wanted me to run from Teddington to Southend, but for me that would have been defeat.

Regardless of what PLA laws might say, I couldn't accept someone telling me I could not swim in the River Thames. Did he and his Authority own the river? Surely a river is a natural resource, owned by the people of a country, and if members of the public wish to swim in the river, they should be entitled to do so. Surely it's not right to say to people you can use the river if you own a boat but you're forbidden if you don't.

We continued to negotiate with Mendoza but it was a waste of time. In the end, we just did it. With the benefit of the swiftly moving tide, we were able to cover big distances and, during one very long day, I swam 75 kilometres. We swam at night, which was magical, and my respect for the young Nic Marshall deepened with every stroke we took. When I was down, he lifted me up. 'See that house, Lewis, we're going to swim down to that. See if you can just do that.' And when we got to the house, he would convince me that I could make it to the bend another 200 metres away. Then, at the end, when it seemed like we were surfing the little waves that sped on the tide towards Southend, the problem was the swarm of jellyfish on the surface of the water. I'd had experience of them in the Sognefjord swim and knew how they stung. 'Let me do this,' Nic said, and he swam directly in front of me, his arms driving in the water as much to scatter the jellyfish as to propel himself forward. He did that for five hours and took a lot of stings for his trouble but he never once mentioned it. You don't find many kids like Nic.

Finally we reached Southend. After twenty-one days I was absolutely shattered. My body ached and my mind was equally exhausted. It was the toughest swim of my life – but it was worth it. It had drawn the public's attention to the dangers posed by climate change.

14

ON TOP OF THE WORLD

Not long before my father died, he and my mother spoke about a swim I had just done. 'He'll kill himself swimming one day,' he said. My mother didn't mention this until very recently and it was a good thing too. In the early days of July 2007 it wouldn't have been at all helpful to know my father feared the worst for me. We were on our way to the North Pole, where I'd planned to do a one-kilometre swim in minus 1.7°C water and it scared me. At Petermann Island off Antarctica a year and a half before, I had swum at zero and I tried to kid myself that the difference between zero and minus 1.7°C wasn't that significant – I tried but didn't really succeed.

Professor Tim Noakes, David Becker and a small but carefully chosen back-up team flew with me from London to Helsinki, and from the Finnish capital on to Murmansk in north-west Russia. The Prof was there to make sure that I didn't die in the water, while David would prepare me for the moment I entered it. Without David, the Prof's task would have been impossible. Without the Prof, I wouldn't have listened to David. My life was in their hands and, though we sometimes joked about that, it was an onerous responsibility. Shortly before we boarded the flight to Murmansk, I sent an email to the Prof and David. The timing was important because they would not be able to pick it up in Murmansk and certainly not at the North Pole. It would be there for them on their return, if they needed it:

Dear Prof and David,
Tomorrow we depart for the North Pole. I am very excited. I want to thank you both for coming with me on this expedition.
 If I don't come back, I would hate it if anyone blamed you. I am doing this swim of my own free will. What you have done for me has been amazing. You have brought me so much happiness and joy and helped me incredibly with my campaigning. Neither my mother nor I would ever want people to point fingers at you if something goes wrong.
 In the event of my not coming back, I want you to show the press this email.
 With kindest wishes,
 Lewis

After the Thames swim, I went with Clare Kerr to the London premiere of Al Gore's film, *An Inconvenient Truth*. By now I'd read much of the literature on climate change and everything confirmed what I'd felt when I was in Antarctica and at Spitsbergen: changes to our climate are now affecting people's lives and will do so to a much greater degree in the near future. Those who question the science and seek to downplay the significance of climate change are not sceptics but deniers.
 Al Gore was preaching to the converted but still I was shocked. Everything we love is threatened by global warming and it is man who has created the potential for his own

destruction. It is now man's responsibility to undo the damage. *An Inconvenient Truth* explained the science in layman's terms and, because I had been in Antarctica, the footage of glaciers retreating made a big impact. But there were things that the film didn't do. I wanted Al Gore personally to take us to the Arctic and Antarctica and to the tops of mountains, to point out graphically what was happening and will continue to happen if we don't reverse the trend of climate change, but stock footage was used. I yearned, too, for guidance about what we can personally do. We know the world's population has jumped from 3.5 billion when I was born in 1969 to 6.8 billion today and it is predicted to reach 9 billion by 2050, but how should we respond to this? Should we have one child or no children?

More than anything, the film left me wanting to do something. 'Clare, I once had an idea that I would do a long swim at the North Pole but I was put off by the danger. I'm going to do it now.' It was the logical place to make a statement about climate change because summer sea ice at the North Pole is melting at an alarming rate and there are predictions that in the not-so-distant future there will be little summer sea ice at the North Pole. If I could do a swim at the North Pole, it would make the point that something weird was happening to the environment. Who would know whether I would find open sea at the North Pole in July? An Aussie who lives at Spitsbergen and who had been to the North Pole seventeen times, Jason Roberts, was the man. If you've seen film of a polar bear in the last ten years, chances are Jason either organized the filming or was the cameraman. He does a lot of work for the BBC Natural History Unit in Bristol and, when I tracked him down, he was on his way there. 'We can talk in London,' he said.

We met at a sandwich shop in Regent Street and we hit it

off straight away. Jason was a clear thinker, experienced and enthusiastic – 'a fair dinkum Aussie' he'd be called back in his home country.

'The only way to get there in summer is to sail. There are two or three sailings from Murmansk, straight between Spitsbergen and a Russian island, Franz Josef. You can see polar bears around there and the ship carrying you to the North Pole, the IB *Yamal*, is the best ice-breaker in the world.'

'Jason, the thing I have to know is will I be able to do a one-kilometre swim at the North Pole?'

'You know I've been there seventeen times and the more times I go, the more open sea I find. I am sure that if you go in July, you will find enough open sea to do your swim. But remember it's the Arctic; there are no guarantees.'

'Could you help me set it up, if I decide to go ahead?'

'I'd love to be involved.'

According to Jason, the biggest danger was that the ship wouldn't make it to the North Pole. 'I've been there, mate, when we kept running into thick multi-year ice, it slowed us down and we didn't have enough time to get to the Geographic North Pole.'

'How much is it going to cost for a berth on this boat?'

'About $25,000 or about £15,000 per berth. Getting to the North Pole is not cheap.'

At that second, I thought, 'Do I really want to do this?' Fundraising will sap my energy and, if I succeed in getting the money, all I do is create the opportunity to do something that frightens me. That moment passed. This was the North Pole and it was a chance to do something for one of the most important places on earth, an opportunity to add my voice to the debate about climate change. I reckoned a minimum of £180,000 must be raised and I had just a couple of months to do it. My first call was to my Thames sponsor, Hendrik du Toit at Investec.

In an ideal world, I would have had a fundraising team behind me and let them get on with that while I trained. But I didn't have the resources to employ anyone. For the Thames swim Tim Toyne Sewell introduced me to Hendrik in the hope that I could get some backing from him. Through the course of a lunch together, I couldn't bring myself to ask for help from his company and instead wrote him an email the following day. 'How much do you need?' he replied, and it was clear he was enthusiastic. My innocence was reflected in the amount I sought.

'What about £3,500 and you become our major sponsor?'

For what would be a three-week expedition on the Thames, I certainly hadn't played hardball. 'I'll write the cheque straight away,' said Hendrik, who must have been hugely relieved.

Of course you don't hire a riverboat, undertake a major PR campaign and feed a team of five people for twenty-one days on £3,500. Fortunately, newspapers, radio and television ran with the story, we had a meeting with Prime Minister Tony Blair at 10 Downing Street and Investec received a staggering return in good publicity for their £3,500 investment. To Hendrik's credit, when the true cost of the Thames rose to £25,000, he immediately wrote a cheque to make up the difference.

One hundred and eighty thousand was a different kettle of fish and Investec felt they couldn't offer more than £80,000. That was generous but insufficient. I begged, pleaded and cajoled them into upping their offer. They went to £120,000 but that was it – no more. It was a major commitment and they made it knowing that all it would take was Israeli soldiers steaming into Gaza or al-Qaeda detonating a bomb on the same day and no one would be interested in Lewis Pugh's North Pole swim.

I'd read about Sir Wally Herbert, who set out on an extraordinary 3,800-mile trek across the Arctic Ocean in 1969 and, amazingly, managed to finish on the same day that Neil Armstrong landed on the moon and that is why, until now, you have probably never heard of him. During the Thames swim, every day had a relevance because it was another step along the journey; it was no less relevant than the previous day's swim or the following day's. At the North Pole, there would be one day, one swim and one opportunity to send ripples south and touch the conscience of people on every continent.

During the search for additional backing, I learned that a great-grand-nephew of Roald Amundsen, the first man to walk to the South Pole, had a watch company in Switzerland called Villemont. His name was Jørgen Amundsen and, after calling him up, I briefly described what I planned to do at the North Pole and that I wanted to come to see him. He agreed to a meeting in Geneva. After I'd made my case, he said that if I wore his watch he would give me £20,000 sponsorship. He also said he would like to make a special commemorative watch for every member of my team. In the end, Jørgen came with us to the North Pole and skied on the ice alongside where I swam. I was thrilled to have a great-grand-nephew of Roald Amundsen on our expedition. Because Amundsen had beaten the British team to the South Pole, there was no way I would give up in front of his great-grand-nephew. Jørgen was also a good guy, he'd skied the last few degrees to the North Pole a few years previously and was an experienced skier and a welcome addition to the team.

Weeks passed and the date for our departure crept up on us. Though I'd pared the costs down to the absolute minimum, there was still a £25,000 shortfall with just one week to go. I began to sweat. We couldn't make the team any smaller. It consisted of Professor Noakes, Marilyn Noakes, Jørgen Amundsen, David Becker, the cameraman Chris Lotz and the photographer Jason Roberts. As far as I was concerned, the trip wouldn't happen without all six. A few days before our departure, there was an unexpected call.

'Hi, Lewis, my name is Stephen Rubin, Chairman of Pentland. We own Speedo and I've heard you're going to swim at the North Pole. How is it going?'

'Good,' I replied, not telling the whole story. 'Actually, could you please help me with some sponsorship?'

'How much do you need?'

'We are £25,000 short.'

'Don't worry. I'm about to jump on a flight to the south of France but you've got my word that we'll take care of that. We're both lawyers, so there's no need for a contract. I will get my accountant to transfer funds to your account in the morning. Please just wear a pair of Speedo swimming trunks. I think what you're doing is very important and I wish you the best of luck. Let me know how it goes.'

And that was it. The following day £25,000 was transferred to my bank account. Speedo's support meant the expedition was finally going to happen. Once that worry was out of the way, I felt much better about what I was taking on. I also liked the fact that I had a small team of highly talented and committed people. No one knew human physiology better than the Prof, Becker knew his way round the inside of my head, Chris Lotz's work for us in Antarctica had been excellent and though Jason Roberts was with us for the first time, everything about the guy encouraged me. I was sure we had a world-class team.

In the months before leaving for the North Pole, my life had changed. Back in Cape Town to make a commercial for one of my sponsors, I'd arranged to meet Chris Lotz at a coffee shop on Kloof Street where I would formally ask him to be part of our team for the North Pole. Before the meeting, while standing on a balcony, I saw a woman on the street whom I had not seen for twenty years. She was not just any woman from my past: she was the one whose pigtails I had tugged from the desk behind during history lessons at Camps Bay High School, the girl I'd wanted to date but hadn't had the courage to ask. We recognized each other and she came up the steps to say hello. Seeing her again startled me. In the excitement, I couldn't remember her first name.

'Malherbe,' I said.

'Antoinette,' she replied.

'You have not changed at all.'

'Lewis, Dad has been telling me about your swims. He and his friends at the Pavilion Pool in Seapoint talk all the time about what you're doing.'

'So what's happened in the last twenty years?'

Standing on a balcony in Kloof Street, Antoinette sprinted through the story of her life. She worked as a make-up artist in the film industry, had been married, had two children and was now living in Hout Bay. She spoke fourteen words to the dozen and all I could think was that she had been the prettiest girl at Camps Bay High School and she had turned into a very beautiful woman. In that ten-minute encounter, it came back to me, that unbearable teenage crush that I hadn't been able to do anything about: I was in her class but not in her league. She was so gorgeous she could have had any of the boys and, at that stage, the jocks a year or two ahead of us were more interesting.

But twenty years on, our lives had moved on. I was no longer the innocent and Antoinette had grown up too. I was a cold-water swimmer and an environmental campaigner and she was a working mother. About the only thing that hadn't changed was how I felt towards her. That crush was merely in hibernation, waiting for this day.

Antoinette was rushing off to a refresher course in hair-styling and, showing more enterprise than was my style in the old days, I suggested we exchange telephone numbers. An hour or so later I sent her a text suggesting we meet for a drink. A couple of days later we met at a cocktail lounge in Camps Bay and we exchanged the stories of our lives since leaving high school. Antoinette had been very close to her mum, who loved music and dreamed her daughter might become a violinist or a concert pianist. From age six, Antoinette was taught music and by the time she was eleven she had her own piano teacher and her own violin teacher and was practising as much as four hours each day. Though she loved music and was talented, Antoinette depended upon her mother's drive. Her mum took her to lessons and listened when she practised. If there were days when Antoinette's enthusiasm flagged, her mum's passion was unrelenting. Then, when Antoinette was fifteen, her mum died and everything changed.

Music remained part of Antoinette's life but not like it had been. There were days when her dad couldn't take her to lessons, and if Antoinette didn't practise no one made her feel guilty about it. After her mother's death, Antoinette's sense of loss led to years of mild rebellion. She no longer focused on her music as she once had and didn't commit to her schoolwork. She went to UCT to do a music degree but it was very academic when all she wanted was to play. After a term, she dropped out and joined a band in which she sang and played the piano. She liked to sing because it was something she chose rather than being her mother's idea, but what she had really wanted was a life in theatre or film and that's how she ended up doing creative make-up. At twenty-two, she got married and had her daughter Taegyn but she was too young and after three years the marriage ended. A few years later, she committed to a new relationship and had her son, Finn, but after eight years that relationship ended too.

I could sense her unease and the battering her confidence had taken from two broken relationships, but when we spoke it was easy and natural and I felt incredibly comfortable. After our meeting at Camps Bay, she called me a couple of days later and asked if I would go swimming with her. We met at Clifton Beach just before sundown. Though the waves were big and the water cold, it didn't stop us from swimming. Antoinette wasn't sure if she wanted to go in but I held her hand and she came with me. That holding of hands was our first physical contact and afterwards we sat on the beach, shared a bottle of wine and watched the sun disappear. Three days later we went kayaking, which was remarkable because Antoinette had never sat in a kayak before, but she is one of those people who are prepared to try things. A few nights later we ran on Table Mountain, saw Cape Town light up beneath us and felt we were about the two luckiest people in one of the world's most beautiful cities.

Instinctively, I felt Antoinette was the one, but the situation scared me. She had a busy job and two young children, while my life had moved from maritime lawyer to cold-water swimmer and now to committed environmentalist. London was where I needed to spend most of my time because it was closer to the politicians and businessmen of those economies that had done most to damage the environment. It is these countries that must spearhead the movement to protect the environment. I wondered how I could be a strong advocate for the environment and also look after Antoinette and her children. I wrestled with this dilemma for months, and though my idea of what I should do often changed, my love for Antoinette was constant.

When I went to Namibia's Skeleton Coast on a pre-North Pole training camp with my friend Simon Blackburn, I persuaded Antoinette to come. Swimming in the ocean, long sessions kayaking and lots of runs on Namibia's magnificent sand dunes were followed by peaceful nights looking at the stars. Off the Skeleton Coast, the sea was about 11 degrees but nowhere near cold enough for someone preparing for the North Pole. After Namibia, I decamped to a small wooden cabin close to Nigards Glacier in Norway and spent two weeks training in the glacial lake where the temperature was two degrees. Antoinette also came to Nigards Glacier and, though we greatly enjoyed being together, I struggled with the training. It was one thing to train systematically at our ice pool on the Cape Town docks, going from eight degrees to six, to four, down to two, reacting to Jonathan Dugas's sergeant-major voice, but quite another to go from comfortable 11-degree swims off Namibia to an icy two degrees in Nigards Glacier Lake.

My first swim at Nigards Glacier Lake showed how ill-prepared I was for extremely cold water. It lasted 50 metres before the pain forced me to stop. Four weeks later I was due to swim one kilometre at minus 1.7°C and, as hard as that first swim was, it was harder to imagine going twenty times further in water four degrees colder. Worries about my preparation were filling my mind on what should have been a magical time for Antoinette and me. This was June in Norway; there were blue skies and lovely long warm days in a part of the world as beautiful as anywhere you've ever seen. Antoinette loved the place, as I knew she would. Like a blue-tinted tongue coming from the face of the mountain, Nigards Glacier reaches down and, at the end, ice-cold fresh-water cascades into a turquoise-blue lake. Chunks of ice drop from the glacier into the lake, bobbing and floating towards the river that carries them to the fjord. To see this on a warm summer's day is something else and it bugged me that I couldn't enjoy it without worrying about my training.

We worked at it and planned our day to start with a tough kayaking session. I had use of a big red bathtub of a kayak, as heavy as the *QE2*, and I would grind up and down the lake each morning. A small ferry taking tourists to the face of the glacier was my rival and I would race it. Soon the captain and his passengers were encouraging me and it made me race hard. My muscles grew and hardened, and my spirits improved. Each afternoon I swam and I always went further than the day before: 50 metres became 100, then 150, but it didn't get any easier and it felt like my body couldn't adjust to the extremely cold water. Was the drop from 11 degrees off the Namibia coast to Nigards' two-degree water too much or had the years of cold-water swimming taken their toll? I missed Jonathan Dugas screaming at me and didn't want to think about how I would ever be able to swim one kilometre in minus 1.7°C.

Antoinette, though, was joyful company. Understanding I was there primarily to train, she became mentor and coach and soulmate. She drove the car along the road next to the lake, watched as I swam and was there to pick me up when I got out gibbering and freezing. Back at the cabin, she would prepare the food while I basked in life-restoring hot water. Midway through, the repetitive torture of the swim got to me and I pretended that what I needed was a long swim in less cold water. We drove all the way down to Lusterfjord, a 50-kilometre journey, for a training session in 12-degree water. There are more subtle ways of kidding yourself and, that evening, wracked by guilt, I asked Antoinette if she'd come with me while I did a proper swim in Nigards Glacier Lake. It was ten o'clock at night. As it was going to be a long swim, I needed Antoinette to kayak alongside me. She had never been in a single kayak in her life, yet she agreed, knowing that if she capsized it was going to be a big problem. She got in one kayak, I got in another and we kayaked to the glacier front, where I did my swim, and we then kayaked the two kilometres back to the car.

After the hot shower, I spoke with the Prof about my training. 'It's going well,' I lied. At Nigards Glacier with General Tim Toyne Sewell a year before, I had knocked out a 1,200-metre swim and spent 25 minutes in the water. Antoinette sensed I was struggling and, to encourage me, she decided to go for a short swim in the glacial water. After a tough run, she jumped in to chest-deep water and, never having experienced anything nearly as cold, she couldn't breathe. 'Concentrate on breathing normally,' I urged her. 'After me, come on: one Mississippi, two Mississippi, three Mississippi.' She calmed herself and began counting; she got to twenty but could bear it no longer than that. Out of the water Antoinette felt the exhilaration that comes after a brief encounter with brutally cold water. She loved it and got in the water every day after that; forty seconds became a minute, a minute became a minute ten and so on. It was inspiring for me and her way of saying, 'I'm with you on this. I can appreciate how hard it is going to be at the North Pole.'

From working with Martin Jenkins and David Becker I'd learned to exercise my mind and get it into shape. So for each swim at Nigards Glacier Lake I played the music I would listen to at the North Pole, I visualized how cold and hostile the water would be and I worked on my aggression, imagining my body's shock at minus 1.7°C and telling myself that the pain was something I would rise above. At other moments I thought of the Prof and David standing in the Zodiac shouting encouragement, driving me on. Towards the end of the two weeks, I did one very tough swim in the river that empties the lake. Attempting to swim upstream, I had to work really hard to stay in the same spot while

Antoinette on the nearby bank was my timekeeper. 'You've done one minute . . . Two minutes, you've done two minutes.' I got it up to fourteen minutes, which was a good effort and my best over the two weeks, but it was nowhere near where I needed to be.

The memory of the trip is one I treasure because Antoinette and I learned so much about each other. She saw me go into military mode when training wasn't good and responded well to that, saying it wasn't much different to a film set when the director gets stressed. Antoinette liked the fact that I was calm under pressure and I loved her willingness to go with the flow and not complain when things got rough. And she was one capable woman. On the first day I threw her the keys of the hired car and asked if she could go to the supermarket in the nearby town and get groceries.

'I've never driven a car on the right-hand side of the road,' she said.

'You'll be fine,' I said. 'What could possibly go wrong?'

'Nothing,' she replied sarcastically, and got in the car and drove off – my kind of woman.

Murmansk was grey, physically and psychologically, that part of Russia untouched by perestroika and glasnost. At the airport a tractor and trailer hauled our luggage from the plane to the terminal, and green-uniformed customs officials pored over our passports and visas and somehow made us feel we were the single greatest threat to the security of Russia. 'Guys, it's over. There is no Soviet Union. Ever heard of Mikhail Gorbachev?' you wanted to scream but this was no country for dissent. All of those travelling to the North Pole on board the IB (Ice Breaker) *Yamal* were on our flight from Helsinki. For a Brazilian couple, Murmansk was where their adventure ended. They had arrived in Helsinki two days before the rest of us and decided to spend the spare day in nearby St Petersburg. At Murmansk they were informed their one-visit visas were no longer valid – the trip to St Petersburg had seen to that. Nor could they reapply for a new one and under no circumstances could they transit Russia without proper documentation. We left for the North Pole and they were on the next flight back to Helsinki. No amount of pleading would help.

Sailing out of Murmansk was a strange experience as there were conflicting emotions. For so long I'd wanted to travel to see the North Pole and felt that excitement but there was also foreboding. That one-kilometre swim in minus 1.7°C water hung like a cloud over my life, refusing to allow in any light. There were about 100 tourists on the IB *Yamal*: lots of Americans but also Swiss, Germans, British and travellers from many countries. The *Yamal* is a nuclear-powered ship and, in terms of its capacity to cut through ice, it was super-efficient. Our Antarctic ship, the *Polar Star*, was ice-strengthened, whereas the *Yamal* was a proper ice-breaker. No ship in the world is better at getting through sea ice.

Worries about my preparation weren't helped by the captain's refusal to make a brief stop on the way to allow me a short acclimatizing swim. Two years before, thick ice prevented him getting to the North Pole and he wasn't prepared to jeopardize his chances of making it. It was hard for me to argue, as I needed the *Yamal* to get to the North Pole as much as anyone.

There was a 15-metre pool on the ship and though I was assured it would be ready for use by the second or third day it wasn't. Refilling it took four days and on the third day concern about not being able to swim had turned to panic. Jason Roberts spoke to the captain on my behalf and eventually persuaded him to allow me a short trial swim in the sea on the fourth day while the engines were being serviced.

Jason and our cameraman Chris Lotz saw this practice swim as their opportunity to test their cameras and see that everything worked in freezing cold conditions. A documentary was to be made from their footage and our sponsors needed certain photographs, so we agreed that we would devote half an hour to getting all of this stuff out of the way before I did my swim. Where we stopped was featureless; with no mountains in the background it could just as easily have been a lake in Siberia. David Becker decided to stick a blue flag with 'North Pole' written on it in the ice with a Norwegian flag 100 metres further on and I would swim between the two flags. The Hampshire Flag Company in England had given us the flags and specially pointed the poles to get them into the ice. But even with sharpened poles, it was a nightmare and we ended up spending far too much time standing around before I got into the water. The Prof measured the water temperature at minus 1.7°C, which was what we expected. Still, it scared me.

'Prof, we are going to do just five minutes,' I said.

He sensed my apprehension. 'Fine, that's no problem.'

I got my music going, David encouraged me and I reminded myself that I had done a one-kilometre, 18-minute swim off Petermann Island when the water was zero. What was there to fear? Five minutes at minus 1.7°C wasn't going to be more difficult than that? Given it was going to be such a short time, we decided not to rig up the heart monitor and thermometer.

What you don't realize until you get deep into the Arctic is that the water is black and I felt like I was diving into a giant pot of ink. They call it the Black Ocean and looking at it makes you shiver. 'Don't think about that,' I said to myself. After four quick steps to the edge of the ice, I dived in. Rising to the surface, one thought overwhelmed all others: the difference between zero-degree water and minus 1.7°C is the difference between heaven and hell, day and night, life and death. I gasped for breath, my goggles misted over and I burned with pain. The voice of reason told me to control the fear but when you can't see and you can't breathe and the pain won't go away, fear is a formidable enemy.

I pulled off my goggles, quickly rinsed them, put them back on and started swimming. But 30 seconds later, the goggles misted over again and were frozen onto my face. I prised them away from my skin, pulled them off my head and swam to the edge of the ice. 'New goggles,' I shouted at David. He rummaged in my kit bag, tossed me a different pair, I put them on and away I went. As well as pain more severe than anything I'd previously experienced, my fingers began to separate and weren't pulling the water through as they should. Ideally, the fingers stay relaxed and you feel the water as it is pushed away by your hands. But on this swim the fingers felt rigid. After five minutes I have covered 400 metres and I just have to get out.

I'm quickly helped out of the water, the goggles are taken off my face and I notice my fingers are as big as large sausages. They look grotesque and I feel a desperate need to warm up. The guys are trying to wrench the flags out of the ice and gather together different bits and pieces. Time is passing and I'm in trouble, I know it. My SAS instincts take over: if there's danger, don't mess around. Without a blanket I sprint across the ice barefoot towards the chopper waiting to pick us up. Because the tail rotor is spinning, I run round to the front and, attracting the attention of the two pilots, I give them a thumbs-up and indicate that I'm climbing aboard. They know how cold it is outside, they realize I've been in the water and I'm standing there in just my swimming trunks, cap and goggles, and they urge me in quickly. Inside the chopper there are hot vents and I crawl right up to one.

With my hands rammed under my armpits, I shiver and try to warm up but this pain, this terrible pain. I've never felt anything like it – ever.

After a couple of minutes, I look again at my fingers – larger sausages. When David gets in the helicopter, I get him to open his jacket and I put my hands under his bare armpits. Virtually crying from the pain, I put my head on his shoulder and close my eyes. Back on the deck of the *Yamal*, passengers wait for me and clap when I get out of the chopper. A weak wave is all I can offer and, with blood flowing from a knee gashed on the ice, I am a miserable sight. In the shower, I put my hands directly under the rose and they sting with unbearable pain but I dare not take them away. Chris Lotz films me in the shower and, though I'm miserable and freezing, I pick up the shock on his face. This from a guy who doesn't show much emotion, so I know things are bad. It takes me fifty minutes to defrost and, even then, my fingers remain in a bad way. They are swollen and splayed and I can't even make fists.

Before the test swim, I was Lewis Gordon Pugh, the best cold-water swimmer in the world. I could deal with extremely cold water because of my mental toughness and because I could raise my body temperature before entering the water. Anticipatory thermo-genesis was the name given to the art of self-heating through the use of psychological stimuli and it was coined to explain what happened with my body before a major swim. Now, after one short test swim in the Arctic, my belief system was splintered. There was a simple and inescapable question: if five minutes in this water had caused so much pain and damage to my hands, what would twenty minutes do? In attempting to swim at minus 1.7°C degrees, had I pushed myself beyond the limit of human endurance? It was less difficult to climb Mount

Everest after Edmund Hillary had done it; it was easier to run the mile in under four minutes after Roger Bannister. No one had done a long-distance swim at minus 1.7°C.

After the hot shower, my negative thoughts held their victory march through the streets of my mind. 'Remember Sir Ranulph Fiennes? He lost the tips of the fingers on his left hand after accidentally falling into that water. He described it as his three-minute mistake . . . And you think you can do a 20-minute swim? He was fully clothed . . . Admiral Robert Peary, the first man to walk to the North Pole, lost eight toes up here . . . You have taken this on but you don't know how your body reacts at minus 1.7°C. This is a swim too far.'

All my life, I'd felt my destiny was to do something in the polar regions and now that the moment had come, I was dreading it. Five hundred metres might be possible, but not double it. Yet I had promised to do a one-kilometre swim and the world's biggest television networks were covering the event. If we reduced the length of the swim, it would look like we'd failed. Then I looked at my fingers, still swollen, with no feeling in the left hand and none in the fingers of the right, and I felt intense desolation – I'd come all this way to discover it wasn't possible to do a long swim at the North Pole. A swimmer's hands are a footballer's legs: they grip the water, they pull it through, their feel for the water propels you – without healthy fingers, it was impossible to envisage a successful swim.

Life on the IB *Yamal* as it ploughed its way north wasn't as dull as you might imagine. There were various activities for the passengers and a resident artist who put on painting classes. He was a young and handsome Canadian and he attracted a devoted class of would-be artists. Marilyn Noakes is a keen and talented botanical artist who enjoyed the opportunity to practise. We gave the Prof a terrible time: 'Hey Tim, Marilyn's spending a lot of time with that young

Canadian artist; she seems to like his classes a lot.' Towards the end of the trip, the teacher/painter put his work on show with a price on every piece. The most beautiful was one of a polar bear and Tim, broadminded and generous, bought it for Marilyn. Hung in a passageway, the paintings looked beautiful and those who had purchased them were asked to leave them where they were until the *Yamal* returned to Murmansk. On the second to last day, the polar bear painting went missing. Laurie Dexter, the expedition leader, spoke on the ship's public address system. 'Could the person who may have accidentally taken the painting of the polar bear please return it?'

Of course, there had been no accident; the painting had been stolen and what made it intriguing was the certainty that it was still on the ship. Even more bizarre was the likelihood that someone who had paid $25,000 for a berth had stolen a painting worth a few hundred dollars. Most of us agreed that no member of the ship's staff would risk losing their job by stealing something so easily discovered. You can't easily hide a painting. Like amateur sleuths, we identified a number of suspects among the passengers and eventually pointed our finger at a couple from Texas. He was a loud Scot who had moved to the US and she was a doctor but we weren't sure about them. When we asked her about her work, she became uneasy and evasive. We decided they had taken the painting. Sadly for Tim and Marilyn, the ship's bosses weren't prepared to search luggage as each passenger disembarked and whoever stole that polar bear still has it. For a couple of days, it had been our Agatha Christie story except that we never found out whodunit and we may have been entirely wrong.

Feeling nothing but hopelessness after the test swim, I spoke with David Becker the next morning, telling him of the dread and my expectation of the calamity that was about to unfold. He'd seen what a mess our trial run had been and witnessed how physically distressed I was afterwards. Unsurprised by my pessimism, he told me how he saw it. 'Lewis,' he said, 'I have been thinking about it and there are things we need to do for you to be able to come through this. First you've got to squeeze every negative thought out of your head. If you allow them to enter, they will destroy the swim before you ever get in the water. You can get them out of your head or you can allow them into your subconscious where they will become ingrained. I am going to give you three anchors, three ideas, and if you embrace them, you will make the swim. Every member of your team still believes you can do it and so do I. But from this moment until you get in the water, you've got to get your head in the right place.'

As David talked, I looked at my swollen fingers and thought, 'Right! I can't feel my hands – no feeling at all. This is something that's never, ever happened before. You can say what you want about believing in me but you don't have to get in that water. What I felt on that stupid test swim wasn't like anything I'd felt before. I don't believe I can do this.' I thought that but I didn't utter a word. I didn't want to knock David off course.

'Lewis, the first thing we're going to do is break this swim down into ten 100-metre chunks and every chunk is going to have a particular significance for you. We have ten national flags and we will plant one at every 100-metre mark and each will represent the people from that country who have helped you to do this swim. When we've worked in the past, we've been motivated by those who doubted you, said you couldn't do it. Now, as you swim past each flag, you're going to focus on those people who believe in you, who have inspired you, and you're going to show them they weren't wrong. Just think about the 100 metres you are doing – no more. Just get to the next flag. Don't think of a one-kilometre swim. It's too far. We have just two days for you to see not just the flags but the people they represent in your team – the Norwegians, the Swede, the Russians, Americans, Canadians, Swiss, South Africans, the New Zealander, the Australian and the Britons – the people who have given so much so you have this opportunity.'

He only had to mention the countries and I knew the people those flags represented. Twenty-nine people in all, each had done something to make the North Pole swim possible. David was right: the last thing I wanted to do was let them down.

'The second thing we're going to do, Lewis, is walk back to the beginning of your life and reflect on where you have come from. You recall sitting on your father's lap and him giving you impromptu history lessons, telling you what great leaders did in the past, and how inspired you were by those men and by him. Your parents took you to the game reserves in South Africa because they knew how much you loved wildlife and you are here because of your love for the environment. There is a meaning in what you're doing and you only have to walk back through your life to see it. After yesterday's experience you're thinking this swim is a leap into the unknown but it is not. Look back, consider what you've done: Robben Island when you were seventeen, Lake Malawi, the English Channel, the Cape Peninsula, the North Cape, Sognefjord, Spitsbergen, Antarctica, the Thames. This is just another step on the same journey and, when it has mattered in the past, you have always had the courage. Why would your courage fail you now? It's not going to.'

At this point, David lightened the tone and spoke of how every person in the team had the courage to believe in me, because each one of them was saying I could do it. 'Lewis, if you die tomorrow, it isn't going to look good on our CVs.' He smiled at that point but I didn't. I'd always been conscious of how people like the Prof and David were putting their entire reputations on the line for me.

'And Lewis,' he said, 'the third thing I want you to do is walk on to the end of your life and turn around and look back. What do you want your legacy to be? You are doing a symbolic swim to show the world what is happening to our environment. You are going to be able to look back and say, "When the moment came, I stood up." Through this swim you will tell leaders around the world they can no longer shirk the issue of climate change. You are going to shake their lapels and make them realize this is the biggest challenge facing all of us. You shouldn't be able to swim across the North Pole. It should be frozen over. There shouldn't be such big open leads of water. This place is changing and it will impact all of us.'

That was the last thing David said and in the 20 minutes that he spoke, everything changed. What he said shook me up and it was what I needed. After listening to him, the idea of abandoning the swim disappeared. I was doing it and it was going to be done properly. As the *Yamal* sped further north, I noticed how much open sea there was so close to the North Pole. This lack of summer sea ice was one of the many symptoms of climate change.

We failed to take the short test swim seriously enough and that contributed significantly to the fiasco. A bad rehearsal can, however, be helpful, as it shows where things can go wrong and it gets rid of complacency. We'd had our warning and we had to act on it. I spoke to the team as a group and said we all had to sharpen up, everything had to be done more quickly and with greater concentration and focus. 'Guys, this has to be a Special Forces-like operation, in and out, not a second more on that ice than we need. The flagpoles have to be put in place quickly. When I get to the ice, we've got to be ready to go. I don't want to be on the ice for longer than is necessary. Every second gets me closer to hypothermia. When the swim is done, I'm out of the water and straight back to the boat. The equipment, the flags, none of that stuff can delay me.'

'Ladies and gentlemen,' Captain Stanislav Rumyantsev, skipper of the *Yamal*, says the next evening, 'we are approaching the Geographic North Pole.'

There is suddenly a buzz as passengers appear on deck. They want to know when I'll be doing the swim and if they can come along. They mean well but this is not a circus and there are no seats for sale. The last thing I need is for one of the passengers to slip into the water or break an ankle or have any of the mishaps you can so easily have on ice. There is an American passenger that I got on very well with who is keen to watch the swim but, unfortunately, I have to say no. A few offer me money and it is easy to decline.

The *Yamal*'s speed drops as the captain tries to get us right over the North Pole. He inches a little this way, then a little that way until, finally, his GPS says he is 90 degrees North. He hoots the horn, people cheer and clap, some passengers have brought champagne to the front of the ship and there is a party atmosphere.

For me and the team this is our moment. We are now at the North Pole and there is plenty of open water. It is now or never, the evening of 14 July, and suddenly time is passing quickly because there are things to do before the swim can take place. One of the ship's crew comes to me with a form I must sign. It is a contract that will exempt the shipping company of all responsibility should I die in the course of the swim. Without any fuss, I sign. It will be midnight before we are ready to swim but, with 24-hour daylight, that doesn't matter. I do not want to swim on 15 July because it the anniversary of my father's death and it would be bitterly cruel for my mother to lose her husband and son on the same date.

When I mention this to David Becker, he gets me to see it differently. 'Lewis, the Captain is not going to wait a day so you can do the swim on the 16th. That's not going to happen. I want you to swim from flag to flag – Norwegian, Swedish, Russian, American, Canadian, Swiss, South African, New Zealand, Australian – and I want you to imagine your father waiting for you by the British flag at the end. I want you to do this swim for your father and you must embrace the fact that you're doing the swim on his anniversary.' David knows how to calm me; he always has.

Following our disastrous test swim, I'm sure I can do much better, but the entire team must up their performance. I spend much of the 14th thinking about what people need to do and then talking them through that. Close to midnight, I gather the team for a final briefing. Standing on the bridge of the *Yamal*, I go through everything for the last time. 'David, your responsibility is to prepare me mentally. This means we will go down to our cabin shortly and you will get me properly revved up. On the ice I am going to hand you my clothes. You will then count me down, using the same commands as the RAF dispatcher when I used to parachute: "One minute to swim. Red on. GREEN ON! GO, GO, GO!" You will then get in the Zodiac with Tim and you will put on the white board the names of the people who have supported me. I want to see those names.'

I then turn to the Prof, who has been through a tough time recently and who almost didn't make this trip. Four months before he'd lost a great friend when the Pakistan cricket coach Bob Woolmer was found dead in his Jamaican hotel room during the Cricket World Cup the day after his team was dramatically knocked out of the tournament by Ireland. At first it was thought Bob was murdered; it was later decided he died from natural causes but suspicions lingered. The Prof and Bob had co-authored a fine book on cricket and he was devastated by Bob's death. He couldn't have contemplated the North Pole expedition without having Marilyn, his wife, with him. 'Tim,' I say, 'your responsibility is my safety. If at any time you do not believe it is safe, it will be your call to get me out of there. If my core temperature dips below 35 degrees, you've got to pull me out but you are the only person who can make this call. Prof, I have the courage to do this swim because you have the courage to believe in me.'

Tim wanted Marilyn to witness the swim, as she had the test swim, but I was against it. If things went wrong, I just didn't want Marilyn to see it, and I thought there was a reasonable chance they would. The Prof was disappointed but accepted the decision and, in time, I would look back and regret it. In her way, Marilyn is an integral part of the team and should have been there.

Tobie van Heerden is here for our major backer, Investec, and has taken on the job of getting our flags into the ice. 'Tobie,' I say, 'I know there were problems with the flags the last time. This evening there can be no hiccups. Whatever it takes, you get them into the ice.'

Jason Roberts is standing close to Tobie. 'Jason, you've got to get the perfect picture, the one that makes the front page of newspapers all over the world. Take a few shots with a fish-eye lens on – it will create the curvature – so it looks like we are actually on the top of the world. Okay, Jason?'

'Chris,' I say to our cameraman Chris Lotz, 'I saw your professionalism as you sat for twelve hours on the front of the ship to get footage of polar bears on our way here. You don't need to prove anything to me. You're going to be in the Zodiac with Jason. You'll film me all the way along and as I'm coming out of the water at the end make sure you are on the ice.'

Jørgen Amundsen was last. 'Jørgen, your job is to ski alongside me with that big stopwatch over your shoulder, positioned so I can see it. I also want you, please, to motivate me with hand signals, thumbs-up, plenty of shouting. Don't underestimate the importance of that encouragement.'

There is one thought that dares not utter its name but it's on my mind and something we must plan for. 'Guys, we haven't discussed what happens if I go under. You know it can happen quickly. And the water is completely black.'

There is a momentary silence and then Jason looks up. 'I will dive in and get you,' he says.

Everyone else nods in admiration and relief that this responsibility is being taken by someone else. I am also relieved because Jason is a former lifeguard, physically strong and obviously very brave. He is the one I would have picked for the job if nobody had volunteered. Before breaking up, I ask if there are any questions. Everyone remains silent.

Before heading to my cabin to begin the last stage of my preparation, I ask Jason to arrange a short meeting with the Russian guards whose job it is to ensure that I won't be eaten by polar bears while in the water. I tell them about the swim and my desire to draw attention to the fragility of the area and do something that will help preserve the North Pole. 'The important thing,' I say, 'is that if a polar bear jumps in, you can frighten it away or you can pull me out of the water – but, please, you can't shoot the bear. That would be a disaster. We are here to help protect polar bears.' I shake their hands and thank them for helping me and I see the warmth and respect in their Russian eyes.

While the team is out marking the course, the Prof notices where the guards will be placed and doesn't like the relatively large distances between them. There is too much room for a polar bear to slip in undetected, so he decides to change the route from two legs of 500 metres to four 250-metre legs. I don't like this, because constant turning breaks up my rhythm and makes the swim harder, but safety comes first.

Back in the cabin I lie on the bunk and put on my earphones. I listen to music chosen for me by my friend the New Zealand tenor Shaun Dixon, who was the only person ever trained by Luciano Pavarotti. I asked him to choose the most evocative pieces of music he'd heard and, from his selection, I play Verdi's 'Chorus of the Hebrew Slaves' because it was so much a part of my childhood.

Listening to it, I am transported back in time: my mother is in the kitchen, a recording of the opera *Nabucco* is playing on the radio and my mother is singing this song with the choir and, carried away by the emotion in the music, she cries but she doesn't stop singing. That memory fills me with energy and love and the feeling that I will do this swim and I will not stop. An ironic thought strikes me: all of my life I have looked up to my father but now, at a desperately important moment, it is to my mother I turn. Reminded of her singing so long ago is somehow all that I need. This swim is my destiny. I am going to swim past every flag. Every stroke will be a thank you to those who have believed in me.

Soon Tim comes to strap on my chest harness and, for the first time ever, he is nervous. The strap runs over my chest and as he tapes it to my body, his hands begin to shake. We are right next to each other. 'Prof,' I say, 'we've got to be brave here. If we are nervous, the rest of the team will pick up on that and it won't help them. We're going to walk out of here like heavyweight champions before a title fight, not betraying one ounce of doubt. And if you must know,' I say, smiling, 'you are not nearly as nervous as I am.' He smiles his goofy smile and I'm happy.

I put on the clothes that I will wear on the ice and leave the cabin. I do feel like a prizefighter as I walk past passengers who have come to see me off. They wish me well. I give them a V–for–victory sign and feel totally confident that I can do it. In 48 hours, my mindset has turned 180 degrees.

David Becker has done his job. I go down the gangplank, onto the ice, into a Zodiac, and now all of the tourists are waving and shouting. 'Go for it, Lewis.'

I think about why I am here, what has been happening to our environment and it makes me strong. On the ice I walk past all the flags and the people they represent: Norway, Jørgen Amundsen, Peder Kjærvik; Sweden, Olle Nordell, who helped put together my website; Russia, the skipper and crew of the *Yamal*, the polar guards, Alexander Brylin; USA, Jonathan Dugas; Canada, Laurie Dexter, who would drive one of our Zodiacs, and Tessa Graham; Switzerland, Olivier Müller, who runs Villemont watches with Jørgen; South Africa, so many people: my girlfriend Antoinette, the Prof, David, Chris, Nic Marshall, my outstanding swim coach Brian Button, Simon Blackburn, Hendrik du Toit; New Zealand, Shaun Dixon; Australia, Jason Roberts; Great Britain, Mum, Dad, Tim Toyne Sewell, Nick Peterson, Emily Lewis-Brown, Stephen Rubin, Martin Jenkins and many others.

I speak to the Russian guard furthest from the start and thank him for doing this. I stretch out my hand and he wraps me in a bear hug. I think of how strong I am and how prepared I am to stay in the water as long as I need to. Martin Jenkins always talks about the power of the made-up mind. I am going to swim a kilometre. I am not going to get out a metre before. You don't plan for victory and defeat at the same time. My mind is made up. I have never felt as empowered as at this moment. Close to where I will start, I thank another guard and then shake Jørgen Amundsen's hand. 'Don't forget to shout, Jørgen.'

In my ear Puff Daddy is talking to me, 'Come With Me'. It is strong, aggressive and I am ready. The thermometer is working and I hear the Prof say, 'Okay, I've got his body temperature. Everything's okay.'

Then I shout, 'Everyone ready. Five seconds to swim.' I run my goggles along the surface of the water.

'Green on,' David shouts, 'GO, GO, GO!' Standing on an ice ledge, knee-deep in icy water, I dive into the black unknown and start swimming. Though severe, the initial shock is not as brutal as it had been two days before. This time I'm ready but the goggles haven't improved. They freeze onto my face, some water gets inside and I try to adjust them but it's hopeless. 'Lewis,' I tell myself, 'you keep thinking about these goggles and you will die right here, before you even get to the Norwegian flag.' The goggles remain in place but they don't exist any more. I look up and the Norwegian flag is there; I've already done 100 metres. 'You're going great,' Jørgen shouts, and I count the strokes to stop my mind wandering. At the Swedish flag I am hyper-ventilating and swallowing too much water. My skin is burning; in ice water it feels like I'm on fire. 'Calm,' I think, 'you've got to be calm. Concentrate on breathing. Come on, Lewis. Stroke, breath; stroke, breath.'

I get to the first turn, 250 metres down, and I feel okay. 'Keep going, keep going,' Jørgen yells. Going back the other way I feel the strength of the current against me. Why is it that we never notice the current when it is with us but always feel when it is against us? Going this way, I can see David and the Prof; they say I'm going well, their thumbs are pointed upwards and I catch a glimpse of my core tempera-ture, 37-something, and I'm encouraged it hasn't dropped too much because this water is murderous. I reach the halfway point but it has been at a cost. I feel wasted.

My fingers are opening up again, splaying outwards, and becoming inefficient in their work. I feel the cold move from my hand into my wrists and there's still 500 metres to go. But the Rottweiler is at the gate, barking, protecting me from negative thoughts. 'Lewis, people give up when they're so close and they regret it their whole lives. Graveyards are full of people with unfinished business. You're not going to be one of those people. Just concentrate, concentrate, concentrate.'

This 250 metres, the third of four, is the hardest. 'JUST GET TO 750 METRES,' I scream silently, 'and remember the people who have believed in you.' At 750 metres I do not think of stopping because the end is in sight. I feel cramp in one leg and know I can't force too much. Looking to my right again, I can see the Prof and David; my temperature is 36, which is fine, but my hateful goggles keep misting over. Now I just want to get there. My hands are useless, just slapping the water like they've never been taught how to swim. The Prof and David keep shouting, 'Brilliant, Lewis, almost there, almost there. Keep going.' I can now see the British flag and I think of my dad.

A large chunk of ice drifts across my path, I slow slightly to veer round it. Through the last 100 metres I keep going but can't think any more, can't enjoy it, can't measure how close I am to the end. 'Just keep going, keep going. Don't stop.'

Then I hear Tim shouting, 'You've made it!!!'

I swim towards the edge of the ice, Jørgen grabs and pulls me out of the water. 'Slow down,' I scream, knowing the ice can cut me open. Jørgen tries to shake my hand but I want him to take the goggles off. Tobie van Heerden is beside me and only by holding on to him can I remain standing. My feet stick to the ice and I know it's time to move. I always have the same thought when I get out of the water: the danger lies in the fifteen minutes after the swim. Get to the hot shower or bear the consequences.

David is trying to get my shoes on but, as my feet have swollen, he struggles. They get me into the Zodiac and deliver me to the ship. David and I jog the last bit to the gangplank. People are crowding round but I desperately need the hot shower. I hear them cheering in the near distance. 'Thank you,' I think but am unable to respond. David is beside me. 'You made it, you made it,' he is saying. While I'm in the hot shower, I hear the shutter of Jason's camera opening and closing but when I try to speak, my lips are still frozen and the words come out slurred.

Hot water improves things – glorious, tingling, restorative hot water. Once the lips have melted, the words at last sound like English. 'How on earth did we do that?' I ask David. Two days before dying seemed a distinct possibility, and the loss of fingers and toes seemed likely but, remarkably, my fingers are not particularly swollen. They are no longer sausages. Five minutes in the water when we weren't prepared caused awful swelling and nerve damage; now because we have done our jobs correctly 18 minutes and 50 seconds has not been nearly as damaging.

Returning to the ship on the second Zodiac, the Prof comes to my cabin. 'Well done, well done,' he says. Jørgen then comes in and the room is full of joy. In the euphoria of having got through the swim, I forget how cold I am. My body doesn't. I stay in the hot shower for 50 minutes and, even then, it is a wrench to leave.

When it comes to taking off the chest monitor, I know exactly what has to be done. Previously I would have removed it carefully, making sure it wasn't damaged. Now I reach for my toilet bag, take out a pair of scissors and cut the harness off my body. It is a symbolic moment, as it is my promise never again to do a swim so dangerous. What I feel is not victory nor vindication but the sense of having survived. After dressing I go to the top of the ship, where there is a satellite phone. I call Antoinette and tell her I've made it. In her voice I hear nothing but relief.

15

THE AFTERMATH

Sailing back from the North Pole, the feeling of having done something worthwhile was deeply satisfying. The time-honoured belief that much in life depends upon timing was borne out by our experience of the Arctic swim. We did it at a time when the public was beginning to demand action on climate change and that was the key to the ultimate success of the expedition. Everyone wanted to speak to the person who had undertaken the first swim across the North Pole. I stood on the deck of the IB *Yamal* just two hours after the swim, clutching my satellite phone, and took countless calls from media outlets all over the world. If the swim had engaged the attention of the world's press, it had also empowered me in a way I had not foreseen.

The Prof talked about this, saying he had twice seen sportsmen changed by a single event in their lives: once when South African rugby player Joel Stransky kicked the winning drop goal in the 1995 World Cup final and again when I did the North Pole swim. Joel kicked the drop goal in the final minute and beat New Zealand. With so much riding on the game — it was South Africa's first major international tournament in the post-apartheid era and President Nelson Mandela had 'adopted' the multiracial rugby union team – this was a monumental moment in the history of the Rainbow Nation. Similarly, the Prof believed the Arctic swim changed me and I felt it had.

Having witnessed the melting sea ice and swum across the North Pole, I felt entitled to speak about the effects of climate change and to demand change from business and political leaders. A month after returning to London I went to Hollywood to appear on NBC's *The Tonight Show* with Jay Leno and it was an experience. I had done many interviews for various British and South African television shows when there were five or six people on the set. Leno's show was very different. I arrived at what looked like a big warehouse. Dozens of people buzzed around the set. Leno is an easy-to-warm-to fellow, friendly and down to earth. He briefed me before going on: 'Lewis, this is what we're gonna do: an eight-minute interview in which I ask you about the swim, the effects on your body, why you did it, and we will try to wrap it up with a bit of humour.' He had considered putting me on the previous day with Jennifer Lopez but decided against that because climate change is serious and J. Lo can be a little earnest; it would be a bad combination. I went on with a comedian, whose company I thoroughly enjoyed, and who brought out the best in me. After Leno, I flew east and did *Good Morning America* with Diane Sawyer, then Jon Stewart's *The Daily Show* on Comedy Central.

You do the TV shows, speak about the importance of protecting the environment and get lulled into thinking the world really does want to do the right thing. Then something happens and you are smashed in the face by reality. Shortly after returning to London, I was walking past a newsagent when I noticed a Russian flag on the front page of one of the more serious newspapers. The picture ran with a story about the Russians planting their flag at the bottom of the seabed at the North Pole. I felt absolute disgust and hopelessness. What the story said was that the Russians had sent a ship to the North Pole, launched a submersible that dropped to the bottom of the Arctic Ocean and, by using a mechanical arm, planted the Russian flag there.

This was early August 2007, oil prices were soaring and Russia was staking a claim to the enormous potential oil and gas fields in the Arctic. With oil and gas reserves dwindling elsewhere in the world, who can be sure the Arctic will not become the world's next great oilfield? As climate change melts more sea ice and makes oil exploration in the Arctic more commercially viable, the natural beauty of the Arctic may not be enough to protect it. The Law of the Sea Convention allows each nation to exploit the natural resources in its 'exclusive economic zone', which extends 200 nautical miles off its coast. Countries are also entitled to resources in their continental shelf, up to 350 nautical miles off the coast. Russia's claim to the Arctic is based on its belief that the Lomonosov Ridge extends from inside its economic zone to near the North Pole and is part of its continental shelf and, therefore, it is legally entitled to drill for oil and gas that far north. It was almost as if we had returned to the days of Christopher Columbus, when you could place a flag in the ground and claim the territory as yours.

Canada complained about what the Russians had done, the US and Denmark demurred but that was about it. The rest of the world paid little attention. Perhaps the possibility of Russia drilling for oil near the North Pole seemed too far into the future for anyone to be bothered. For me, Russia's determination to stake this claim was grim confirmation that man continues to see the environment as nothing other than a well from which he can continue to draw finite resources. What matters is having more oil and gas than our neighbours while leaving the protection of the planet to others. In planting that flag at the North Pole, Russia made an aggressive statement that should have drawn strident disapproval from the rest of the world – should have but did not. If, in forty or fifty years, the Russians start mining the vast oil and gas reserves in the Arctic seabed and fifty years after that the Arctic's reserves have been used up, where will the economic powers then turn for their next source? They'd turn to Antarctica, of course, because the international treaty protecting that region from drilling and mining can be amended in 2041. In a world dependent upon oil and gas, Antarctica will become a target. I looked at that newspaper photograph and wanted to weep. When are we going to see that our children's futures will not be secure until we agree to concentrate all our efforts on developing renewable sources of energy?

After returning to England there were good moments. An unexpected highlight followed on from an invitation Jørgen Amundsen and I received to a banquet at Hampton Court Palace in West London. Approximately 300 guests gathered for a black-tie occasion. When Jørgen and I checked the seating plan, we were astounded to find we were positioned on either side of Prince Charles. That made it a hugely enjoyable evening because Prince Charles is passionate about protecting the environment; he is also a charming dinner companion. He delivered an address about the need to protect the Amazon rainforest. The more serious parts of the evening were lightened by a spectacular exhibition of samba dancing by stunning Brazilian girls which, I must say, the Prince appeared particularly to enjoy.

At different moments during the evening we spoke about the Arctic swim and he was curious about which part of my body most felt the cold during the swim. With the invisible computer inside my head doing the calculations, the choice for me was straightforward: it was either my hands or my 'you know what'. Without any doubt, the most severe pain I'd felt was in my 'you know what'. As my body heats up through the effects of anticipatory thermo-genesis, I felt the need to drink a lot before getting into the water and therefore I needed to pee shortly before the swim. When entering extremely cold water, it is important to make sure that when you wee there is absolutely nothing left in the nozzle after you've emptied your bladder. I was sure I had done that but I was wrong. Some remained and after a few minutes in the freezing water, it froze and expanded. The pain caused by this stalactite was something else. Until I got into the shower and melted it, the pain was excruciating. I thought of telling the Prince this sorry saga but decided against it.

'My hands, your Royal Highness,' I said. 'I couldn't feel them for four months after returning from the North Pole.'

Inspired by what I'd seen at the North Pole, I wanted to continue working for the environment and to be a voice for the Arctic. It was a question of what to do next. I decided I'd go on an ambitious expedition kayaking north from the island of Svalbard to try to get as close to the North Pole as I could. Not so long ago it would have been impossible to do this but with so much ice melting during the summer, I reckoned on getting fairly close. The expedition was planned for late August 2008, almost fourteen months after the North Pole swim. Though I had done some kayaking, I was not at the level that was necessary to survive paddling in the freezing temperatures of the Arctic Ocean. Luckily, one of the world's foremost canoeists, Robert Hegedüs, was training the South Africa team for the Beijing Olympics and I persuaded him to be my coach. And that's how I came to know the remarkable Robert.

When he was competing for Hungary, Robert won seven world titles as a sprint canoeist and was a hugely successful and popular sportsman in his home country. He was thirty-five when we met. He had retired from competition but he was still an extraordinary physical specimen: he was almost 6ft 4in but with an even bigger wingspan of 6ft 9in and a zest for life that was infectious. We would do pull-ups and, though that exercise should have been difficult for a man so tall and so broad, Robert would do a hundred without a break whereas I would do twenty-five and die. Very fit, very competitive and an exceptional athlete in his chosen sport, Robert was also a very gentle man whose supreme confidence was married to a natural humility and that made him a special character. Normally confidence and humility do not go hand in hand – certainly not in someone so young. But he didn't spare me when we trained and he was determined I would learn to paddle correctly: if that meant endless repetition of a particular technical point, then that's what he would put me through and I liked him for it.

After a few months of working together, I wanted Robert not just to be my trainer but to do the Arctic kayak with me. It didn't surprise me in the slightest that he jumped at the opportunity. He was technically brilliant. When we trained in a two-man surf ski (an ocean-going open kayak), he would sit at the front and knew exactly what mistakes I was making even though he couldn't see me or how I was paddling. 'Your left arm is not going far enough forward, stretch it more,' he would say, and he was always right. Soon he got me to train with the South African Olympic team that he was coaching and arranged for me to travel with the team to Hungary for specialist pre-Beijing training. That was tough because the weather was particularly hot and the proximity of the Olympics meant everyone was training to their maximum. There was a subtle pressure on me to keep up but there were days when it was so hot and I just had to hold back and stay within my limits.

A week after I left, there was a shocking tragedy as the 36-year-old Hungarian double Olympic champion György Kolonics collapsed on a jetty after training with Robert. After apparently suffering a massive heart attack, he died. He and Robert had long been good friends and it was devastating for Robert. Recriminations followed as the canoeing people accused the ambulance service of taking too long to show up and then not having a defibrillator; the ambulance people said they found tightly wrapped bandages on György's body, which could have been used to reduce muscle fatigue and would not have helped someone experiencing a heart attack. In the end, they agreed not to blame each other because nothing was going to change what had happened; it would only make things worse for György's family and friends.

It was a tough time in Robert's life because his marriage was also breaking up and he was deeply affected by that. To his credit, he did not allow his personal sadness to intrude upon the work he was doing to make me a better paddler. The opposite was true: he remained an excellent trainer and brought out the best in me. We went to Spitsbergen for two weeks' training in the conditions we would experience during the expedition and Robert fell in love with the Arctic. I watched him react and was reminded of how I'd felt when I'd first come to this desolate but majestic part of the world. Jason Roberts got us a little hut on a beach just outside Spitsbergen's main town, Longyearbyen, and almost every evening Robert would go to the kennels, where a big pack of huskies were housed. In winter they pulled sledges through the snow but now, in summer, they were tied up and Robert would spend over an hour with them. He patted and made each one feel special; the essence of his character came through in his frequent visit to the huskies.

The wind howled at different times when we were in Spitsbergen and it was clear that if we got bad weather when we were paddling north, we would be in for a very unpleasant ride. One day Robert decided to go out in his surf ski when the wind was blowing strong.

'Robert,' I said, 'that wind is howling. It's dangerous out there. What happens if you fall out or get blown out to sea?'

'Lewis, we've got to see how the surf ski performs in bad conditions.'

'The water is three degrees.'

'That's why I am not going to fall out,' he replied with a smile.

There was no point in my talking to him because once Robert decided to do something that was it. In normal weather he would routinely paddle 13 kilometres in an hour but in these conditions it took him an hour to do just two kilometres. I watched as the white water blasted across his bow and got so concerned that I jumped into the pick-up Jason had left us and drove along the coastal road, keeping as close to Robert as I could. After an hour of punishment, he turned back on himself and just flew the return journey to his starting point. In the gusting wind we had a hell of a job carrying the surf ski over some rocks and back to the hut. Robert was wasted and frozen from the effort and just flopped down onto a sofa.

'Lewis, we have totally underestimated the strength of the wind here.'

I didn't disagree. We had but it was also true that if I'd considered everything that could have gone wrong, I wouldn't have undertaken most of what I'd done in the previous six years. I did have particular worries about the Arctic Kayak, as we came to call this expedition, because it wasn't a swim and this wasn't the ocean you'd recommend to a man taking his first long journey in a single surf ski. Furthermore there was the customary stress of raising the money to fund the trip, which was all the more difficult than it had been for previous years, as the credit crunch was in full swing.

In the hostile conditions of our training camp at Spitsbergen, I questioned whether I was biting off more than I could chew. Fortunately, Martin Jenkins came with us to Spitsbergen. He is one of the world's top performance coaches, and he knows his way round the human mind. Once he heard my expressions of doubt, he sorted things out straight away. 'Lewis, you must make up your mind. You are paddling next month. No ifs, no buts. You are doing it. Period. Fix your mind on that. The rest will follow.'

While Robert and I were training, a luxurious cruise ship docked at the island. However impressive the ship, it was nothing compared to its A-list of passengers. Former US President Jimmy Carter, former US Secretary of State Madeleine Albright, Google founder Larry Page, media tycoon and philanthropist Ted Turner and others were visiting the Arctic while holding a climate change conference on the ship. They'd heard I was in the area and the organizer called to ask if I would deliver a short speech on climate change to the conference about what I'd seen on my trips to the Arctic. 'You've got fifteen to twenty minutes,' she told me. With a week to prepare, I did a lot of preparation and was all set the day before, when another call from the organizer brought the news that there was no time for me to speak but I was welcome to join the guests at a cocktail reception on the ship.

During the reception, the Captain mentioned me in his introduction. 'At the back of the room there is a very special person, Lewis Pugh, the first man to swim across the North Pole and a man who did so much to bring attention to the disappearing Arctic sea ice. Lewis, would you make yourself known?'

It was a mistake to give me this opportunity because I was still annoyed at having prepared a speech and then being told it wasn't wanted. Looking round the room, I could see Carter and Albright and I knew there were a few US senators and congressmen among the audience as well. It was too good an opportunity to let slip past. Walking towards the front, I stretched out my hand to the Governor of the Island of Spitsbergen, who had just spoken, and he kindly handed me the microphone. To all present, except the lady in charge, it would have seemed normal: Lewis Pugh is introduced and then comes up to deliver his speech. From the corner of my eye, I caught an expression of fury on the organizer's face as she stood at the back of the room, but she couldn't do anything.

I spoke for ten minutes and told those assembled about the times I had been in the Arctic, the changes I had seen and the desperate need for action from the major Western countries. As I walked back to my place, Ted Turner stood up, gave me a high-five and asked, 'You free for dinner this evening?' That night we had dinner and discussed what needed to happen to protect the Arctic.

Before and after our two weeks in Spitsbergen, I trained in London, kayaking from Tower Bridge to Greenwich Village and back. At the time I shared a grotty apartment near Tower Bridge with a friend, Damien Forrest, and such was the awfulness of the place that it was relief to get out on the Thames. The flat's attraction was its low rent and central location but after a time even that ceased to be any consolation. Damien and I had separate rooms but we might as well have been sharing because the paper-thin wall dividing us vibrated with the unrelenting rhythm of his snoring. Little wonder then that the early morning kayak down to Greenwich became so important and I grew to love the old maritime town with its museum and Christopher Wren's magnificent Old Royal Naval College. Later I would get emails from people who didn't believe in climate change and thought people like Al Gore and I were in it for the money. 'Come visit me at the Tower Bridge apartment,' I wanted to reply.

Robert and I didn't get as far north on our kayaking expedition as we had hoped. The clear water we needed to make good progress never materialized. Instead we had ice floes coming at us, making our journey north hazardous and slow. Nevertheless it was a hugely satisfying trip for us. Tom Hall, an equity partner from a company called Apax Partners whom I'd met when I'd given a speech there, contributed greatly to the expedition and it was reassuring to have him in charge of the support boat. And I will always regard it as a privilege that I got to know Robert so well. I have always considered myself enthusiastic and energetic: if there's a job to do the next day, I will be up for it and early. Robert is in a different class. No matter how cold or how hostile the conditions, it was he who came into my cabin at six o'clock every morning. 'Lewis,' he would say with the biggest smile, 'it's time to paddle!' In its way, it was inspiring because this was something he had done all of his life and yet his desire to keep doing it seemed greater than ever. His enthusiasm was totally infectious. I like to think it was the beauty of the Arctic that inspired Robert. I will always remember something he said: 'Lewis, compared to this place, the Olympics, the world titles, the gold medals are nothing – absolutely nothing.'

Ironically, global warming played no small part in undermining the entire expedition. We believed that the greater melting of summer ice would open up large areas of sea and allow us to paddle north at a good speed. What we didn't fully appreciate was that to the north of us there was a widespread melting of sea ice off the coast of Alaska and the New Siberian Islands and the ice was being pushed south towards us.

Julia Thomas came with us as a physio and, when she wasn't trying to put life back into our aching backs, she would stand on the deck with Tom Hall and shout instructions to Robbie and me.

'Move left five metres, Robert!'

'Lewis, ice coming left, move right.'

If it wasn't ice floes, it was logs, which had once been trees in Alaska or Canada but got caught up in currents, and they, too, wanted to torpedo us. Julia designed small steel-and-foam guards that she attached to the fronts of our surf skis and these helped to reduce the damage to our boats.

The evidence of climate change was stark. Fourteen months before I'd sailed north and I'd seen a preponderance of multi-year ice about three metres thick north of Spitsbergen, but this time most of the ice was just a metre thick. That shocked me.

Concerned by the changes and outraged that so few seemed to be getting the message, I got on our satellite phone and called the Prime Minister's office in London.

'Could I please speak to the PM?' I asked.

They put me through to his press secretary, who said it wouldn't be possible because the PM was in Belfast.

'Okay,' I said, 'this is my satellite phone number, would you please ask the Prime Minister to call me as soon as he gets back? It's really important.'

The next day our satellite phone rang. It was a lady from Downing Street.

'Will you please take a call from the PM?'

'Sure,' I replied.

There was then a click, as the call was transferred to another extension.

'Good morning, Lewis,' said Gordon Brown.

'Morning, Prime Minister,' I said.

'Lewis, we have been watching you on the news in the evenings. We are all very proud of you here in Great Britain. You are carrying on the fine tradition of British exploration. And I am especially pleased you are raising so much awareness about climate change. It's a crucial issue. What have you seen on this trip, Lewis?'

It was an invitation and an opportunity that I wasn't going to let pass. 'Prime Minister, I have visited the Arctic for the past six summers and I have witnessed this ecosystem change. I have just kayaked 135 kilometres through the Arctic sea ice and I can tell you there has been a significant melting of the ice since I was in this vicinity last summer. Most of the ice I saw last summer was around three metres thick; this year the only ice I have seen was just one metre thick.'

There was deathly silence on the other end of the phone. 'Right. What are the implications of that?'

'First, what I've seen tallies with data from the NSIDC [National Snow and Ice Data Center in Colorado], which shows that the sea ice in the Arctic is at its thinnest and lowest volume on record. This week the North-west Passage and the North-east Passage opened for the first time together. My concern is that we are totally underestimating the speed of climate change. I also believe that governments are basing their policies on a "best-case scenario" rather than a "most-likely case scenario".

'Prime Minister, all the work you are doing in developing countries in terms of debt relief and foreign aid will be rendered useless if the Arctic melts. This will affect everyone and will have devastating consequences for many of the world's poorest and least developed areas. Great Britain needs to lead the world on climate change and I believe you have to appoint a minister specifically tasked to deal with climate change. Furthermore, the bill now going through Parliament on climate change has to be toughened. Many scientists are convinced that a 60 per cent cut in CO_2 emissions by 2050 is simply not enough to halt runaway climate change and that there must be an 80 per cent cut over this period.'

Perhaps it was going to happen anyway, but less than a month later Ed Miliband was appointed Secretary of State for Energy and Climate Change and the Climate Change Bill that eventually went through Parliament had a target of an 80 per cent cut in CO_2 emissions by 2050. Of course I wasn't the only person calling for these changes but, when that very progressive piece of legislation went through Westminster, I hoped that my symbolic expeditions deep in the Arctic had made the difference.

16

TIME TO BELIEVE

Public speaking is something I have learned to do and it has become my principal means of support. Mostly it is in the corporate world and it has been encouraging for me to see that so many business people are interested in the fragility of places such as the Arctic and Antarctica. There is now a general acceptance that though you work in an office in London, New York or Johannesburg, your life and the lives of your children will be affected by what happens at the two ends of the earth. I have grown to love public speaking and was delighted when a speech on leadership I recently gave at an influential conference in the United States was voted as one of the seven most inspiring videos on the Web.

In 2008 I was asked to do a speaking tour of some South African schools. The prospect excited me, as it would take me into the world of young people and into some of the country's poorest townships. I spoke in the ganglands of the Cape Flats in Cape Town, in Soweto, and in many other townships with low employment and high crime rates. Yet it was a life-affirming experience: the kids were interested and appreciative, their teachers enthusiastic and idealistic. I spoke, too, at England's most prestigious private school, Eton College, and at its South African equivalent and, remarkably, the kids in these institutions of privilege didn't seem as interested in the dangers posed by climate change or the thinness of the ice at the Arctic Circle. Don't ask me why because I haven't been able to figure it out. Perhaps Eton pupils felt it was someone else's problem while their counterparts in African townships were just excited that someone from another world had come to speak with them.

Speaking to young people has been an education for me. In talking to them about the environment and telling them about my life I've got to know myself better. They ask all kinds of things:

Are you married?

I tell them about how Antoinette and I knew each other at high school in Cape Town and how we met twenty years later and realized we had more in common than we'd realized as teenagers. We got married on 10 October 2009 in St Peter the Fisherman's Church in Hout Bay and it was one of the happiest days of my life. One of the hymns we chose for our wedding ceremony was C. F. Alexander's wonderful 'All Things Bright and Beautiful':

    All things bright and beautiful,
    All creatures great and small,
    All things wise and wonderful,
    The Lord God made them all.

The children sometimes ask if I can sing it for them and I reply that, while I am of Welsh descent and love singing, now would not be the best time!

What is the key to achieving things?

Self-confidence, I tell them. If you've got that, everything is easier. It can come from many sources: from within, because some people are born with confidence, but it is generally instilled by parents and teachers. There is an expression in Gaelic that says: '*mol an óige agus tiocfaidh sí*' ('praise the young and they will come'). I believe that. Sir Roger Bannister, the athlete immortalized for being the first to run a mile in less than four minutes, was asked where he got the belief to break that barrier. He replied it was from his coach, Franz Stampfl, telling him he could do it. You get the best out of people when you expect the best from them.

What is the most beautiful thing you've seen?

Maybe the peace and harmony of Sami herdsmen caring for their reindeer at North Cape in Norway, or the colonies of penguins we saw in Antarctica, or the beautiful wildlife I came across at the many game reserves that my parents took me to see when I was a boy. A particular favourite was a recent walk enjoyed in the Umfolozi Game Reserve in Zululand. My companion was an 80-year-old man, Baba Gumedi, and we camped on a rock overlooking a river at night. With an extraordinarily clear sky, we savoured the twinkling stars. The river was home to crocodiles and hippos and the first thing we saw the next morning was elephants strolling down to the edge of the water to get their fill. The crocodiles have been in this region since the age of the dinosaurs and, as Baba and I watched, we talked about all the humans who'd passed through this little corner of Africa but despite that the place had not been spoiled. The relationship between man and nature need not be destructive.

What is the worst thing you've seen on your expeditions?

I tell the kids about the thousands of whalebones I saw in Deception Island and the fact that they'd been dumped in Antarctica, one of the most beautiful places on the planet. I have been haunted by that swim through the whale graveyard and haven't been able to get the image of the bones out of my head. Man hunted whales almost to the point of extinction, not seeming to care that we could lose one of the wonders of the sea world forever. It is the coldness of the water in Antarctica that preserves the bones and makes it look like they were left there yesterday but I like to think they are there as a reminder of man's potential for folly.

Another troubling image is closer to where I often train. In Hout Bay there is a statue of a lone leopard looking out to sea and it commemorates the last Cape Leopard to be shot in the bay in 1933. Hout Bay ('Wood Bay' in Afrikaans) was woodlands 200 years ago; now most of the trees are gone and Cape Leopards are on the verge of extinction.

And what is the thing that worries you the most?

I tell the kids that it's the explosion in human population.

I believe passionately that we must protect the environment and not just man's interests. In 2009 I sat on a panel with the inspirational Archbishop Desmond Tutu and two scientists during Pan-African Climate and Poverty Hearings. One by one, ordinary African people recounted stories about climate change making their lives impossible. A tea-farmer told of the endless cycles of drought and flood and how she had to travel 40 kilometres for water – something her people never had to do in the past. We heard other terrible testimonies from women whose farming livelihoods have been taken away by droughts and floods and how some had even resorted to prostitution to feed their children. Mary Robinson, the former President of Ireland and former UN High Commissioner for Human Rights, was at the hearings in her capacity as Honorary President of Oxfam International. After listening to the testimonies of the poor, she said, 'I think we need to care a little bit less about polar bears and a little bit more about humans.' I disagree, because you can't separate one from the other. We are totally dependent on nature for our survival. The global warming that causes ice to melt in the Arctic also causes drought in Africa. In one place it hurts people; in the other it threatens polar bears. I fear I will outlive polar bears. It is not just polar bears that need protection but the ecosystems that support them and all other forms of life.

Desmond Tutu is one of my favourite people. His love of life and his joyous, booming laughter are inspiring and he retains all of his mental alacrity. 'How do we stop climate change?' he said at the Pan-African hearings. 'With love. It's all about love – about loving people and respecting people and loving nature and respecting it.' I could not have agreed more. If you care for your fellow man, how can you build an enormous house or buy a huge car because we know what excessive energy consumption is doing to the environment, especially in those parts of the world where the poorest live?

People argue about the science of climate change but, for me, there are no arguments. In the last six summers I have spent time in the Arctic, each year I have seen less sea ice. We have reached a pivotal moment in history. I firmly believe that unless we take the right direction from here, there may be no future for our children's children. A friend told a story about a discussion with his twelve-year-old daughter during which he suggested that maybe climate change wasn't as great an issue as it was said to be in the media. 'Daddy,' she said, 'you're just hoping the worst effects will not happen in your lifetime and you're not looking further than that.' Out of the mouths of babes indeed! My friend admitted his daughter had struck a chord. My experiences speaking to schoolchildren around the world have shown that young people are aware and very concerned about the dangers of climate change and they are determined to be part of a generation that has a more sympathetic relationship with the environment. But will we, the current generation, do enough to ensure our children don't have an even bigger mess to sort out?

So far, the developed world has not offered true leadership on climate change. It is prepared to go so far, but no further. It wants developing countries, such as China and India, to do more but there is a basic inequality that must be considered: Western countries have built their prosperity on industries and consumerism that have done the most damage to the environment, yet they now need much less-developed countries to reduce their CO_2 output significantly. With their huge populations and low average income, it is easy to understand the reticence of poor countries to accept measures that will slow down their development. They believe the West has created the problem and now wants them to pay for it. So the Chinese and Indians come to the negotiating table but without the necessary resolve. The Americans, the British and other developed countries don't truly acknowledge their part in the creation of the problem and, ultimately, Nero is fiddling while Rome burns.

But the problem doesn't go away; in fact, it grows. Many politicians think not of our children's children but of getting re-elected. The world desperately needs a charismatic leader – a Nelson Mandela or an Abraham Lincoln – but the promise offered by the election of Barack Obama to the White House seems a long way away. Perhaps we're looking in the wrong places. In his play *Julius Caesar*, William Shakespeare wrote:

> The fault, dear Brutus, is not in our stars
> But in ourselves, that we are underlings.

We must be part of the change we wish to see. Something the Chinese premier, Wen Jiabao, said in a different context brings meaning to the challenge of climate change. He said if you take a problem and multiply it by 1.3 billion people (his country's current population), then it becomes a very big problem. But if you take a problem and divide it by 1.3 billion people, it can be solved. We have to accept individual responsibility for what is happening to the environment.

What hope is there for our generation?

More than at any moment in our history, this is the time to believe – to believe we can make the necessary changes. When children ask me, 'What hope is there for our generation?' I tell them about visiting the British Museum and being riveted by a stone tablet from 600BC that fills a number of walls and depicts the Pharoahs capturing lions, herding them into an enclosure and then charioteers, with bows and arrows, killing them for their sport. The images are so vivid. You can see the anger and terror on the lions' faces. That's what man once did and, though we sometimes forget, we live in more enlightened times now. We *can* change.

From the many lessons contained in the story of Nelson Mandela's life, there is one about his treatment of Percy Yutar, the unscrupulous prosecutor in the 1964 trial that saw Mandela and other ANC members sentenced to long prison terms. Yutar tried every trick in the book, and some that weren't in the book, to get Mandela and his colleagues the death sentence, but a skilled defence team saved them. Thirty-one years later Mandela invited the then 82-year-old Yutar to his inauguration and would later have him to lunch at the President's residence. On that latter occasion they shook hands and, for the remaining eight years of his life, Yutar used that handshake as proof that he bore no responsibility for the apartheid regime. He was 'just doing his job'. Some of Mandela's legal team during the trial found it hard to understand why Mandela should have been so conciliatory towards Yutar. Joel Joffe, a key defence lawyer and a great friend of Mandela, asked how he could be so generous. 'In reconciling the different races in South Africa,' Mandela replied, 'I could not afford the luxury of revenge.'

Similarly, we cannot afford the luxury of cynicism or even pessimism in our reaction to climate change. The situation is too serious. We must tackle it head on – and immediately. I have long considered myself a realistic optimist and liked having those types of people on my expedition teams. In facing the battles to protect our planet we're going to need optimism. There is a scene from *The Lord of the Rings: The Two Towers* that mirrors my feelings about the struggle to protect the environment. Sam is speaking to Frodo:

> 'It's like in the great stories, Mr Frodo. The ones that
> really mattered, full of darkness and danger, they were.
> And sometimes you didn't want to know the end.
> Because how could the end be happy? How could the
> world go back to the way it was when so much bad had
> happened? . . . Folk in those stories had lots of chances
> of turning back, only they didn't. They kept going.
> Because they were holding on to something.'
>   'What are we holding on to, Sam?'
>   'That there's some good in this world, Mr Frodo, and
> it's worth fighting for.'

Some people thought my swimming one kilometre in minus 1.7°C water at the North Pole was an act of utter reckless-ness. They said it was an irresponsible form of protest. I never saw it like that and, through the prism of hindsight, I regard it as one of the most satisfying things I have done. Yes, it was dangerous. I will never forget the thought that if it all went wrong and I sank the 4.2 kilometres to the bottom of the Arctic Ocean, there would have been no way to recover my body. I accepted the risks, knowing my symbolic swim would draw attention to something that mattered to me – a fair trade is no robbery. In many respects the swim was the ultimate experience of my life because it brought together my two great passions: the desire to see the world's most spectacular places and my desire to help protect them.

After the North Pole swim, there was an immediate decision never to do anything like that again, but time blurs the recollection of danger and recharges the engine. Right now I am preparing for a May 2010 expedition to the Himalayas, where I will attempt a one-kilometre swim in the 0–2°C water in a lake on the Khumbu Glacier on Mount Everest. Since Sir Edmund Hillary first climbed Everest in 1953, this glacier has retreated significantly and scientists predict it and many other glaciers in the region will melt away in the not too distant future. For China, India, Bangladesh and Pakistan, who depend upon the Himalayas for their constant water supply, the consequences will be catastrophic. By swimming one kilometre under the summit of Mount Everest, I hope to draw attention to the impact it will have on all of us, not just in the region, and on peace.

Two and a half years have passed since I last swam in cold water and I've never swum at high altitude. In January 2010 Antoinette and I flew to Mendoza in Argentina for a three-week training camp. Our plan was to climb the first 3,300 metres of Mount Aconcagua, the highest mountain in the southern hemisphere at nearly 7,000 metres, and to swim in a lake at that point. I was told there was a lake there. We had a mule to carry our rucksacks but it was still a tough climb, especially as the lake wasn't to be found – all that was left was a dried-up basin where it had once been. There was a river so we built a small dam wall with rocks and, for two days, I submerged myself at regular intervals in an attempt to reintroduce my body to cold water.

After descending Aconcagua, we travelled 250 kilometres south to Lagua del Diamante at 3,300 metres in the Andes.

Translated, it means 'Diamond Lake' and gets its name from the extinct volcano Maipo that stands in the background; when the sun shines, the reflection of Maipo looks like a diamond in the lake. To call the terrain and conditions in that part of the Andes tough is to understate the case: they were hostile. Temperatures rose to 35 degrees during the day, which isn't exactly climbing weather, and then dropped to minus 10°C at night, which isn't exactly camping weather. But it was the howling wind, the bleakness of the landscape and the blasting we took from the wind-driven sand that were the really torturous bits. I panted from early morning to late in the evening on our first day but coped a little better on succeeding days. Thankfully, Lagua del Diamante had plenty of water and, at 5°C, it was a good place to pick up the thread of my cold-water swimming life.

Of course, the renewal of this relationship had to be gradual. On the first day, all I could manage was a two-minute submersion. The second day I rose to a four-minute submersion in the morning followed by fourteen minutes of breaststroke in the afternoon. What was surprising was the relative ease with which I was able to do the swim. At this altitude, I was ready to die after a 50-metre jog, yet the swim didn't tire me. On the third day I walked around the Maipo volcano and up to 4,200 metres, a seven-hour trek that completely wasted me. Even the descent back to the lake was murderous. Then, a couple of hours later, I breezed through a 200-metre swim and was baffled by the ease of it. On the fourth day, I couldn't wait to get back in the water and, again, it was a breeze – I swam 1 kilometre with so much comfort that I felt that I had to be cheating.

I've thought about it a lot and the only conclusion I can come to is that when you are in the horizontal position, as you are when swimming, altitude sickness does not affect you to the same degree as when you are in the vertical position. It's a case for the Prof and, no doubt, he will do some tests and explain it to me. But I should never forget that the lake on Mount Everest will be much higher, and as I learned on the test swim near the North Pole – never, ever underestimate the unknown.

THANK YOUS

If you've been to the places I've been, done the things I did and survived to tell the stories, it is only because *a lot* of good people helped me. Without them there would have been no swims, no expeditions, no campaigns to draw attention to vulnerable ecosystems and no opportunity to realize my dreams. Their efforts were appreciated at the time and I remember each one now in alphabetical order.

Thanks to **Steinar Aksnes** for ensuring that however Robert Hedegus and I die, it's now not going to be because of some grumpy walrus . . . to **Jørgen Amundsen** who helped me get to the North Pole and whose great-great-uncle Roald was the first to the South Pole in 1911 . . . to **Kevin Andersson** who was there when the sometimes murderous waters of the Cape Peninsula threatened to overwhelm me . . . to **Dr Terry Babcock-Lumish** for showing me how to deal better with the challenge of public speaking . . . to **Kay** and **Peter Bales** for being pillars of the swimming community in Cape Town . . . to **Mark Barratt** for singing *Gaudeamus Igitur* at the most wonderfully appropriate moment . . . to **Paul Barrett Smith** for taking a kid under his wing and helping him to fly . . . to **Allison Bassett** for reminding me that if a dog is a man's best friend, the woman who looks after his dog has to be his second-best friend . . . to **David Becker** for being such a wonderful and generous friend and for always being there for me – both in good times and hard times . . . to **Commander William Bisset** who made me want to go to university . . . to **Simon** and **Cheryl Blackburn** for beautiful days on the Skeleton Coast and at Three Trees Lodge . . . to **Margaret Brady** who, among other things, got me on Jay Leno . . . to **Sam Branson** for a fondly remembered sense of humour . . . to **Charlie Britz**, **Arryn Eldon** and **Sophia Schelin** for making a beautiful film . . . to **Sarah Brunwin**, a fine woman in a worthy organization . . . to **Alexander Brylin** for being a great Russian and a great friend – Alex, one day I will come to eastern Russia and we will race down the Amur River . . . to **Arianne Burnette** for doing such a fine job with editing my manuscript . . . to **Brian Button**, one heck of a swimming coach . . . to **Alice Byers**, who cut through the ice on a memorable Norwegian day with the General . . . to the **Cape Long Distance Swimming Association** . . . to **Matthew Carlson** for the wise ideas . . . to **Eddie Cassar** for guiding me ashore at the end of the very first swim . . . to **Oscar Chalupsky** for building outstanding surf skis . . . to **Sigal Chiles**, who taught me the value of great slides when speech-making . . . to **Tony Concagh** for trusting me . . . to **Nigel Cones**, who provided the acid test as to whether I was ready for a swim . . . to **Cherryl Curry** for her help and that of the **Wilderness Leadership School** . . . to **Barry Cutler**, without whom I might have been another Great White statistic . . . to **Alan Danker**, who showed me running up Table Mountain is easier when there's company . . . to **Patrick Deane** for believing and then backing me . . . to **Professors Derry Devine** and **James**

Crawford, who taught me International Law . . . to **Laurie Dexter** for staying close to me at the North Pole . . . to **Shaun Dixon**, who shared his love for singing . . . to **Rupert Douglas**, who got me through a swim on Mount Snowdon . . . to **Jonathan** and **Lara Dugas** for giving so much and making it fun . . . to **Hendrik du Toit** for being the first sponsor to write a cheque with my name on it . . . to **Stephan du Toit**, who did more than his share on the tough Cape Peninsula swim . . . to the **English Channel Swimming Association** . . . to **Jack Eggum** for always giving me the finest room in the hotel . . . to **Terje Eggum** for being a great photo-journalist and a fine Norwegian . . . to **Terry Elliot** for that sodden Bakewell tart . . . to **Judge Hannes Fagan** for showing me that without personal responsibility, efforts to protect the environment won't work . . . to **Kevin Fialkov**, who took me swimming when it was neither fashionable nor profitable (it still isn't!) . . . to **Laurie Fialkov**, who was there when the going to Cape Point got tough . . . to **Martin Finegold** for backing me . . . to **Damien Forrest** for helping me with difficult decisions in 2008 . . . to **Gary Freeling** for getting up so early in the winter of 2005 . . . to **Jeremy Gardiner** for being generous . . . to **Laila Gjerde**, who ensured I put on the necessary 10kg – rather quickly I might add . . . to **Zac Goldsmith** for helping with the Arctic Kayak . . . to **Ted Graham**, the legal eagle who kept me in the Thames and out of prison in the summer of 2006 . . . to **Tessa Graham** for guiding me to the next level . . . to **Marie Grey** for giving me the break I needed . . . to **Grif Griffiths** for the wonderful weekends in Erwood . . . to **Olav Grov** for making the Nigards Glacier experience even better . . . to **Baba Gumedi** for showing me the true wilderness . . . to **Sarah Jane Hails** for seeing Sognefjord as the world's most beautiful swimming pool . . . to **Tom Hall** for generosity, good company, excellent writing and taking the best cabin on the MV *Havsel* . . . to **Paul Hamiliton**, who never failed to make me laugh . . . **Professor John Hare**, who was the best kind of teacher . . . to **Murad Hassan**, who helped me across the Maldives . . . to the **Captain of the MV *Havsel***, a smiler, a dancer and our guide through the sea ice around Spitsbergen, and **his crew** . . . to **Robert Hegedüs**, the greatest athlete I have ever worked with and a pretty special human being . . . to **John Ince**, who did so much to make Camps Bay High School a fine place to grow up . . . to **Eva Jeanbart-Lorenzotti** for being a generous supporter . . . to **Martin Jenkins** for showing me how to believe . . . to **Shane Jenkins** for refusing to think only of himself on a very tough forty-eight hours in the Brecon Beacons . . . to **Fred Kalborg** for taking great photos . . . to **Ted Kalborg**, who wasn't afraid to back me . . . to **Daniel Kantor**, who was there for the early swims . . . to **Martin Karlsen** for taking me south . . . to **Nick Keller** and the **Beyond Sports Team** for being generous supporters . . . to **Clare Kerr** for switching on an important light . . . to **Peder Kjærvik**, another reason why I like Norway . . . to **Steven Klugman** for helping me from Seal Island to Kommetjie . . . to **Prue Leith** for believing in the cause . . . to **Guy Lether** for helping me when I most needed it . . . to **Dr Moeketski Letseka** for being such a good companion on runs through Regent's Park . . . to **Barbara Levy** for calmness and good judgement . . . to **Motti Lewis** for designing my cold-water training facility on the V&A Waterfront; without it the swims in the Arctic and at Antarctica couldn't have happened . . . to **Emily Lewis-Brown**, who helped me to understand better what needs to be done to protect our environment . . . to the Cape Point **lighthouse man** who kept his eye on me . . . to **Brian Linden** for backing me . . . to **Chris Lotz** for extraordinary dedication to the job . . . to

Colonel Vladimir Lutov for helping to make Oulu a joyful experience . . . to **Lionel Lynch**, who explained the mysteries of map-reading and helped me to get my SAS beret . . . to **Big Mac** for knowing how to make a great sandwich . . . to **Ben McGuire**, who took me into Sydney Harbour and kept me from being deported from Australia . . . to **Matthew Mansfield** for giving me a second chance with the SAS . . . to **Kerry-Ann Marais**, who helped keep me in one piece on that Thames swim . . . to **Nic Marais** for offering true friendship . . . to **Nic Marshall** for many things, especially for taking so many jellyfish stings on the final leg of the Thames odyssey . . . to **Commander** and **Mrs Wally Maxwell** for Christmases away from home . . . to **James Mayhew**, who was always supportive and who so bravely fought the Thames swans on my behalf . . . to **Sandi Merwitz** for keeping me going to the end in the Maldives . . . to **Peter Morrissey**, who offered good stories, a big smile and wise counsel . . . to **Celia Muir**, who was generous . . . to **Olivier Müller,** who was also generous . . . to **Simon Murie** for helping me towards London . . . to **Andre Nel**, who found a way to introduce me to many of South Africa's townships and to whom I remain indebted . . . to **Marilyn Noakes** for being herself and, of course, the Prof's inspiration . . . to **Professor Tim Noakes**, who challenged assumptions and always believed it was possible . . . to **Olle Nordell** for beautiful writing . . . to **Dave Painter** for great work with the camera . . . to **Adam Parfitt** for stepping in to help . . . to **Tasch Petersmann** for a super website . . . to **Nick Peterson**, a great SAS friend, companion at North Cape, Sognefjord and Sydney, who loves life so much . . . to **Al Petrie**, who got me in the mood for racing at those World Winter Swimming Championships . . . to **Louise Plank**, who did so much to get the messages out there through the last five years . . . to **Dr Ian Player** for being an inspiration . . . to **Geir Ivar Ramsli**, my guide on the magical Norwegian night in the Sognefjord . . . to **David Richter** for paddling day after day . . . to **Jason Roberts** – so much to say but above all the one who volunteered to come and get me if I went under at the North Pole . . . to **Dave Robinson**, who provided the best swimming kit on the planet . . . to **Patsy Rodenburg** for being an illuminating teacher . . . to **Bronwen Rohland**, who believed and supported me so much . . . to **Stephen Rubin** for being there on the bad days . . . to **Hugo Salamonsen**, who enabled me to swim around North Cape . . . to **Maxine Scalabrino** for paddling alongside me on that first swim from Robben Island . . . to **Tony Scalabrino**, skipper on the support boat for the first swim from Robben Island . . . to **Craig Scarpa** for getting me in shape . . . to **Lucy Scott** for being a star on the Thames and for hanging over the Albert Bridge . . . to **Bernard Sellmeyer** for those wonderful paddles on the Atlantic seaboard . . . to **Tony Sellmeyer**, who raised my spirits and helped me get round the Cape of Good Hope . . . to **Kerri Sharp** for sticking with me when things got very difficult . . . to **Helen Siverstol**, whose enthusiasm made all things possible in Sognefjord . . . to **Anthony Smit** for understanding the value of good boots on long marches . . . to **Dean Smith** for saying yes . . . to the wonderful people of **Sognefjord** and **Lusterfjord** who made me feel so welcome . . . to the men of **Special Air Service** wherever you may be serving . . . to **Gill Stramrood** for accompanying me through the fog in Saldanha Bay . . . to **Ryan Stramrood**, who got me from Sandy Bay to Duiker Island . . . to **Dr Damon Stanwell-Smith** for keeping the leopard seals away long enough . . . to **Tim Tacchi** for generous backing . . . to **Mr Tattoo** for not being my opponent in the SAS milling and for breaking sweat with me on the first day of the Thames swim that was actually a Thames run . . . to **Kim Teichmann** for comforting a sun-roasted swimmer in Malawi . . . to **Daniel Terreblanche** for sound advice . . . to **Dr Otto Thaning**, who showed me how a human being can glide majestically through the water and so much more . . . to **Julia Thomas** for revitalizing my limbs and keeping a lookout for logs in the ice . . . to **Jenny Toyne Sewell** for always finding the General's glasses and nursing the malingerers . . . to **Major General Tim Toyne Sewell** for breaking the ice in Nigards Glacier Lake and, later, at a minute's notice in the Maldives, putting Roman Abramovich's yacht at our disposal . . . to **Hugh Tucker**, who helped get me around the Cape . . . to **Johan van Berck** for keeping us all calm when the Great White was under us . . . to **Vince van der Bijl**, who, for me, was not just a fantastic cricketer . . . to **Tobie van Heerden** for getting those flags to stand tall and strong at the North Pole . . . to **Julie van Rijswijk**, who helped to make our Antarctica expedition set sail . . . to **Jeremy Venniker** for coaxing me metre by metre down that muddy river . . . to **Guiseppe Vitali** for getting Otto and me round Robben Island . . . to **Michael Walker**, who shot great photos in the Namibian Desert and the Maldives . . . to **David Walsh** for so much, but especially your beautiful writing, for believing in the cause and for the advice you gave me in that cold winter of 2008 . . . to **Mary** and **Molly Walsh** for your wonderful Irish hospitality . . . to **Alan Weir** for being a kind teacher . . . to **Melissa Weldrick** for helping me to make my time in the townships even more rewarding . . . to **Graham Wilkinson** for the most beautiful flags in the world . . . and to **Mariia Yrjö-Koskinen** who put some fun back into sport at the World Winter Swimming Championships . . .

And thanks to those no longer with us: **Richard Armstrong**, who skippered me across the English Channel . . . **Stuart**

Grant and **Justas Chirwa**, who were with me in Malawi . . . **James Maxwell**, a fine SAS soldier and a dearly missed friend . . . **Daantjie Truter**, who got me round the whole Cape Peninsula . . . **Chris van Jaarsveld** – thank you for not scolding me when I kept looking out of your classroom window across the ocean . . . and to **Tony Wortham**, a very special headmaster who made my childhood so happy.

Finally, heartfelt thanks to those who provided most of the inspiration and are continuing to inspire: my wife **Antoinette**, my sister **Caroline**, my mother **Margery**, my eight-month-old Jack Russell puppy **Nanu,** who has me around her little paw, and of course my beloved late **father**.

INDEX

(key to initials: AP = Antoinette Pugh; PDGP = Patterson David Gordon Pugh; LGP = Lewis Gordon Pugh; MP = Margery Pugh)